"*The Best Democracy Mo*... among progressives."

—*The Village Voice*

"Greg is one of the last of a dying breed of real investigative re-porters. He has more courage than most, and exposes the truth be-hind so many of the things we *never* get to hear about. From the stolen election in 2000 to Lobbygate, Greg mixes documents, facts, and his own particular brand of humor in one excellent book. A must."

—Meria Heller, www.meriaheller.com

"Palast is angry, opinionated, and armed with a tireless desire to expose the truth. His stories about Bush's election theft and intel-ligence agency cover-ups—backed with smoking-gun documents, inside sources, and candid interviews—will shock even the most informed reader."

—WorkingForChange.com

"Palast, who now reports for *The Guardian* and *The Observer* in London, as well as the BBC, distinguishes himself from many other advocacy journalists both left and right with his near-obsession with documentary evidence—memos, correspondence, e-mail, briefing reports and raw data, much of it stamped confiden-tial—and his painstaking research methods."

—*Chicago Tribune*

"Dare we call this loose network the new shadow media? And can it do the job the mainstream press could do—if it only would—with Greg Palast's brand of investigative journalism?"

—*The Baltimore Chronicle*

PLUME
Published by the Penguin Group
Penguin Putnam Inc., 375 Hudson Street, New York, New York 10014, U.S.A.
Penguin Books Ltd, 80 Strand, London WC2R 0RL, England
Penguin Books Australia Ltd, 250 Camberwell Road, Camberwell, Victoria 3124, Australia
Penguin Books Canada Ltd, 10 Alcorn Avenue, Toronto, Ontario, Canada M4V 3B2
Penguin Books (N.Z.) Ltd, Cnr Rosedale and Airborne Roads, Albany, Auckland 1310,
New Zealand

Penguin Books Ltd, Registered Offices: Harmondsworth, Middlesex, England

Published by Plume, a member of Penguin Putnam Inc.
The first edition of this book was originally published by Pluto Publishing Ltd.,
345 Archway Road, London, United Kingdom, N6 5AA.

First Plume Printing, February 2003
10   9   8   7   6   5   4   3

Ⓟ REGISTERED TRADEMARK—MARCA REGISTRADA

LIBRARY OF CONGRESS CATALOGUING-IN-PUBLICATION DATA
Palast, Greg.
      The best democracy money can buy : an investigative reporter exposes
the truth about globalization, corporate cons, and high-finance
fraudsters / Greg Palast.
        p.   cm.
      Includes index.
      ISBN 0-7453-1846-0 (hc.)
      ISBN 0-452-28391-4 (pbk.)
      1. Political corruption.   2. Corporations—Corrupt practices.   I. Title.
JF1081 .P35   2003
364.1'323—dc21

                                                              2002192673

Printed in the United States of America

Designed by Leonard Telesca

PUBLISHER'S NOTE
Publisher is not affiliated with author's websites and/or newsletters, and assumes no responsibility
for their information or use. Although the author has made every effort to provide accurate telephone numbers and Internet addresses at the time of publication, neither Publisher nor author
assumes any responsibility for errors or changes.

BOOKS ARE AVAILABLE AT QUANTITY DISCOUNTS WHEN USED TO PROMOTE
PRODUCTS OR SERVICES. FOR INFORMATION PLEASE WRITE TO PREMIUM
MARKETING DIVISION, PENGUIN PUTNAM INC., 375 HUDSON STREET, NEW
YORK, NEW YORK 10014.

THE BEST DEMOCRACY MONEY CAN BUY

★ $ ★ $ ★ $ ★ $ ★ $ ★ $ ★

AN INVESTIGATIVE REPORTER EXPOSES THE TRUTH ABOUT GLOBALIZATION, CORPORATE CONS, AND HIGH-FINANCE FRAUDSTERS

★ $ ★ $ ★ $ ★ $ ★ $ ★ $ ★

GREG PALAST

A PLUME BOOK

For

LINDA LEVY,

whose work is here plagiarized without mercy

We cannot trust some people who are nonconformists.
　　　　—Ray Kroc, Chairman,
　　　　　　McDonald's Corp., deceased

*The thing about the Golden Straitjacket is, the tighter you
wear it, the more gold it produces.*
　　　　　—Thomas Friedman on globalization

I don't have to be nice to the spirit of the Anti-Christ.
　　　　—Dr. ("Reverend") Pat Robertson

Contents

In the days following the presidential election, there were so many
stories of African Americans erased from voter rolls you might
think they were targeted by some kind of racial computer program.
They were.

Who owns America? How much did it cost? Was the transaction
cash, check or credit card?

Jake Horton borrowed the company plane to confront his
company's board of directors over accounting games and illegal
political payments. Minutes after takeoff, the plane exploded.

THE BEST DEMOCRACY MONEY CAN BUY

Who Gives a Shit?
An Introduction to the
New American Edition

You read the papers and you watch television, so you know the kind of spider-brained, commercially poisoned piece-of-crap reporting you get in America.

You could call this book *What You Didn't Read in the* New York Times *and What You Can't See on* CBS. For example:

> Five months before the November 2000 election, Governor Jeb Bush of Florida moved to purge 57,700 people from the voter rolls, supposedly criminals not allowed to vote. Most were innocent of crimes, but the majority were guilty of being Black.

I wrote that exposé for page one of the nation's top newspaper. But it was the wrong nation: Britain. It ran in the *Guardian* of London and its Sunday sister paper, the *Observer.* You could see it on television too—in Europe, on BBC TV's *Newsnight,* which airs my investigate reports. (If you want to know what was in that diseased sausage called a presidential election, read Chapter 1, "Jim Crow in Cyberspace.")

Something else you didn't read: After the American electorate booted the senior Bush from the White House, he landed
softly on the board of a gold-mining company originally funded by
the Saudi Arabian Adnan Khashoggi, arms dealer to the Axis of
Evil. The former president's gold-digger friends made a billion off
changes in rules courtesy of the outgoing Bush administration.
From there, the story gets more brutal and much bloodier (see
Chapter 2, "The Best Democracy Money Can Buy," new to this
American edition).

Then there's the story of Monsanto's genetically modified
milk-making hormone. The stuff caused company test cows to drip
pus into milk buckets. Yummy. Monsanto fixed that problem the
easy way—by burying test data. U.S. officials helped out, slipping
the company confidential regulatory documents. American journals couldn't cover that. They were too busy licking the loafers of
Monsanto's Robert Shapiro, GE's Jack Welch and Enron's Ken Lay
to write something not cribbed off a company press release (see
Chapter 5, "Inside Corporate America").

And you didn't read how the "Reverend" Dr. Pat Robertson
secretly, illicitly used his Christian Crusade *jihad* assets to boost his
berserker get-rich-quick business schemes (see Chapter 6, "Pat
Robertson").

Nor did you get the news about Aníbal Verón. In August
2000, Verón, a bus driver who hadn't received his pay for nine
months, protested and was shot dead. Argentines believe the
World Bank had a secret plan to force the nation to cut wages.
Antiglobalization conspiracy fantasy? I'll show you the document.

Instead, American-style journalism gives you proglobalization
gurus like Thomas Friedman. It tells you the new international financial order is all about the communications revolution and cell
phones that will call your broker and do your laundry at the same
time. Golly. And if you're against globalization, you're against the
future. The kids protesting in the streets are just a bunch of unsophisticated jack-offs. And in the United States especially, there's
no dissent from this slaphappy view. I'm not going to argue with

Friedman and guys in favor of The Future. What I will do is take you through Country Assistance Strategies, Article 133 diplomatic letters and GATS committee memos. Most are marked "confidential" and "not for public disclosure"—having walked out of filing cabinets inside the IMF, World Bank, World Trade Organization. And there's nothing in there about cell phones for Incas.

If you read the original hardcover edition of this book, you'll see here a substantially different text. An awful lot has happened since we last met between these covers, and new material arrives daily. There were letters like this: *You are a freak liberal asshole! [signed] A Reasonable American.* That is not news. However, there was an extraordinary note from Florida. Katherine Harris, secretary of state, wrote that my reporting was "twisted." Again, no news there; but I was astonished by the evidence she provided me in her lengthy high-volume screed. In this book's first edition, I disclosed that Governor Jeb Bush's office had knowingly blocked 40,000 legal voters from registering. Coincidentally, over 90 percent of those voters were Democrats. Bush's office stone-cold denied it. Now, his buddy Harris faxed me the proof (unwittingly, I presume). You'll see the documents in this new American edition.

In addition, there's the latest on how Governor Jeb fixed his own race for reelection in 2002 and how Republicans are finagling the machinery for 2004.

The first edition of this book included ten pages introducing you to a company named Enron. "This is Enron. You've never heard of them." Presumably, by now, you've heard. But if you think the truth has come out about Enron, Arthur Andersen, Global Crossing, Reliant and the host of other sharks in CEO clothing, don't kid yourself: The U.S. media is still peeing on your leg and telling you it's raining. You're now being told that Harry Potter–magical accounting is a new, short-lived game limited to a couple of corporate rogues, a few bad apples. New? Limited? The apples are dropping because the U.S. corporate tree is rotten—root and branch. Andersen should have been indicted a decade ago. If you want to know why they weren't, ask our president's daddy—and read the new section on the Power Pirates in Chapter 3.

Also in this edition, new information indicating that U.S. financial institutions helped Argentina's ruling families speculate on their nation's death spiral. That opens the door to more tales of Enron, the kidnapping of the president of Venezuela and the Bush-Bush's gold mine, all new to this edition.

Some of you may be wondering why I'd bother with a revision. After all, in 2002 the U.S. Congress passed campaign finance reform. Our president signed it into law. The election process is "reformed." Bush signed another law promising to jail corporate bad guys. But if we look closely, reform consists of *doubling* the amount of so-called "hard" contributions politicians may legally harvest, eliminating only "soft" contributions. Stiffening flaccid contributions may be Congress's idea of progress, but the financial poisoning of our body politic continues. And the corporate governance reforms, like the elections reforms, are simply covers for new mischief.

Am I a bit too rough on the Republicans? I recognize that the selling of America is a bipartisan business. If I spill more ink here on the Bushes than the Clintons, it's primarily because a journalist's first job should be to discomfit those *in* power. Regarding the Democrats, my policy is to let sleeping dogs lie and lying dogs sleep.

Words in Exile

So why have you not seen these stories, or very few of them, in the mainstream media? Take that story of the theft of the U.S. election. In America, editors looked at their shoes and whistled—and hoped it would go away. Not everyone ignored it, of course—I got lots of letters like this one: *"Stay out of our politics, you English pig!"* I hate to quibble, but I'm not British.

I'm from Los Angeles. Actually, the scum end of L.A., in the

San Fernando Valley, raised in a pastel house between the power plant and the city garbage dump. It was not as glamorous as abject poverty, but not far above it. Half the kids in my school were Mexican American and, brown or white, we were pretty much tagged as America's losers. You graduated, worked minimum wage at Bob's Big Boy on Van Nuys Boulevard, and got your girlfriend pregnant. If Vietnam didn't kill you, overtime at the Chevy plant would.

America was a carnivore and we were just food. Anyway, I got out and so did my sister—how we did is neither interesting nor remarkable.

Am I bitter? Why shouldn't I be when I look at the privileged little pricks that call the shots on this planet, whose daddies could make the phone calls, write the checks, make it smooth? Daddy Bush, Daddy Koch, Daddy bin Laden—I've got a list.

As a scholarship kid at the University of Chicago, I witnessed the birth of the New World Globalization Order. It was the mid-1970s and I'd worked my way into Milton Friedman's postgraduate seminar and into a strange clique, which later became known as the "Chicago Boys." That was the little cabal of South America's budding dictators and right-wing economists who would turn Chile into an experiment in torture and free markets.

Even then I was undercover, working for Frank Rosen, head of the United Electrical Workers Union, and Eddie Sadlowski, the dissident steelworkers' leader, for a greater purpose I could understand dimly at best.

I avoided journalism. Starting in 1975, from a desk in the basement of the electrical workers' union hall, I began grinding through U.S. corporate account books. Using their own abstruse financial codes, I challenged gas company heating charges. I negotiated contracts for steel and iron workers. I was broke and I was in heaven.

My dad had been a furniture salesman. He hated furniture. If it were up to him, we would have eaten sitting on the floor. Mom worked in the school cafeteria (you know, hairnet and creamed corn) until she became a hypnotist for McDonald's (really—see Chapter 7). From them, I gained a deep and abiding fear of working for a living.

Bang: One minute I was this dead-broke anticorporate scourge with his head buried in bureaucratic file cabinets, and the next I was "America's number one expert on government regulation bar none" (wrote one kind newspaper). My office, on the fiftieth floor of the World Trade Center, was bigger than an L.A. bowling alley.

Still, I kept my nose in dusty files. I found things like this: Executives of a megalithic power company, Long Island Lighting of New York, swore under oath that their nuclear plant would cost $1.8 billion. Internal confidential memos said the plant would cost $3.2 billion. I convinced the government to charge them with civil racketeering, and a jury said they should pay $4.8 billion. Then, the governor of New York, a slick operator named Mario Cuomo, reached the chief federal judge in New York—and poof!—the jury's verdict was thrown out. That's when I learned about love, and that there is no love greater than the love of politicians for the captains of finance.

So am I bitter? See above.

I finally quit. It was during my investigation of the *Exxon Valdez* crack-up (see Chapter 6). I was working for the Chugach natives of Alaska. Our team quickly discovered the oil spill was no accident: Before the tanker's grounding, Exxon shut off the ship's radar to save money and a British Petroleum affiliate had faked the safety equipment reports.

How could I get the real story out? From a kayak in the Prince William Sound, *who can hear you scream?* The press had f'd up the *Exxon Valdez* story something awful. That was six years ago. I decided from then on I'd write these stories myself, an idea immediately encouraged by the British *Guardian* and *Observer* papers and BBC's *Newsnight*.

While American journalists spent those years smothered in

Monica Lewinsky's panties, I had the luxury of diving into the filing cabinets of the Reverend Pat Robertson, the World Trade Organization and George Bush's favorite billionaires.

I began in earnest in 1997 and my work quickly attracted a little more attention than I'd expected. On July 8 of that year, the entire front page of the *Mirror*, one of Britain's biggest-selling papers, was taken up by a picture of this nasty-looking bald guy—me—under a four-inch-tall headline: THE LIAR (figure i.1). And I thought, *"Damn, it doesn't get any better than this."* The *Mirror*—and the man they loved, Britain's prime minister, Tony Blair—did not like a story I had written with Antony Barnett for the *Observer*. To get the story, "Lobbygate," I'd gone undercover and exposed a stinky little deal-making operation running through Blair's cabinet. That story and the others to follow grew out of this idea: *Why not apply the techniques of investigations I've conducted in government racketeering cases to news reporting?* This would be a quantum leap in dig-out-the-facts methodologies rarely used even by "investigative" journalists. That's what makes these writings a bit different—lots of facts, many from documents thought by their writers to be hidden away in desk drawers, from missent faxes and from tape recordings made when big mouths didn't know whom they were talking to.

If Britain's government was selling its nation, corporate America was buying. That's my main beat: "Inside Corporate America," the title of my column in the *Observer*. Those columns—updated, all fresh material—are in Chapter 5. There you will get, for example, the skinny on Wal-Mart ("What Price a Store-gasm?") and the tale of the strange little deal cut by a big-time environmental group and the number-one lobbyist representing polluters ("How the Filth Trade Turned Green").

This book is largely a compendium of the investigations printed and broadcast overseas, expanded, with the newest information, plus substantial new material for this special edition for the United States.

Fig. i.1. In July 1997, I was in London and caught the front page of the *Mirror,* one of Britain's biggest-selling papers. On the front page was this nasty-looking bald guy—me. Britain's prime minister, Tony Blair, was unhappy with the *Observer*'s undercover investigation into the U.S. corporate purchase of favors from his cabinet members.

*   *   *

The question remains, why were these stories (and their author) exiled to Europe? Where are you, America? Don't you want to know how your president was elected? How the IMF spends your money?

Mike Isikoff, a *Newsweek* reporter, suggested an answer. A couple of years ago, he passed me some truly disturbing information on President Clinton, not the usual intern-under-the-desk stuff. I said, "Mike, why don't *you* print this?" And he said, *"Because no one gives a shit."*

But if you're one of the few who do, here's your book.

CHAPTER 1

JIM CROW IN CYBERSPACE:
The Unreported Story of How They Fixed the Vote in Florida

In the days following the presidential election, there were so many stories of African Americans erased from voter rolls you might think they were targeted by some kind of racial computer program. They were.

I have a copy of it: two silvery CD-ROM disks right out of the office computers of Florida Secretary of State Katherine Harris. Once decoded and flowed into a database, they make for interesting, if chilling, reading. They tell us how our president was elected—and it wasn't by the voters.

Here's how it worked: Mostly, the disks contain data on Florida citizens—57,700 of them. In the months leading up to the November 2000 balloting, Florida Secretary of State Harris, in co-ordination with Governor Jeb Bush, ordered local elections supervisors to purge these 57,700 from voter registries. In Harris's computers, they are named as felons who have no right to vote in Florida.

Thomas Cooper is on the list: criminal scum, bad guy, felon, *attempted* voter. The Harris hit list says Cooper was convicted of a felony on January 30, 2007.

2007?

You may suspect *something's wrong* with the list. You'd be right. At least 90.2 percent of those on this "scrub" list, targeted to lose their civil rights, are innocent. Notably, over half—about 54 percent—are Black and Hispanic voters. Overwhelmingly, it is a list of Democrats.

Secretary of State Harris declared George W. Bush winner of Florida, and thereby president, by a plurality of 537 votes over Al Gore. Now do the arithmetic. Over 50,000 voters wrongly targeted by the purge, mostly Blacks. My BBC researchers reported that Gore lost at least 22,000 votes as a result of this smart little black-box operation.

The first reports of this extraordinary discovery ran, as you'd expect, on page one of the country's leading paper. Unfortunately, it was in the wrong country: Britain. In the USA, it ran on page *zero*—the story was simply not covered in American newspapers. The theft of the presidential race in Florida also grabbed big television coverage. But again, it was the wrong continent: on BBC Television, broadcasting from London worldwide—everywhere, that is, but the USA.

Was this some off-the-wall story that the British press misreported? Hardly. The chief lawyer for the U.S. Civil Rights Commission called it the first hard evidence of a systematic attempt to disenfranchise Florida's Black voters. So why was this story investigated, reported and broadcast only in *Europe*, for God's sake? I'd like to know the answer. That way I could understand why a Southern California ho'daddy like me has to commute to England with his wife and kiddies to tell this and other stories about my country.

In this chapter, I take you along the path of the investigation, step by step, report by report, from false starts to unpretty conclusions. When I first broke the story, I had it wrong. Within weeks of the election, I said the Harris crew had tried to purge 8,000 voters. While that was enough to change the outcome of the election (and change history), I was way off. Now, after two years of peeling the Florida elections onion, we put the number of voters wrongly barred from voting at over 90,000, mostly Blacks and Hispanics, and by a wide majority, Democrats.[1]

That will take us to the Big Question: Was it *deliberate*, this purge so fortunate for the Republicans? Or just an honest clerical error? Go back to the case of Thomas Cooper, Criminal of the Future. I counted 325 of these time-traveling bandits on one of Harris's scrub lists. Clerical error? I dug back into the computers, the e-mail traffic in the Florida Department of Elections, part of the secretary of state's office. And sure enough, the office clerks were screaming: They'd found a boatload like Mr. Cooper on the purge list, convicted in the future, in the next century, in the *next millennium*.

The jittery clerks wanted to know what to do. I thought I knew the answer. As a product of the Los Angeles school system, where I Pledged my Allegiance to the Flag every morning, I assumed that if someone was wrongly accused, the state would give them back their right to vote. But the Republican operatives had a better idea. They told the clerks to *blank out* the wacky conviction dates. That way, the county elections supervisors, already wary of the list, would be none the wiser.[2] The Florida purge lists have over 4,000 blank conviction dates.

You've seen barely a hair of any of this in the U.S. media. Why? How did 100,000 U.S. journalists sent to cover the election *fail* to get the vote theft story (and preferably *before* the election)?

---

[1]Two years into the investigation, we are still uncovering evidence. The stories of Thomas Cooper and the thousands of other "felons" convicted in the future are new to this edition.

"We" are a team. There's no way on earth I could have conducted this investigation without scores of researchers, some the top names in their technical fields, some inspired amateurs, and many unpaid volunteers. Cyber-wizard Fredda Weinberg of Delray Beach, Florida, deserves special praise for cracking the disks and for indefatigable fact-mining; as do my colleagues at the *Guardian*, BBC, *The Nation*, and Salon.com; database expert Mark Swedlund and so many others. I regret I cannot list them all.

[2]E-mail from Janet Mudrow (Florida Department of Elections), "Subject: Future Conviction Dates," to Marlene Thorogood (Database Technologies), cc: Bucky Mitchell (Florida Department of Law Enforcement); dated June 15.

Part I: SILENCE OF THE LAMBS: American Journalism Hears No Evil, Sees No Evil, Reports No Evil

Investigative reports share three things: They are risky, they upset the wisdom of the established order and they are *very expensive* to produce. Do profit-conscious enterprises, whether media companies or widget firms, *seek* extra costs, extra risk and the opportunity to be attacked? Not in any business text I've ever read. I can't help but note that Britain's *Guardian* and *Observer* newspapers, the only papers to report this scandal when it broke just weeks after the 2000 election, are the world's only major newspapers owned by a not-for-profit corporation.

But if profit lust is the ultimate problem blocking significant investigative reportage, the more immediate cause of comatose coverage of the election and other issues is what is laughably called America's "journalistic culture." If the Rupert Murdochs of the globe are shepherds of the New World Order, they owe their success to breeding a flock of docile sheep—snoozy editors and reporters content to munch on, digest, then reprint a diet of press releases and canned stories provided by government and corporate public-relations operations.

Take this story of the list of Florida's faux felons that cost Al Gore the presidential election. Shortly after the U.K. story hit the World Wide Web, I was contacted by a CBS TV network news producer eager to run a version of the story. The CBS hotshot was happy to pump me for information: names, phone numbers, all the items one needs for your typical quickie TV news report.

I freely offered up to CBS this information: The office of the governor of Florida, Jeb Bush, brother of the Republican presidential candidate, had illegally ordered the removal of the names of felons from voter rolls—real felons who had served time but obtained clemency, with the right to vote under Florida law. As a result, *another 40,000 legal voters* (in addition to the 57,700 on the purge list), almost all of them Democrats, could not vote.

The only problem with this new hot info is that I was still in the midst of investigating it. Therefore, CBS *would have to do some actual work*—reviewing documents and law, obtaining statements.

The next day I received a call from the producer, who said, "I'm sorry, but your story didn't hold up." And how do you think the multibillion-dollar CBS network determined this? Answer: "We called Jeb Bush's office." Oh.

I wasn't surprised by this type of "investigation." It is, in fact, standard operating procedure for the little lambs of American journalism. One good, slick explanation from a politician or corporate chieftain and it's *case closed*, investigation over. The story ran on television, but once again, in the wrong country: I reported it on the BBC's *Newsnight*. Notably, the BBC is a publicly owned network—I mean a *real* public network, with no "funds generously provided by Archer Mobil Bigbucks."

Let's understand the pressures on the CBS TV producer that led her to kill the story simply because the target of the allegation said it ain't so. The story demanded massive and quick review of documents, dozens of phone calls and interviews—hardly a winner in the slam-bam-thank-you-ma'am school of U.S. journalism. Most difficult, the revelations in the story required a reporter to stand up and say that the big-name politicians, their lawyers and their PR people were *freaking liars*.

It would be much easier, a heck of a lot cheaper and no risk at all to wait for the U.S. Civil Rights Commission to do the work, then cover the commission's report and press conference. No one ever lost their job writing canned statements from a press release. Wait! You've watched *Murphy Brown* so you think reporters hanker to uncover the big scandal. Bullshit. Remember, *All the President's Men* was so unusual they had to make a movie out of it.

The Election Fix Story Steals Into the States

In London the *Guardian* and *Observer* received about two thousand bless-you-Britain-for-telling-us-the-truth-about-our-elections letters from U.S. Internet readers circulating the *samizdat* presidential elections coverage. I also received a few like this:

> *You pansey brits seem to think that the average American is as undereducated and stupid as the average british subject. Well comrad* [sic], *I'm here to tell you . . .*

. . . which ended with some physically unfeasible suggestions of what to do with the Queen (figure 1.1).

My *Observer* report went to print within three weeks of the election. The vote count in Florida was still on. Watching the vote-count clock ticking, Joe Conason, the most determined of American investigative reporters, insisted to his editors at Salon.com, the Internet magazine, that they bring my story back to America. Salon posted "Florida's Ethnic Cleansing of the Voter Rolls" to the Net on December 4, 2000. It wasn't exactly "print," but at least it was American. Still not one U.S. news editor called, not even from my "sister" paper, the *Washington Post*, with whom the *Guardian* shares material and prints an international weekly.

From a news perspective, not to mention the flood of site hits, this was Salon's biggest politics story ever—and they named Part I their political story of the year. But where was Part II? On their Web site and on radio programs the magazine was announcing Part II would appear in two days . . . and in two days . . . and in two days . . . and *nothing appeared*. Part II was the story blown off by the *CBS Evening News* about an additional 40,000-plus voters whom Jeb Bush barred from voting. The fact that 90 percent of these 40,000 voters were Democrats should have made it news . . . because this maneuver alone more than accounted for Bush's victory.

I was going crazy: Gore had not yet conceded . . . the timing of

---

Re: YOUR SOCIALIST SLANTED NEWS/REPORTING
Date: 1/7/01 2:20:41 PM GMT Standard Time
From: wild.bill@mtaonline.net (wildbill)
To: Gregory.Palast@guardian.co.uk

hey greg,
Let me begin by saying that your "article"on the Florida "black
list" is so transparently a socialist/democrat attempt to help your
socialist cousins in the states that it laughable.You pansey brits
seem to think that the average American is as undereducated
and stupid as the average british subject.Well comrad, I'm here
to tell you that that is not the case. While your average british
male was chasing his classmates around the dorms trying to get
a little buggery time in, The Average American male was in class
paying attention to the subject matter at hand. One of the first
things I learned was to spot a liar,and in your case it was'nt hard.
Yor story is so full of outright lies and half truths that a 6th
grader here in the states could find you out.You claim to be
places and to have spoken to people that would be extreemly
hard if not impossible to a member of the legitimate press and a
genuine miracle for a representative of a thirdworld (yes greg,
britain is considered here in the states to be a third world
country,and one populated by fourth rate acedemics) socialist
rag. We yanks have kicked your worthless limey butts twice so
far,is that what has your panties in a twist? Does'nt matter
anyway, I just wanted to drop you a line to tell you to say hi to
prince chuck for me,you know who I'm talking about don't you?
He's the one member of the boil family that is squatting in
Buckingham palace,the one that from head on looks like a
volkswagon with both doors open. Oh,and I almost forgot, tell
that bitch the Queen the next time you bugger her that she
needs to lose some weight & Stay out of our politics you english
pigs. <>

Fig. 1.1. Fan letter.

Part II was crucial. Where the hell was it? Finally, an editor told
me, "The story doesn't check out. You see, we checked with Jeb
Bush's office and they said . . ."

Argh! It was déjà vu all over again.

Another staffer added, as a kind of explanation, "The *Washington Post* would never run this story."

Well, he had me there. They hadn't, they didn't. Not yet. At least Salon helped me sneak the first report past the border patrols. So God bless America.

While waiting for the United States to awaken, I took my BBC film crew to Florida, having unearthed a smoking-gun document: I had a page marked "confidential" from the contract between the State of Florida and the private company that had purged the voter lists. The document contained cold evidence that Florida knew they were taking the vote away from thousands of innocent voters, most of them Black.

It was February. I took my camera crew into an agreed interview with Jeb Bush's director of the Florida Department of Elections. When I pulled out the confidential sheet, Bush's man ripped off the microphone and did a fifty-yard dash, locking himself in his office, all in front of our cameras. It was killer television and wowed the British viewers. We even ran a confession from the company that was hired to carry out the purge operation. Newsworthy? Apparently not for the United States.

My program, BBC *Newsnight,* has a film-trading agreement with the ABC television network. A record twenty thousand Net-heads in the United States saw the BBC Webcast; and several banged on the door of ABC TV's *Nightline* to run our footage, or at least report what we found. Instead, *Nightline* sent its own crew down to Florida for a couple of days. They broadcast a story that ballots are complex and Blacks are not well educated about voting procedures. The gravamen of the story was, *Blacks are too frigging dumb to figure out how to vote.* No mention that in white Leon County, machines automatically kicked back faulty ballots for voter correction; whereas in Gadsden County, very Black, the same machines were programmed to *eat* mismarked ballots. That was in our story, too.

Why didn't ABC run the voter purge story? Don't look for some big Republican conspiracy. Remember the three elements of investigative reporting: risk, time, money. Our BBC/*Guardian* stories required all of those, in short supply in U.S. news operations.

Finally, in February, my Part II—the report that was too scary and difficult for Dan Rather's show—found asylum in the *Nation* magazine, that distant journalistic planet not always visible to the naked eye.

And then, mirabile dictu, the *Washington Post* ran the story of the voter purge on page one, including the part that "couldn't stand up" for CBS and Salon . . . and even gave me space for a by-lined comment. Applause for the *Post's* courage! Would I be un-grateful if I suggested otherwise? The *Post* ran the story in *June*, though they had it at hand seven months earlier when the ballots were still being counted. They waited until they knew the findings of the U.S. Civil Rights Commission Report, which verified BBC's discoveries, so they could fire from behind that big safe rock of Official Imprimatur. In other words, the *Post* had the courage to charge out and shoot the wounded.

Part II: THE REPORTS

These are the stories you weren't supposed to see: from reports that ran in Britain's *Observer* and *Guardian*, bits of script from the BBC Television investigation and, to help set out the facts, the U.S. stories from Salon, the *Nation* and the *Washington Post*—fol-lowed by new material, never before printed or broadcast on either continent. Documents keep bubbling up from the cesspool of the Florida state offices. I've saved them for you here, having run out of the patience needed to knock heads with "respectable" U.S. pa-pers and networks.

How did British newspapers smell the Florida story all the way across the Atlantic? At the time, I was digging into George Bush Sr.'s gold-mining business (see next chapter), when one of my re-searchers spotted a note on the *Mother Jones* Internet bulletin board flagging a story in the *Palm Beach Post* printed months before the election. The *Post's* back pages mentioned that 8,000 voters had been removed from the voter rolls by mistake. That's one heck of a mistake. Given the Sturm und Drang in Florida, you'd think that an American journalist would pick up the story. Don't hold your breath. There were a couple of curious reporters, but they were easily waylaid by Florida's assurances that the "mistake" had been *corrected*, which the *Post* ran as truth.

But what if the Florida press puppies had been wrong? What if they had stood on their hind legs and swallowed a biscuit of bullshit from state officials—and the "mistakes" had *not* been corrected?

It was worth a call.

From London, I contacted a statistician at the office of the county elections supervisor in Tampa. Such an expert technician would have no reason to lie to me. The question at the top of my list: "*How many of the voters on the scrub list are* BLACK?"

And the statistician said, "You know, I've been waiting for someone to ask me that." From his leads, I wrote:

"Black-Out in Florida"

The Observer, London, November 26, 2000

Vice-President Al Gore would have strolled to victory in Florida if the state hadn't kicked up to 66,000 citizens off the voter registers five months ago as former felons. In fact, not all were ex-cons. Most were simply guilty of being African-American. A top-placed election official told me that the government had conducted a quiet review and found—surprise!—that the listing included far more African-Americans than would statistically have been expected, even accounting for the grievous gap between the conviction rates of Blacks and Whites in the U.S.

One list of 8,000 supposed felons was supplied by Texas. But these criminals from the Lone Star State had committed nothing more serious than misdemeanors such as drunk driving (like their governor, George W. Bush).

The source of this poisonous blacklist: Database Technologies, acting under the direction of Governor Jeb Bush's frothingly partisan secretary of state, Katherine Harris. DBT, a division of ChoicePoint, is under fire for misuse of personal data in state computers in Pennsylvania. ChoicePoint's board is loaded with Republican sugar daddies, including Ken Langone, finance chief for Rudy Giuliani's aborted Senate run against Hillary Clinton.

Voting with the Alligators

When the *Observer* report hit the streets (of London), Gore was still in the race.

Reporter Conason pushed Salon.com to pick up my story and take it further. But that would not be easy. The Texas list error—8,000 names—was corrected, said the state. That left the tougher question: What about the 57,700 *other* people named on that list? The remaining names on the list were, in the majority, Black—not unusual in a nation where half of all felony convictions are against African Americans. But as half the names were Black, and if this included even a tiny fraction of *innocents*, well, there was the election for Bush.

The question was, then, whether the "corrected" list had in fact been corrected. Finding the answer would not be cheap for Salon. It meant big bucks; redirecting their entire political staff to the story and making hotshot reporters knuckle down to the drudgery of calling and visiting county elections offices all over Florida. But they agreed, and Salon's Alicia Montgomery, Daryl Lindsey and Anthony York[3] came back with a mother lode of evidence proving that, by the most conservative analysis, Florida had

---

[3] Thank you all.

purged enough innocent Black voters—several thousand—to snatch the presidency from Al Gore.

At that time the presidential race was wide open. Word was, Gore's camp was split, with warriors fighting the gray-heads of the Establishment who were pushing him to lie down and play dead, advice he'd ultimately follow. Just before we hit the electronic streets with it, someone called a key player in the White House and Gore's inner circle about the story Salon would soon break. The Big Insider said, "That's fantastic! Who's the reporter?" The tipster said, "This American, he's a reporter in Britain, Greg Palast."

Mr. White House Insider replied, "Shit! We *hate* that guy."

But that's another story.

On December 4, 2000, I sent this to Salon:

"Florida's Ethnic Cleansing of the Voter Rolls"

From *Salon.com*

If Vice President Al Gore is wondering where his Florida votes went, rather than sift through a pile of chads, he might want to look at a "scrub list" of 57,700 names targeted to be knocked off the Florida voter registry by a division of the office of Florida Secretary of State Katherine Harris. A close examination suggests thousands of voters may have lost their right to vote based on a flaw-ridden list of purported "felons" provided by a private firm with tight Republican ties.

Early in the year, the company ChoicePoint gave Florida officials the names of 8,000 ex-felons to "scrub" from their list of voters.

But it turns out none on the list was guilty of felonies, only misdemeanors.

The company acknowledged the error, and blamed it on the original source of the list—the state of Texas.

Florida officials moved to put those falsely accused by Texas back on voter rolls before the election. Nevertheless, the large number of errors uncovered in individual counties suggests that thousands of other eligible voters have been turned away at the polls.

Florida is the only state that pays a private company that promises to provide lists for "cleansing" voter rolls. The state signed in 1998 a $4 million contract with DBT Online, since merged into ChoicePoint, of Atlanta. The creation of the scrub list, called the central voter file, was mandated by a 1998 state voter fraud law, which followed a tumultuous year that saw Miami's mayor removed after voter fraud in the election, with dead people discovered to have cast ballots. The voter fraud law required all 67 counties to purge voter registries of duplicate registrations, deceased voters and felons, many of whom, but not all, are barred from voting in Florida. In the process, however, the list invariably targets a minority population in Florida, where 31 percent of all Black men cannot vote because of a ban on felons.

If this unfairly singled out minorities, it unfairly handicapped Gore: in Florida, 93 percent of African-Americans voted for the vice president.

In the ten counties contacted by Salon, use of the central voter file seemed to vary wildly. Some found the list too unreliable and didn't use it at all. But most counties appear to have used the file as a resource to purge names from their voter rolls, with some counties making little—or no—effort at all to alert the "purged" voters. Counties that did their best to vet the file discovered a high level of errors, with as many as 15 percent of names incorrectly identified as felons.

News coverage has focused on some maverick Florida counties that rejected the scrub lists, including Palm Beach and Duval. The *Miami Herald* blasted the counties for not using the lists; but local officials tell us they had good reason to reject the scrub sheets from Harris's office. Madison County's elections supervisor, Linda Howell, had a peculiarly personal reason for distrusting the central voter file. She had received a letter saying that since she had committed a felony, she would not be allowed to vote.

Howell, who said she has never committed a felony, said the letter she received in March 2000 shook her faith in the process. "It really is a mess," she said.

"I was very upset," Howell said. "I know I'm not a felon." Though the one mistake did get corrected and law enforcement officials were quite apologetic, Howell decided not to use the state list because its "information is so flawed."

She's unsure of the number of warning letters that were sent out to county residents when she first received the list in 1999, but she recalls that there were many problems. "One day we would send a letter to have someone taken off the rolls, and the next day, we would send one to put them back on again," Howell said. "It makes you look like you must be a dummy."

Dixie and Washington counties also refused to use the scrub list. Starlet Cannon, Dixie's deputy assistant supervisor of elections, said, "I'm scared to work with it because [a] lot of the information they have on there is not accurate."

Carol Griffin, supervisor of elections for Washington, said, "It hasn't been accurate in the past, so we had no reason to suspect it was accurate this year."

But if some counties refused to use the list altogether, others seemed to embrace it all too enthusiastically. Etta Rosado, spokeswoman for the Volusia County Department of Elections, said the county essentially accepted the file at face value, did nothing to confirm the accuracy of it and doesn't inform citizens ahead of time that they have been dropped from the voter rolls.

"When we get the con felon list, we automatically start going through our rolls on the computer. If there's a name that says John Smith was convicted of a felony, then we enter a notation on our computer that says convicted felon—we mark an 'f' for felon—and the date that we received it," Rosado said.

"They're still on our computer, but they're on purge status," meaning they have been marked ineligible to vote.

"I don't think that it's up to us to tell them they're a convicted felon," Rosado said. "If he's on our rolls, we make a notation on there. If they show up at a polling place, we'll say, 'Wait a minute, you're a convicted felon, you can't vote.' Nine out of ten times when we repeat that to the person, they say 'Thank you' and walk away. They don't put up arguments." Rosado doesn't know how many people in Volusia were dropped from the list as a result of being identified as felons.

Hillsborough County's elections supervisor, Pam Iorio, tried to make sure that the bugs in the system didn't keep anyone from voting. All 3,258 county residents who were identified as possible felons on the central voter file sent by the state were sent a certified letter informing them that their voting rights were in jeopardy. Of that number, 551 appealed their status, and 245 of those appeals were successful. (By the rules established by Harris's office, a voter is assumed guilty and convicted of a crime and conviction unless and until they provide documentation certifying their innocence.) Some had been convicted of a misdemeanor and not a felony, others were felons who had had their rights restored and others were simply cases of mistaken identity.

An additional 279 were not close matches with names on the county's own voter rolls and were not notified. Of the 3,258 names on the original list, therefore, the county concluded that more than 15 percent were in error. If that ratio held statewide, *no fewer than 7,000* voters were incorrectly targeted for removal from voting rosters.

Iorio says local officials did not get adequate preparation for purging felons from their rolls. "We're not used to dealing with issues of criminal justice or ascertaining who has a felony conviction," she said. Though the central voter file was supposed to facilitate the process, it was often more troublesome than the monthly circuit court lists that she had previously used to clear her rolls of duplicate registrations, the deceased and convicted felons. "The database from the state level is not always accurate," Iorio said. As a consequence, her county did its best to notify citizens who were on the list about their felony status.

"We sent those individuals a certified letter, we put an ad in a local newspaper and we held a public hearing. For those who didn't respond to that, we sent out another letter by regular mail," Iorio said. "That process lasted several months."

"We did run some number stats and the number of Blacks [on the list] was higher than expected for our population," says Chuck Smith, a statistician for the county. Iorio acknowledged that African-Americans made up 54 percent of the people on the original felons list, though they constitute only 11.6 percent of Hillsborough's voting population.

Smith added that the DBT computer program automatically transformed various forms of a single name. In one case, a voter named "Christine" was identified as a felon based on the conviction of a "Christopher" with the same last name. Smith says ChoicePoint would not respond to queries about its proprietary methods. Nor would the company provide additional verification data to back its fingering certain individuals in the registry purge. One supposed felon on the ChoicePoint list is a local judge.

While there was much about the lists that bothered Iorio, she felt she didn't have a choice but to use them. And she's right. Section 98.0975 of the Florida Constitution states: "Upon receiving the list from the division, the supervisor must attempt to verify the information provided. If the supervisor does not determine that the information provided by the division is incorrect, the supervisor must remove from the registration books by the next subsequent election the name of any person who is deceased, convicted of a felony or adjudicated mentally incapacitated with respect to voting."

But the counties have interpreted that law in different ways. Leon County used the central voter file sent in January 2000 to clean up its voter rolls, but set aside the one it received in July. According to Thomas James, the information systems officer in the county election office, the list came too late for the information to be processed.

According to Leon election supervisor Ion Sancho, "there have been some problems" with the file. Using the information received in January, Sancho sent 200 letters to county voters, by regular mail, telling them they had been identified by the state as having committed a felony and would not be allowed to vote. They were given 30 days to respond if there was an error. "They had the burden of proof," he says.

He says 20 people proved that they did not belong on the list, and a handful of angry phone calls followed on election day. "Some people threatened to sue us," he said, "but we haven't had any lawyers calling yet." In Orange County, officials also sent letters to those identified as felons by the state, but they appear to have taken little care in their handling of the list.

"I have no idea," said June Condrun, Orange's deputy supervisor of elections, when asked how many letters were sent out to voters. After a bit more thought, Condrun responded that "several hundred" of the letters were sent, but said she doesn't know how many people complained. Those who did call, she said, were given the phone number of the Florida Department of Law Enforcement so that they could appeal directly to it.

Many Orange County voters never got the chance to appeal in any form.

Condrun noted that about one-third of the letters, which the county sent out by regular mail, were returned to the office marked undeliverable. She attributed the high rate of incorrect addresses to the age of the information sent by DBT, some of which was close to 20 years old, she said.

Miami-Dade County officials may have had similar trouble. Milton Collins, assistant supervisor of elections, said he isn't comfortable estimating how many accused felons were identified by the central voter file in his county. He said he knows that about 6,000 were notified, by regular mail, about an early list in 1999. Exactly how many were purged from the list? "I honestly couldn't tell you," he said. According to Collins, the most recent list he received from the state was one sent in January 2000, and the county applied a "two-pass system." If the information on the state list seemed accurate enough when comparing names with those on county voter lists, people were classified as felons and were then sent warning letters. Those who seemed to have only a partial match with the state data were granted "temporary inactive status."

Both groups of people were given 90 days to respond or have their names struck from the rolls.

But Collins said the county has no figures for how many voters were able to successfully appeal their designation as felons.

ChoicePoint spokesman Martin Fagan concedes his company's error in passing on the bogus list from Texas. ("I guess that's a little bit embarrassing in light of

the election," he says.) He defends the company's overall performance, however, dismissing the errors in
8,000 names as "a minor glitch—less than one-tenth of
1 percent of the electorate" (though the total equals 15
times Governor George W. Bush's claimed lead over
Gore). But he added that ChoicePoint is responsible only
for turning over its raw list, which is then up to Florida
officials to test and correct.

Last year, DBT Online, with which ChoicePoint would
soon merge, received the unprecedented contract from
the state of Florida to "cleanse" registration lists of ineligible voters—using information gathering and matching
criteria it has refused to disclose, even to local election
officials in Florida.

Atlanta's ChoicePoint, a highflying dot-com specializ-
ing in sales of personal information gleaned from its
database of four billion public and not-so-public records,
has come under fire for misuse of private data from government computers.

In January 2000, the state of Pennsylvania terminated a contract with ChoicePoint after discovering the
firm had sold citizens' personal profiles to unauthorized
individuals.

Fagan says many errors could have been eliminated
by matching the Social Security numbers of ex-felons on
DBT lists to the Social Security numbers on voter registries. However, Florida's counties have Social Security
numbers on only a fraction of their voter records. So
with those two problems—Social Security numbers
missing in both the DBT's records and the counties' records—that fail-safe check simply did not exist.

Florida is the only state in the nation to contract the
first stage of removal of voting rights to a private company. And ChoicePoint has big plans. "Given the outcome of our work in Florida," says Fagan, "and with a
new president in place, we think our services will expand
across the country."

Especially if that president is named "Bush." Choice-Point's board, executive suite and consultant rosters are packed with Republican stars, including former New York Police Commissioner Howard Safir and former ultra-Right congressman Vin Weber, ChoicePoint's Washington lobbyist.

More Votes Fished Out of the Swamps

Following the Salon investigation I was confident that at least 7,000 innocent voters had been removed from voter rolls, half of them Black, and that swung the election. But my investigation was far from over—and I found yet another 2,834 eligible voters targeted for the purge, almost all Democrats.

It was December 10, 2000—Gore was still hanging in there—when I wrote this for British readers:

"A Blacklist Burning for Bush"

The Observer, London, December 10, 2000

Hey, Al, take a look at this. Every time I cut open another alligator, I find the bones of more Gore voters. This week, I was hacking my way through the Florida swampland known as the Office of Secretary of State Katherine Harris and found a couple thousand more names of voters electronically "disappeared" from the vote rolls. About half of those named are African-Americans.

They had the right to vote, but they never made it to the balloting booths.

On November 26, we reported that the Florida Secretary of State's office had, before the election, ordered the elimination of 8,000 Florida voters on the grounds that they had committed felonies in Texas. None had.

For Florida Governor Jeb Bush and his brother, the

Texas blacklist was a mistake made in Heaven. Most of those targeted to have their names "scrubbed" from the voter roles were African-Americans, Hispanics and poor white folk, likely voters for Vice-President Gore. We don't know how many voters lost their citizenship rights before the error was discovered by a few skeptical county officials before ChoicePoint, which has gamely 'fessed-up to the Texas-sized error, produced a new list of 57,700 felons. In May, Harris sent on the new, improved scrub sheets to the county election boards.

Maybe it's my bad attitude, but I thought it worthwhile to check out the new list. Sleuthing around county offices with a team of researchers from Internet newspaper Salon, we discovered that the "correct" list wasn't so correct.

Our ten-county review suggests a minimum 15 percent misidentification rate. That makes another 7,000 innocent people accused of crimes and stripped of their citizenship rights in the run-up to the presidential race, a majority of them Black.

Now our team, diving deeper into the swamps, has discovered yet a third group whose voting rights were stripped. The state's private contractor, ChoicePoint, generated a list of about two thousand names of people who, earlier in their lives, were convicted of felonies in Illinois and Ohio. Like most American states, these two restore citizenship rights to people who have served their time in prison and then remained on the good side of the law.

Florida strips those convicted in its own courts of voting rights for life. But Harris's office concedes, and county officials concur, that the state of Florida has no right to impose this penalty on people who have moved in from these other states. (Only 13 states, most in the Old Confederacy, bar reformed criminals from voting.)

Going deeper into the Harris lists, we find hundreds more convicts from the 37 other states that restored their rights at the end of sentences served. If they have the right to vote, why were these citizens barred from the polls? Harris didn't return my calls. But Alan Dershowitz did. The Harvard law professor, a renowned authority on legal process, said: "What's emerging is a pattern of reducing the total number of voters in Florida, which they know will reduce the Democratic vote."

How could Florida's Republican rulers know how these people would vote?

I put the question to David Bositis, America's top expert on voting demographics.

Once he stopped laughing, he said the way Florida used the lists from a private firm was "a patently obvious technique to discriminate against Black voters." In a darker mood, Bositis, of Washington's Center for Political and Economic Studies, said the sad truth of American justice is that 46 percent of those convicted of felony are African-American. In Florida, a record number of Black folk, over 80 percent of those registered to vote, packed the polling booths on November 7. Behind the curtains, nine out of ten Black people voted for Gore.

Mark Mauer of the Sentencing Project, Washington, pointed out that the "White" half of the purge list would be peopled overwhelmingly by the poor, also solid Democratic voters.

Add it up. The dead-wrong Texas list, the uncorrected "corrected" list, plus the out-of-state ex-con list. By golly, it's enough to swing a presidential election. I bet the busy Harris, simultaneously in charge of both Florida's voter rolls and George Bush's presidential campaign, never thought of that.

Thursday, December 7, 2 a.m. On the other end of the line, heavy breathing, then a torrent of words too fast for me to catch it all. "Vile . . . lying . . . inaccurate . . . pack of nonsense . . . riddled with errors . . ." click! This was not a ChoicePoint whistleblower telling me about the company's notorious list. It was Choice-Point's own media communications representative, Marty Fagan, communicating with me about my "sleazy disgusting journalism" in reporting on it.

Truth is, Fagan was returning my calls. I was curious about this company that chose the president for America's voters.

They have quite a pedigree for this solemn task. The company's Florida subsidiary, Database Technologies (now DBT Online), was founded by one Hank Asher. When US law enforcement agencies alleged that he might have been associated with Bahamian drug dealers—although no charges were brought—the company lost its data management contract with the FBI. Hank and his friends left and so, in Florida's eyes, the past is forgiven.

Thursday, 3 a.m. A new, gentler voice gave me ChoicePoint's upbeat spin. "You say we got over 15 percent wrong—we like to look at that as up to 85 percent right!" That's 7,000 votes-plus—the bulk Democrats, not to mention the thousands on the faulty Texas list. (Gore lost the White House by 537 votes.)

I contacted San Francisco–based expert Mark Swedlund. "It's just fundamental industry practice that you don't roll out the list statewide until you have tested it and tested it again," he said. "Dershowitz is right: they had to know that this jeopardized thousands of people's registrations. And they would also know the [racial] profile of those voters."

"They" is Florida State, not ChoicePoint. Let's not get confused about where the blame lies. Harris's crew lit this database fuse, then acted surprised when it blew up. Swedlund says ChoicePoint had a professional responsibility to tell the state to test the list; ChoicePoint says the state should not have used its "raw" data.

Until Florida privatized its Big Brother powers, laws kept the process out in the open. This year, when one county asked to see ChoicePoint's formulas and back-up for blacklisting voters, they refused—these were commercial secrets.

So we'll never know how America's president was chosen.

Yet Another 40,000 Located. I Repeat: 40,000

Now it gets weird. Salon was showered with praise—by columnists in the *New York Times*, *LA Times*, *Washington Post* and *Cleveland Plain Dealer* (almost to a one Black or Jewish), who were horrified by, as Bob Kuttner of the *Boston Globe* put it, Florida's "lynching by laptop." And still no *news* editor from print or television called me (except the *CBS Evening News* producer who ran away with tail tucked as soon as Governor Jeb denied the allegations).

My work was far from over. On a tip, I began to look into the rights of felons in Florida—those actually convicted.

Every paper in America reported that Florida bars ex-criminals from voting. As soon as every newspaper agrees, you can bet it probably isn't true. Someone *wants* the papers to believe this. It did not take long to discover that what everyone said was true was actually false: *some* ex-cons could vote, thousands in fact. I knew it . . . and so did Governor Jeb Bush. Was Jeb Bush involved?

So I telephoned a clerk in First Brother Jeb's office, who whispered, "Call me tomorrow before official opening hours." And when I did call the next morning, this heroic clerk spent two hours explaining to me, "The courts tell us to do *this*, and we do *that*."

She referred to court orders that I'd gotten wind of, which ordered Governor Bush to stop interfering in the civil rights of ex-cons who had the right to vote.

I asked Jeb's clerk four times, "Are you telling me the governor knowingly violated the law and court orders, excluding eligible voters?"

And four times I got, "The courts tell us to do *this* [allow certain felons to vote] and we do *that* [block them]."

But Salon, despite a mountain of evidence, stalled—then stalled some more.

Resentment of the takeover of the political coverage by an "alien" was getting on the team's nerves. I can't blame them. And it didn't help that Salon was facing bankruptcy, staff were frazzled and it was nearly Christmas.

The remains of the year were lost while I got hold of legal opinions from top lawyers saying Bush's office was wrong; and later the Civil Rights Commission would also say Bush was wrong. But the political clock was ticking and George W. was oozing toward the Oval Office.

E. J. Dionne of the *Washington Post* told me, *"You have to get this story out, Greg, right away!"* Notably, instead of directing me to the *Post*'s newsroom, E. J. told me to call *The Nation*, a kind of refugee center for storm-tossed news reports.

After double-checking and quintuple-checking the facts, the *Nation* held its breath and printed the story of the "third group" of wrongly purged ex-felon voters (numbering nearly three thousand), and a *fourth* group of voters wrongly barred from registering in the first place—*yet another 40,000 of them, almost all Democratic voters.*

It was now February 5, 2001—so President Bush could read this report from the White House:

"Florida's Disappeared Voters"

The Nation, *February 5, 2001*

In Latin America they might have called them *votantes desaparecidos,* "disappeared voters." On November 7, 2000, tens of thousands of eligible Florida voters were wrongly prevented from casting their ballots—some purged from the voters registries and others blocked from registering in the first instance.

Nearly all were Democrats, nearly half of them

African-American. The systematic program that disfranchised these legal voters, directed by the offices of Florida's Governor Jeb Bush and Secretary of State Katherine Harris, was so quiet, subtle and intricate that if not for George W. Bush's 500-vote eyelash margin of victory, certified by Harris, the chance of the purge's discovery would have been vanishingly small.

The group prevented from voting—felons—has few defenders in either party.

It has been well reported that Florida denies its nearly half a million former convicts the right to vote. However, the media have completely missed the fact that Florida's own courts have repeatedly told the governor he may not take away the civil rights of Florida citizens who have committed crimes in other states, served their time and had their rights restored by those states.

People from other states who have arrived in Florida with a felony conviction in their past number "clearly over 50,000 and likely over 100,000," says criminal demographics expert Jeffrey Manza of Northwestern University.

Manza estimates that 80 percent arrive with voting rights intact, which they do not forfeit by relocating to the Sunshine State. In other words, there are no fewer than 40,000 reformed felons eligible to vote in Florida.

Nevertheless, agencies controlled by Harris and Bush ordered county officials to reject attempts by these eligible voters to register, while, publicly, the governor's office states that it adheres to court rulings not to obstruct these ex-offenders in the exercise of their civil rights. Further, with the aid of a Republican-tied database firm, Harris's office used sophisticated computer programs to hunt those felons eligible to vote and ordered them thrown off the voter registries.

David Bositis, the Washington, DC, expert on voter demographics, suggests that the block-and-purge program "must have had a partisan motivation. Why else spend $4 million if they expected no difference in the ultimate vote count?"

White and Hispanic felons, mostly poor, vote almost as solidly Democratic as African-Americans. A recently released University of Minnesota study estimates that, for example, 93 percent of felons of all races favored Bill Clinton in 1996. Whatever Florida's motive for keeping these qualified voters out of the polling booths on November 7, the fact is that they represented several times George W. Bush's margin of victory in the state. Key officials in Bush's and Harris's agencies declined our requests for comment.

The disfranchisement operation began in 1998 under Katherine Harris's predecessor as secretary of state, Sandra Mortham. Mortham was a Republican star, designated by Jeb Bush as his lieutenant governor running mate for his second run for governor. (A financial scandal caused Jeb to replace her with Harris.)

Six months prior to the gubernatorial contest, the Florida legislature passed a "reform" law to eliminate registration of ineligible voters: those who had moved, those who had died and felons without voting rights. The legislation was promoted as a good government response to the fraud-tainted Miami mayoral race of 1997.

But from the beginning, the law and its implementation emitted a partisan fragrance. Passed by the Republican legislature's majority, the new code included an extraordinary provision to turn over the initial creation of "scrub" lists to a private firm. No other state, either before or since, has privatized this key step in the elimination of citizens' civil rights.

In November 1998 the Republican-controlled office of the secretary of state handed the task to the single bidder, Database Technologies, now the DBT Online unit of ChoicePoint Inc. of Atlanta, into which it merged last year.

The elections unit within the office of the secretary of state immediately launched a felon manhunt with a zeal and carelessness that worried local election professionals. *The Nation* has obtained an internal Florida State Association of Supervisors of Elections memo, dated August 1998, which warns Mortham's office that it had wrongly removed eligible voters in a botched rush "to capriciously take names off the rolls." However, to avoid a public row, the supervisors agreed to keep their misgivings within the confines of the bureaucracies in the belief that "entering a public fight with [state officials] would be counterproductive."

That November, Jeb Bush had an unexpectedly easy walk to the governor's mansion, an election victory attributed, ironically, to his endorsement by Black Democratic politicians feuding with their party.

Over the next two years, with Republicans in charge of both the governorship and the secretary of state's office, now under Harris, the felon purge accelerated. In May 2000, using a list provided by DBT, Harris's office ordered counties to purge 8,000 Florida voters who had committed felonies in Texas.

In fact, none of the group was charged with anything more than misdemeanors, a mistake caught but never fully reversed. ChoicePoint DBT and Harris then sent out "corrected" lists, including the names of 437 voters who had indeed committed felonies in Texas. But this list too was in error, since a Texas law enacted in 1997 permits felons to vote after doing their time. In this case there was no attempt at all to correct the error and re-register the 437 voters.

The wrongful purge of the Texas convicts was no one-of-a-kind mishap. The secretary of state's office acknowledges that it also ordered the removal of 714 names of Illinois felons and 990 from Ohio—states that permit the vote even to those on probation or parole. According to Florida's own laws, not a single person arriving in the state from Ohio or Illinois should have been removed.

Altogether, DBT tagged for the scrub nearly 3,000 felons who came from at least eight states that automatically restore voting rights and who therefore arrived in Florida with full citizenship.

A ChoicePoint DBT spokesman said, and the Florida Department of Elections confirms, that Harris's office approved the selection of states from which to obtain records for the felon scrub. As to why the department included states that restore voting rights, Janet Mudrow, Florida's liaison to ChoicePoint DBT, bounced the question to Harris's legal staff. That office has not returned repeated calls.

Pastor Thomas Johnson of Gainesville is minister to House of Hope, a faith-based charity that guides ex-convicts from jail into working life, a program that has won high praise from the pastor's friend, Governor Jeb Bush. Ten years ago, Johnson sold crack cocaine in the streets of New York, got caught, served his time, then discovered God and Florida—where, early last year, he attempted to register to vote. But local election officials refused to accept his registration after he admitted to the decade-old felony conviction from New York. "It knocked me for a loop. It was horrendous," said Johnson of his rejection.

Beverly Hill, the election supervisor of Alachua County, where Johnson attempted to register, said that she used to allow ex-felons like Johnson to vote.

Under Governor Bush, that changed. "Recently, the [Governor's Office of Executive] Clemency people told us something different," she said. "They told us that they essentially can't vote."

Both Alachua's refusal to allow Johnson to vote and the governor's directive underlying that refusal are notable for their timing—coming after two court rulings that ordered the secretary of state and governor to recognize the civil rights of felons arriving from other states. In the first of these decisions, *Schlenther v. Florida Department of State,* issued in June 1998, Florida's Court of Appeal ruled unanimously that Florida could not require a man convicted in Connecticut twenty-five years earlier "to ask [Florida] to restore his civil rights. They were never lost here." Connecticut, like most states, automatically restores felons' civil rights at the end of their sentence, and therefore "he arrived as any other citizen, with full rights of citizenship."

The *Schlenther* decision was much of the talk at a summer 1998 meeting of county election officials in Orlando. So it was all the more surprising to Chuck Smith, a statistician with Hillsborough County, that Harris's elections division chief Clayton Roberts exhorted local officials at the Orlando meeting to purge all out-of-state felons identified by DBT. Hillsborough was so concerned about this order, which appeared to fly in the face of the court edict, that the county's elections office demanded that the state put that position in writing—a request duly granted.

The Nation has obtained the text of the response to Hillsborough. The letter, from the Governor's Office of Executive Clemency, dated September 18, 2000, arrived only seven weeks before the presidential election. It orders the county to tell ex-felons trying to register that even if they entered Florida with civil rights restored by another state's law, they will still be "required to make application for restoration of civil rights in the state of Florida," that is, ask Governor Bush for clemency—the very requirement banned by the courts. The state's directive was all the more surprising in light of a second ruling, issued in December 1999 by another Florida court, in which a Florida district court judge expressed his ill-disguised exasperation with the governor's administration for ignoring the prior edict in *Schlenther.*

Voting rights attorneys who reviewed the cases for

The Nation explained that the courts relied on both Florida statute and the "full faith and credit" clause of the U.S. Constitution, which requires every state to accept the legal rulings of other states. "The court has been pretty clear on what the governor can't do," says Bruce Gear, assistant general counsel for the NAACP. And what Governor Bush can't do is demand that a citizen arriving in Florida ask him for clemency to restore a right to vote that the citizen already has.

Strangely enough, the governor's office does not disagree. While Harris, Bush and a half dozen of their political appointees have not returned our calls, Tawanna Hayes, who processes the requests for clemency in the governor's office, states unequivocally that "we do not have the right to suspend or restore rights where those rights have been restored in another state." Hayes even keeps a copy of the two court decisions near her desk and quotes from them at length. So, why have the governor and secretary of state ordered these people purged from the rolls or barred from registering? Hayes directed us to Greg Munson, Governor Bush's assistant general counsel and clemency aide.

Munson has not responded to our detailed request for an explanation.

A letter dated August 10, 2000, from Harris's office to Bush's office, obtained under Florida's Freedom of Information Act, indicates that the chief of the Florida State Association of Supervisors of Elections also questioned Harris's office about the purge of ex-cons whose rights had been restored automatically by other states. The supervisors' group received the same response as Hillsborough: strike them from the voter rolls and, if they complain, make them ask Bush for clemency.

While almost all county supervisors buckled, Carol Griffin did not. Griffin, Washington County's elections chief, concluded that running legal voters through Jeb

Bush's clemency maze would violate a 1993 federal law, the National Voter Registration Act, which was designed to remove impediments to the exercise of civil rights. The law, known as "motor voter," is credited with helping to register 7 million new voters. Griffin quotes from the Florida section of the new, NVRA-certified registration form, which says: "I affirm I am not a convicted felon, or if I am, my rights relating to voting have been restored." "That's the law," says the adamant Griffin, "and I have no right stopping anyone registering who truthfully signs that statement. Once you check that box there's no discussion." Griffin's county refused to implement the scrub, and the state appears reluctant to challenge its action.

But when Pastor Johnson attempted to register in Alachua County, clerks refused and instead handed him a fifteen-page clemency request form. The outraged minister found the offer a demeaning Catch-22. "How can I ask the governor for a right I already have?" he says, echoing, albeit unknowingly, the words of the Florida courts.

Had Johnson relented and chosen to seek clemency, he would have faced a procedure that is, admits the clemency office's Hayes, "sometimes worse than breaking a leg." For New Yorkers like Johnson, she says, "I'm telling you it's a bear." She says officials in New York, which restores civil rights automatically, are perplexed by requests from Florida for nonexistent papers declaring the individual's rights restored. Without the phantom clemency orders, the applicant must hunt up old court records and begin a complex process lasting from four months to two years, sometimes involving quasi-judicial hearings, the outcome of which depends on Jeb Bush's disposition.

Little wonder that out of tens of thousands of out-of-state felons, only a hardy couple of hundred attempted to run this bureaucratic obstacle course before the election. (Bush can be compassionate: he granted clemency

to Charles Colson for his crimes as a Watergate con-
spirator, giving Florida resident Colson the right to vote
in the presidential election.)

How did the governor's game play at the ballot box?
Jeb Bush's operation denied over 50,000 citizens their
right to vote. Given that 80 percent of registered voters
actually cast ballots in the presidential election, at least
40,000 votes were lost. By whom? As 90 percent or
more of this targeted group, out-of-state ex-cons, votes
Democratic, *we can confidently state that this little twist
in the voter purge cost Al Gore a good 30,000 votes.*
Was Florida's corrupted felon-voter hunt the work of
cozy collusion between Jeb Bush and Harris, the
president-elect's brother and state campaign chief, re-
spectively? It is unlikely we will ever discover the motives
driving the voter purge, but we can see the consequences. Three decades ago, Governor George Wallace
stood in a schoolhouse door and thundered, "Segregation now! Segregation tomorrow! Segregation forever!"
but failed to block entry to African-Americans. Governor
Jeb Bush's resistance to court rulings, conducted at
whisper level with high-tech assistance, has been far
more effective at blocking voters of color from the
polling station door. Deliberate or accidental, the error-
ridden computer purge and illegal clemency obstacle
course function, like the poll tax and literacy test of the
Jim Crow era, to take the vote away from citizens who
are Black, poor and, not coincidentally, almost all Democrats. No guesswork there: Florida is one of the few
states to include both party and race on registration files.

Pastor Johnson, an African-American wrongfully
stripped of his vote, refuses to think ill of the governor
or his motives. He prefers to see a dark comedy of bureaucratic errors: "The buffoonery of this state has cost
us a president." If this is buffoonery, then Harris and the
Bushes are wise fools indeed.

Part III: FROM PLANNING TO EXECUTION TO INAUGURATION: What They Knew, and When They Knew It

And that *Nation* story would be the last investigative report on the matter in the U.S. press for a year. An editor at one of the biggest newspapers in the United States told me, "The committee has decided not to continue printing stories about the presidential vote. We think it's over. We don't want to look partisan."

I thought, what "committee"? And I picked up that I wasn't supposed to ask.

America had, as Katherine Harris requested, "moved on."

But I hadn't.

It was now February, and here's what we knew so far. The *Observer*/Salon stories told us that Harris's elections office had wrongly ordered over 50,000 voters stripped from the rolls, thousands of them wrongly. From the *Nation* report we knew that Governor Bush's office had barred the registration of another 40,000—Democrats by a wide margin. That was the election.

Maybe Governor Bush had simply misread the court orders, and maybe Harris's office had no idea the purge list was wildly wrong; maybe the computer firm DBT simply flubbed the algorithms. One man's mistake is another man's inauguration. Tough, but no criminal intent.

A loose clue still nagged me. As always, it was the money. When I looked into state files, I discovered that ChoicePoint's DBT was not the first contractor on the job. In 1998, this first firm, Professional Service Inc., charged $5,700 for the job. A year later, the Florida Department of Elections terminated their contract, then gave the job to DBT for a first-year fee of $2,317,800— no bidding! Then I found out that indeed there had been an open bid for the job. However, when the offers were unsealed, DBT's was the *costliest*—several thousand percent over competitors'. The state ignored the bids and grabbed for DBT, in the end signing a deal for *more* than DBT's original astronomical bid. Hmm.

When I contacted database industry experts about the fee paid DBT by Florida their eyes popped out—*"Wow!" "Jeez!" "Scandalous!"* The charge of twenty-seven cents per record was easily *ten times* the industry norm.

Something else bothered me: It was the weird glee, the beaming self-congratulations, from the ChoicePoint public-relations man over my *Salon* report that 15 percent of the names on his purge list were wrong (even though the error turned around an election). To ChoicePoint, my story was good news: In effect, they said, I reported their list was "85 percent correct." But was it?

The Killer Stats

The list was 85 percent "accurate," said DBT ChoicePoint's PR man, because they used Social Security numbers. That was convincing—until I checked the felon scrub lists themselves and *almost none* of them listed a voter's Social Security number. Floridians, until recently, did not have to provide their Social Security number when registering to vote.

Four days after I ran my first report in England, on November 30, 2000, the Bloomberg business news wire interviewed Marty Fagan of ChoicePoint, one of the PR men who'd spoken to me. Based on the big "success" of its computer purge in Florida, ChoicePoint planned to sell its voter-purge operation to every state in the Union. This could become a billion-dollar business.

Fagan crowed to Bloomberg about the accuracy of Choice-Point's lists. The company, he said, used 1,200 public databases to cross-check "a very accurate picture of an individual," including a history of addresses and financial assets.

That was impressive. And indeed, every database expert told me (including DBT's vice president), if you want 85 percent accuracy or better, you will need at least these three things: Social Security numbers, address history and a check against other databases. But over the ensuing weeks and months I discovered:

- ChoicePoint used virtually *no* Social Security numbers for the Florida felon purge;
- of its 1,200 databases with which to "check the accuracy of the data," ChoicePoint used exactly *none* for cross-checking;
- as to the necessary verification of address history of the 66,000 named "potential felons," ChoicePoint performed this check in exactly *zero* cases.

There was, then, not a chance in hell that the list was "85 percent correct."

One county, Leon (Tallahassee), carried out the purge as the law required. But with doubts in the minds of their in-house experts, the county did the hard work of checking each name, one by one, to verify independently that the 694 named felons in Tallahassee were, in fact, ineligible voters. They could verify only 34 names—a 95 percent error rate. *That is killer information.* In another life, decades ago, I taught "Collection and Use of Economic and Statistical Data" at Indiana University. Here's a quicky statistics lesson:

The statewide list of felons is "homogeneous" as to its accuracy. Leon County provides us with a sample large enough to give us a "confidence interval" of 4.87 at a "confidence level" of 99 percent. Are you following me, class? In other words, we can be 99 percent certain that *at least 90.2 percent of the names on the Florida list are not felons—52,000 wrongly tagged for removal.*

Okay, you want to argue and say not everyone tagged was actually removed. Maybe 52,000 did not have their vote swiped, but 42,000 or 22,000. Al Gore "lost" by 537 votes.

Now I was confident the list was junk—it had to be, because ChoicePoint did not use the most basic tools of verification. But why didn't they? Is ChoicePoint incompetent, hasn't a clue of the methodology for verifying its output? That's unlikely—this is the company hired by the FBI for manhunts, and the FBI doesn't pay for 90.2 percent wrong.

And why would ChoicePoint lie about it? Their list was bogus and they had to know it. Did someone *want* it wrong? Could someone, say, want to swing an election with this poisoned list? That's when I went back to a stack of documents from inside Harris's office—and to one sheet in particular, marked, "DBT CONFIDENTIAL AND TRADE SECRET."

"When the going gets weird," Hunter Thompson advises journalists, "the weird turn pro." In London, I showed this "CONFIDENTIAL" sheet to the ultimate pro, Meirion Jones, producer with BBC Television's *Newsnight*. He said, "How soon can you get on a plane to Florida?"

Mr. Roberts Does a Runner

Our BBC *Newsnight* broadcast began with a country-and-western twang off the rental car radio:

"After hundreds of lies . . . fake alibis . . ."

Newsnight's camera followed me up to the eighteenth floor of the Florida Capitol Building in Tallahassee for my meeting with Clayton Roberts, the squat, bull-necked director of Florida's Division of Elections.

Roberts, who works directly under Secretary of State Katherine Harris, had agreed to chat with me on film. We sat on the reception sofa outside his office. His eyes began to shift, then narrowed as he read the heading of the paper on the sofa next to me: "CONFIDENTIAL."

He certainly knew what I had when I picked up the paper and asked him if the state had checked whether DBT (the ChoicePoint company) had verified the accuracy of a single name on the purge list before they paid the company millions.

"No, I didn't ask DBT. . . ," Roberts sputtered, falling over a few half-started sentences—then ripped off his lapel microphone, jumped up, charged over the camera wires and slammed his office

Fig. 1.2. Clayton Roberts, Katherine Harris's elections division chief, runs for cover, caught on video by my BBC Television crew and by filmmaker Danny Schechter. These shots are taken from his film *Counting on Democracy*. (© 2001 Globalvision)

door on me and the camera crew giving chase. We were swiftly escorted out of the building by very polite and very large state troopers (figure 1.2).

Before he went into hiding and called the Smokies, Roberts whipped around and pointed an angry finger at the lens, saying, "Please turn off that camera!" Which we did—BBC rules. But he didn't add, "and turn off the microphone," so our lawyers ruled we could include his parting shot, "You know if y'all want to hang this on me that's fine." I will. Though not him alone. By "this" he meant the evidence in the document, which I was trying to read out to him on the run.[4]

What was so terrifying to this Republican honcho? The "CONFIDENTIAL" page (figure 1.3), obviously not meant to see the light of day, said that DBT would be paid $2.3 million for their lists and "manual verification using telephone calls and statistical sampling." No wonder Roberts did a runner. He and Harris had testified to the U.S. Civil Rights Commission—under oath—that verification of the voter purge list was left completely up to the county elections supervisors, not to the state or the contractor, Choice-Point DBT.

It was the requirement to verify the accuracy of the purge list that justified ChoicePoint's selection for the job as well as their astonishingly high fee. Good evening, Mr. Smith. Are you the same Mr. John Smith that served hard time in New York in 1991? Expensive though that is to repeat thousands of times, it is necessary when civil rights are at stake. Yet DBT seemed to have found a way to cut the cost of this procedure: not doing it. There is no record of

---

[4]On the Internet, a self-proclaimed video expert on a pro-Bush Web site wrote that I had faked the Roberts film, "unethical as you can get," because we clearly must have hidden away "the two-hour interview that preceded" Roberts's running away—fantasy footage that would have made Roberts look honest. Not so. You can watch the film of the Roberts run for yourself at www.news.bbc.co.uk/olmedia/cta/progs/newsnight/palast.ram.

EXHIBIT A

(DBT CONFIDENTIAL AND TRADE SECRET INFORMATION)

Pricing Structure:

1. Phases I-IV (1998-1999)* $2,197,800
   (includes manual verification using
   telephone calls and statistical sampling)   120,000

                                                 Total $2,317,800

   * Based on the processing of 8,140,000 CVF Records @ $.27/record

2. Year Two (Optional Renewal) (1999-2000) $1,024,000
   (includes manual verification using
   telephone calls and statistical sampling)

3. Year Three (Optional Renewal) (2000-2001) $1,024,000
   (includes manual verification using
   telephone calls and statistical sampling)

Fig. 1.3. Contract secrets. This is a photocopy of a page from the contract that won the election for George W. Bush—between the State of Florida and DBT Online to identify "felon" voters to remove from registration rolls. DBT was paid $2,317,800 for the first year's work to include "manual verification using telephone calls." The work was paid for but not done—with the approval of the state. Why?

DBT having made extensive verification calls. It is difficult for DBT to squirm out of this one. If they had conducted manual verification as contracted, you'd think they would have noticed that every single record on the Texas felon list was wrong.

I took my camera crew to DBT's Boca Raton, Florida, office complex to confront them about the verification calls, but they barred our entry. On our return to London, we received a call from one of their executives explaining that "manual verification by telephone" did not "require us to actually make telephone calls" to anyone on the list. Oh, I see.

Based on this new evidence, BBC broadcast that the faux

felon purge and related voting games cost Al Gore at least 22,000 votes in Florida—forty times Bush's margin of victory as certified by Harris. Quibble with that estimate, tweak it as you will, we now knew the rightful winner of the election. Or at least the *British* public knew.

New Unreported Evidence: Wrong Is Good, Right Is Bad

I now began to understand the brilliant deviltry of the purge game. It did not matter if, on Day One of the purge process, Republicans had some grand plan, some elaborate conspiracy, to eliminate the vote of African-American innocents. Rather, document after document suggested that, once the operatives saw the demographics of the raw lists—tens of thousands of names of mostly Democratic voters—they moved heaven and earth to prevent its reduction. A list of 57,000 voters, mostly Black, erased with the flick of a switch was just fine with Mr. Roberts and crew. Make verification phone calls? Have statisticians check the findings? Correct the methods? Why, that would only cut the list . . . by 90 percent at least. Why should a Republican administration pay for *that?*

It's not "conspiracy," but opportunism. The Department of Elections Republicans began to act like a bank customer who accidentally receives a million-dollar deposit that is not theirs: To fail to correct the error, to actively conceal the error, is theft in any court. Only here the crime was far bigger: the theft of our democracy.

Opportunism does not require planning and conspiracy; it does require a cover-up. In any investigation, I try to imagine myself in the perps' shoes. If I had a magic list falsely accusing my opponents' voters of crime, how would I prevent the discovery that it is bogus? First, don't dare verify the list; not one phone call. Second, don't correct the methodology: Ignore every warning about crap inputs, crap methods, crap results. And third, *for God's sake, don't allow any independent statistician near it.*

The Case of the Missing Statistician

Florida's contract with DBT states:

> During the verification phase, DBT shall use academically-based and widely utilized statistical formulas to determine the exact number of records necessary to represent a valid cross-section [sample] of the processed files. DBT shall consult a professional statistician. . . . Upon the return of the processed data, DBT shall supply the formulas and mathematical calculations and identify the professional statistician used during the verification process.

The 8,000-name Texas list had a 100 percent error rate—which seemed a wee bit high to me. What kind of "academically-based formula" was used to verify the accuracy of these data? Who was the consulting "professional statistician"? Inscrutably silent on whether he or she exists, ChoicePoint DBT referred me back to Clay Roberts. His minions could not name this Man of Mystery either, although the contract requires DBT to provide evidence of the statistician's hiring and analysis. Neither the name nor the calculations were filed as required.

Eventually, I found this: a letter dated March 22, 1999, from DBT to the state. "Our" statistician, said the one-page note, "certified" their list as 99.9 percent "accurate"! I can imagine why "our" statistician would remain nameless: 99.9 percent accurate but almost every name an eligible voter. No backup. *Nada*.

How convenient. No independent technician, no expert to see things go rotten, no one to blow the whistle.

Evidence of Innocence: "Don't Need"

I turned back to the question of Florida hiring DBT for $2.3 million, booting the company charging $5,700. When questioned, George Bruder, ChoicePoint DBT's senior vice president, said, "a little birdie" told him to enter that astonishing bid. What else did the little birdie tell him?

What happened to the 1,200 databases, the millions and millions of records that DBT used in its Carl Saganesque sales pitch to the state? In fact, the state paid for this vital cross-check—or at least DBT's bid said that for their two-million-dollar fee, they would use artificial intelligence for "cross-referencing linked databases . . . simultaneously searching hundred of data sources, conducting millions of data comparisons, compiling related data for matching and integration."

In all, they had *four billion* records to check against. Under "Offer and Bid" it read:

DBT will process total combined records from:

8,250,000 Criminal Conviction Records
69,000,000 Florida Property Records
62,000,000 National Change of Address Records
12,590,470 Florida Driver License Records. . . .

And so on. The phone calls, the massive data crunching, it all justified the big payoff to DBT and scared away competitors who could not match DBT's database firepower. DBT's offer promised "273,318,667 total records to be processed." But they didn't do it.

Once the contract was nailed, it seems a little birdie in the state told DBT not to bother with all that expensive computing work. In the state files, on the DBT bid, I found a handwritten notation, *"don't need,"* next to the listing of verification databases (the 62 million address histories, etc.), though this work was included in the price.

Each pass would have cut the list by thousands, thereby letting thousands more Democrats vote. So when the state said, "Don't need," the underlying motive was, "Don't *want*."

*   *   *

Take a look at the scrub list itself, figure 1.4. I picked a random piece of the scrub sheet for a magazine illustration,[5] then took a careful look at each name. And, unlike DBT and the state, I dialed the phone.

Besides Thomas Cooper, whose crime is still in the future, there's Johnny Jackson Jr., thirty-two years of age. He was on the purge list because his name *partially* matched that of a man convicted in Texas, John Fitzgerald Jackson. Johnny Jr.'s never been to Texas, and his mama swears to me he never had the middle name Fitzgerald. Neither is there any evidence that John Fitzgerald Jackson, the felon, ever left Texas—or ever left his jail cell. There are 638 John and Johnny Jacksons (and permutations thereof) in the Florida phone book. How did the state know they had the right Johnny? They didn't; and it looks like they didn't *want* to know. Using the address history database, as the state was promised, would have saved Jackson, a Black man, his right to vote.

Then there's Wallace McDonald, age sixty-four. Wallace tells me how in 1959 he fell asleep on a bus-stop bench and was busted. Even for a Black man in then-segregated Florida, that was a misdemeanor, not a felony. He never lost his right to vote; and the state agrees he was wrongly "scrubbed." Had DBT checked the databases, as promised, they would not have named Wallace.

Willie Dixon is on the list, too. The Reverend Dixon was convicted decades ago, and has received *full executive clemency*. That would have been an easy one to catch if the state had checked and verified the clemency records as per the contract.

Mismatches Made in Heaven

Read down the list and mismatches jump out at you. Note they have taken voting rights away from Randall Higginbotham, age

---

[5]*Harper's* magazine, March 2002.

1	Source	Method	Voter Full Name	Voter DOB		Voter Race	Felon State	Felon Full Name	Felon DOB		Convicted	n Race
346	DOE	NAM	SMITH , JC	5/25/1978	M	BLA	FL	SMITH , JC	5/25/1978	M	8/12/1997	BLA
347	DOE	SSB	NETTLES , MARY ANN	11/14/1959	F	BLA	FL	DOE , JANE	11/14/1959	F	7/11/1996	WHI
348	DOE	NAM	STEWART , ROBERT N	8/19/1948	M	WHI	FL	STEWART , ROBERT NORMAN	8/19/1948	M	2/5/1987	WHI
349	DOE	NAM	SEWELL , IMOGENE	8/14/1951	F	BLA	FL	SEWELL , IMOGENE BREWTON	8/14/1951	F	7/18/1988	BLA
350	DOE	NAM	WOODBERRY , MARIE	4/8/1908	F	BLA	FL	WOODBERRY , MARIE	4/8/1908	F		BLA
351	DBT	NAM	REEDER , WILLIAM T	9/10/1927	M	WHI	SC	REEDER , WILLIAM THOMAS	9/10/1927	M		WHI
352	DOE	NAM	FAULK , JOSEPH CURTIS	9/29/1930	M	WHI	FL	FAULK , JOSEPH CURTIS	9/29/1930	M		WHI
353	DOE	SDL	HIGGINBOTHAM , RANDALL J	8/28/1960	M	WHI	FL	HIGGINBOTHAM , SEAN DAVID	6/16/1971	M	12/22/1994	WHI
354	DBT	NAM	JACKSON JR, JOHNNY	8/8/1969	M	BLA	TX	JACKSON , JOHN FITZGERALD	8/8/1969	M		BLA
355	DOE	NSD	WOODS , LAWRENCE LAMAR	3/31/1949	M	WHI	FL	WOODS , CLARENCE L	3/31/1949	M	2/3/1992	WHI
356	DOE	NAM	ROBERTS , DUSTY EDWARD	11/21/1954	M	WHI	FL	ROBERTS , DUSTY EDWARD	11/21/1954	M	10/12/1987	WHI
357	DBT	NAM	BUTLER JR, DAVID RUSSELL	9/17/1959	M	WHI	IL	BUTLER , DAVID	9/17/1959			
358	DBT	NAM	DIXON JR, WILLIE G	10/3/1931	M	BLA	FL	DIXON , WILLIAM G	10/3/1931	M	11/20/1981	WHI
359	DOE	NAM	THOMPSON , DOYLE TRAVIS	3/23/1962	M	WHI	FL	THOMPSON , DOYLE TRAVIS	3/23/1962	M	8/8/1983	WHI
360	DOE	NAM	ALDRIDGE , LOYAL EDDIE	4/26/1953	M	BLA	FL	ALDRIDGE , LOYAL EDDIE	4/26/1953	M	7/18/1988	BLA
361	DBT	NAM	COOPER , THOMAS ALVIN	9/5/1973	M	WHI	OH	COOPER , THOMAS	9/5/1973	M	1/30/2007	BLA
362	DOE	NAM	RAMOS , MIGUEL ANGEL	12/19/1956	M	WHI	FL	RAMOS , MIGUEL	12/19/1956	M	5/30/1997	WHI
363	DOE	NAM	HALL , ARTHUR LEE	6/3/1943	M	BLA	FL	HALL , ARTHUR LEE	6/3/1943	M	5/7/1970	BLA
364	DOE	NAM	BARNES , SHANDA L	12/26/1973	F	BLA	FL	BARNES , SHANDA LATAIN	12/26/1973	F	6/3/1997	BLA
365	DOE	NAM	MCDONALD , WALLACE	2/11/1937	M	BLA	FL	MCDONALD , WALLACE	2/11/1937	M	6/12/1959	BLA
366	DOE	NAM	MARTIN , MARY A	2/17/1971	F	WHI	FL	MARTIN , MARY A	2/17/1971	F	11/2/1993	WHI
367	DOE	NAM	WILLIAMS JR, FRANK DEE	5/13/1975	M	BLA	FL	WILLIAMS , FRANK DEE	5/13/1975	M	7/26/1999	BLA
368	DBT	NAM	RODRIGUEZ , MICHAEL A	6/23/1976	M	UNK	NJ	RODRIGUEZ , MICHAEL	6/23/1976	M	6/29/1998	

Fig. 1.4. Scrub list. Florida "felon" scrub list. This is one screen page from the computer "scrub" list of thousands tagged for removal from voter registration rolls.

forty-one, because of the crimes of Sean Higginbotham, age thirty. The list is lousy with suspicious matches: pairing voter David Russell Butler Jr. of Florida to convict David Butler of Ohio. No question why David R. registered with his full name and appended the Junior. There are sixty-six other David Butlers listed in the Florida phone book and they must get one another's mail all the time. It is disturbingly improbable that they purged the right Butler. That should have been a no-brainer to correct.

The wrong Butlers, Smiths and Jacksons remained on the list because of DBT's "matching logic" and "matching criteria." Credit card companies can require thirty-five matches for verification before they will issue you plastic. The State of Florida was content with a partial match of four: names (the first four letters were good enough), date of birth, gender and race. Not even the address or state mattered in the mad dash to maximize the number of citizens stripped of their civil rights.

Rather than add matching criteria to verify the list, the state told DBT to *remove* criteria. For example, Messrs. Butler and Jackson so carefully added "Jr." to their official names to avoid such confusion. Tough luck. I found an internal mail in Roberts's office, dated June 14, 2000, in which clerks fretted about what they called "tweaked" data, allowing "matches" between Edward and Edwin (and Edwina!); deliberately ignoring middle names and initials; and skipping the "Jr." and "Sr." suffixes.

I met with a Willie D. Whiting of Tallahassee. The Reverend Whiting confessed he had a speeding ticket a decade ago, but doubted that should cost him his right to vote. But there he was: on the purge list, matched with Willie J. Whiting—no "Jr."—whose birthday was two days different from Willie D.'s.

Our experts looked at the paltry number of match criteria and were horrified. One, Mark Hull, told me the state and Choice-Point could have chosen criteria that would have brought down the number of "false positives" to less than a fragment of 1 percent. He said it made him ill to learn what the company had agreed to do. These revelations were especially upsetting to him; he had been the senior programmer for CDB Infotek, a Choice-Point company.

"Wanted More Names Than We Can Verify . . ."

DBT's "expertise" in obtaining data justified their hiring. But it was a con. Janet Mudrow, the state's liaison with DBT, confessed to me that DBT merely downloaded lists from eleven states that make the data available publicly, such as Texas. Any high school kid with a Mac and a credit card could have grabbed the names off the Internet. And that was okay with Florida, even though eight of those states do not take away an ex-felon's voting rights, and therefore should not have been used at all.

DBT's negligence in handing Florida the bogus Texas list cost

Florida and its counties a pretty penny when they tried to reverse that error. Yet Mudrow, in Harris's office, says the state neither demanded reimbursement nor sought any penalty as permitted under the contract. In fact, the state awarded DBT *another* contract renewal, bringing total fees to over $4 million.

Why didn't the state complain, sue, or withhold payment?[6] Following my first reports, when the stats hit the fan, ChoicePoint DBT agreed to a one-year extension of their contract without charge. But why didn't the watchdog bark?

One can only conclude that Harris's office paid an awful lot of money for either (a) failed, incomplete, incompetent, costly, disastrous work that stripped innocent citizens of their rights, or (b) services performed exactly as planned.

Was DBT paid to get it wrong? Every single failure—to verify by phone, to sample and test, to cross-check against other databases—worked in one direction: to increase the number of falsely accused voters, half of them Black.

How could ChoicePoint, such an expert outfit, do such a horrendous job, without complaint from their client? You'd think their client, the state, *ordered* them to get it wrong.

They did. Just before we went on air in February 2000, ChoicePoint vice president James Lee called us at the BBC's London studios with the first hint that the state of Florida *instructed* the company to give them the names of innocents. The state, he said, "wanted there to be more names than were actually verified as being a convicted felon." What an extraordinary statement.

When ChoicePoint saw the story with their own words— "more names than were actually verified"—printed across the

---

[6]Florida Attorney General Bob Butterworth told me our evidence suggested contractor fraud against the state. I asked him if, as chief law enforcement officer for the state, he'd be investigating. Butterworth explained that Florida is unique in limiting his powers. The investigation would have to be conducted by the secretary of state, Ms. Harris.

screen, the company went ballistic. They demanded in writing to my network chiefs that we retract it all. The BBC wouldn't back down an inch.

McKinney Nails the Confession

Following the February 15, 2001, broadcast, only one member of the U.S. Congress called BBC to ask for our evidence: Congress-woman Cynthia McKinney. This lady is trouble, the kind of trouble I like. A Black single mom and doctoral candidate at Princeton's Fletcher School of Diplomacy, she is always asking questions. And in the world of politics, that makes her dangerous—"radioactive," as a staffer from the Democratic National Committee describes her. Unusual for a member of Congress, she reads the detailed memos and evidence herself, not delegating the research to underlings. She knows her stuff.

McKinney represented Atlanta, ChoicePoint headquarters. She demanded their executives appear before a special hearing. As usual, she had some questions she wanted answered, in public. So I handed McKinney—and ChoicePoint—the evidence. Choice-Point was shoveling a lot of nonsense my way, but I figured the company might hesitate about shucking and jiving a member of the U.S. Congress.

On April 17 ChoicePoint VP James Lee opened his testimony before the McKinney panel with notice that, despite its prior boast, the firm was getting out of the voter purge business. Then the company man, in highly technical, guarded language, effectively confessed to the whole game. Lee fingered the state.

Lee said that, for example, the state had given DBT the truly insane directive to add to the purge list people who matched 90 percent of a last name—if Anderson committed a crime, Andersen lost his vote. DBT objected, knowing this would sweep in a huge number of innocents. The state then went further and ordered DBT to shift to an *80 percent* match. It was programmed-in inaccuracy. Names were reversed—felon Thomas Clarence could knock out the vote of Clarence Thomas. He confirmed that middle initials were skipped, "Jr." and "Sr." suffixes dropped. Then, nicknames and aliases were added to puff up the list. "DBT told state officials," testified Lee, "that the rules for creating the [purge] list would mean a significant number of people who were not deceased, not registered in more than one county or *not a felon* would be included on the list. Likewise, DBT made suggestions to reduce the numbers of eligible voters included on the list."

Correct the list? Remove those "not a felon"? The state, says DBT, told the company, *Forget about it.*

Hunting the Black Voter—the June 9 Letter

Florida was *hunting* for innocents and, it seems, the Blacker the better. To swing an election, there would be no point in knocking off thousands of legitimate voters if they were caught randomly—that would not affect the election's outcome. The key was color. And here's where the computer game got intensely sophisticated. How could it be that some 54 percent of the list were Black? There is no denying that half of America's felons are African Americans, but how could it be that the *innocent* people on the list were mostly Blacks as well?

In November, ChoicePoint's PR men jumped up and down insisting in calls to me that "race was not part of the search criteria." The company repeated this denial in press releases after they were sued by the NAACP for participating in a racist conspiracy against citizens' civil rights. DBT complained to my producers and to federal investigators: Race was not a search criterion, period! Then, I obtained a letter dated June 9, 2000, signed by Choice-Point DBT's Vice President Bruder written to all county elections supervisors explaining their method:

"The information used for the matching process included first, middle, and last name; date of birth; *race;* and gender; but not Social Security Number."

They had *not* lied to me. Read closely. They used race as a *match* criterion, not a *search* criterion. The company used this confusion between "match" and "search" criteria to try to pull the BBC off the track. They tried to slide the race question by the U.S. Civil Rights Commission. However, on the morning of February 16, the day after our broadcast, I faxed to the commission the June 9 letter. Later that day, the commission questioned Bruder.

COMMISSION: Was race or party affiliation matching criterion in compiling that list?

BRUDER: [under oath] No. . . .

COMMISSION: [June 9 letter read into record.] Did you write this letter? It has your signature on it.

BRUDER: Can I see it, please?

COMMISSION: So, you misinformed the Florida supervisors of elections that race would be used as a matching criterion?

BRUDER: Yes.

Wise answer, Mr. Bruder. Misleading elections officials is not a crime; perjury would be. He pleaded confusion. So if race was not a match criterion, how did Black people get matched to felons? I was perplexed by this until I looked again at the decoded scrub sheets: There were columns for *felon race* and *voter race.* How could DBT deny that? (See figure 1.4, Scrub List.) However, DBT had simply *identified* race for every real felon, and the secretary of state provided the race of the voters. It was left to the county supervisors to finish the Jim Crow operation: They would accept racial matches as "proof" that the right person was named. Therefore, a Black felon named Willie Whiting wiped out the registration of an innocent Willie Whiting (Black) but not the rights of an innocent Will Whiting (white).

The Pre-clearance Deception

The U.S. Voting Rights Act of 1965 assumes something very unkind about Florida, that the Old South state will twist the process to stop African Americans from voting. Florida cannot be trusted to change voting procedures on its own. So, with the handful of other states named in the act, Florida must "pre-clear" voting operations changes with the U.S. Justice Department. The state must certify any new voter registration process will have no "disparate impact" on Black voters.

How in the world did Florida zing this racially bent felon purge scheme past the Feds? In 1998, the Justice Department smelled something rotten and asked a few questions, including, Why did Florida need to hire an outside contractor?

On July 21, 1998, a lowly state legislative aide drafted a soothing memorandum of law to the Justice Department, dismissing the purge operation as mere administrative reform. The aide—Clayton Roberts—worked with a state senator—Katherine Harris. In 1998 they sowed; in 2000 they reaped.[7]

Voting Machine Apartheid

Mary Frances Berry, chairperson of the U.S. Civil Rights Commission, said the real horror of the 2000 election was not the vote count that so transfixed our media, but what she calls "the no-count"—the means of keeping citizens from voting or having their ballots voided.

---

[7]The intensely complex research unraveling Florida's deceptive moves to obtain pre-clearance was conducted by Paul Lukasiak.

And Florida used more than the voter purge in their "no-count" bag of tricks. In February 2001, I found a doozy.

This fact caught my attention: In a presidential race decided by 537 votes, Florida simply *did not count* 179,855 ballots. And whether your vote counted depended a lot on your color. In Leon (Tallahassee), a primarily white county, only 1 in 500 ballots was uncounted, "spoiled," as they say in the vote biz, that is, voided for one reason or another. In neighboring Gadsden, with a high population of Black voters, *1 in 8 ballots* was never counted.

Here's the breakdown of ballots not counted in Florida's Blackest and whitest counties:

BLACK COUNTIES		
Population 25+% African American		
	Black residents	Ballots not counted
Gadsden	52%	12%
Madison	42%	7%
Hamilton	39%	9%
Jackson	26%	7%
WHITE COUNTIES		
Fewer than 5% African American		
Citrus	2%	1%
Pasco	2%	3%
Santa Rosa	4%	1%
Sarasota	4%	2%

Detect a pattern?

How could this happen? Exactly how do votes "spoil"? And why do Black votes spoil so easily?

I found the answer in the Tallahassee office of Leon County Supervisor of Elections Ion Sancho. Like many other counties, Sancho's used paper ballots. These ballots are read by machine, "optically scanned." He had set up a voting machine to demonstrate its use. I tried it out, voting for Pat Buchanan *and* Ralph Nader—a deliberate error as a gag for a documentary film crew. I marked the ballot, then put it into a slot in the machine and— *grrrr-zunt!*—it shot back into my hands, recognizing my error. You *cannot* make a voting mistake on this machine, called an "Accu-vote." Mighty cool. But if you can't make a mistake, how did so many votes "spoil" in paper ballot counties? I asked a clerk: Does every county using paper ballots have this machine? The answer— yes and no—was disturbing. The adjoining county, Gadsden, also had machine-read paper ballots, *but did not activate the reject mechanism.* Make one wrong mark on your ballot in Gadsden and your ballot disappears into the machine—it will not be counted. For example, some voters had checked off and written in the name "Al Gore"—yet their vote did not count for Gore.

So I asked what I call The Florida Question: "By any chance, do you know the racial profile of counties where machines accept bad ballots?"

Then I got The Florida Answer: "We've been waiting for someone to ask us that." The clerk then pulled out a huge multi-colored sheet, listing, for every Florida county, the number of ballots not counted. The proportion of uncounted ballots to the Black population, county by county, was a nearly perfect match. But Ted Koppel's *Nightline* tells us this was because Blacks were too ignorant to figure out the ballot. Could Ted have gotten it wrong? As the Tallahassee officials demonstrated to me, whether a ballot was counted or not had almost nothing to do with the voter's education or sophistication—but an awful lot to do with the type of machine deployed and *how the buttons were set.*

Then I got to the 64 Dollar questions: What did Harris and the governor know and when did they know it? Was either aware of this racially loaded technical problem? Harris's office and Jeb's are literally a stone's throw away from Sancho's. The technicians told me, "That's why we set up this machine, so they could see it—*before* the election."

Cover-up and Counterspin

While virtually none of the new investigate material reached America's shores, the counterspin machine was in full throttle. The *Wall Street Journal*, usually unbiased, ignored the racial demographics of the mountains of spoiled ballots and proclaimed that there was no racial difference in the geographic division of sophisticated voting machines.

My felon purge reports got Florida's press poodles up in arms. Months after the election, the *Palm Beach Post*, ChoicePoint DBT's hometown paper, announced dramatically, "thousands of felons voted in the presidential election last year. . . . It's likely they benefited Democratic candidate Al Gore." Wow! Thousands! The *Post*'s FELONS VOTED! shock-horror story ran one week before the U.S. Civil Rights Commission aimed to blast the state/DBT purge list as garbage.

What did the *Post*'s sleuths use to hunt for felons? The DBT list. They then looked for voters who matched, by name, birthday, race and gender, "felons" among the 6 million Florida voters. It was DBT Lite. They failed to do even the lame cross-checks done by the state and counties.

The *Post* did not find "5,643 felons voted," or anything close to it. Rather, they simply had a list of common names (for example, John Jackson) and birthdays, maybe some misdemeanor violators or felons with clemency. (Think of this: If every birthday were a city, America would have 365 cities with 750,000 people in each. How many in that city's phone book would have the name "Joe White"?)

This was not just bad journalism, it smacked of a disinformation campaign.

There's good reason to suspect the motive and method of the *Post's* story. This is the paper, remember, that began to sniff the fake purge before the election, but then swallowed what an internal preelection memo from the state to DBT's Bruder called the "Department of Elections News Coverage Game Plan."[8] In that memo, discovered after the election by our researchers, the Department of Elections gloated that they had gotten the *Palm Beach Post* to "correct" their story and had successfully planted happy-talk stories in the *Sun-Sentinel* and other papers.

The Ultimate Measure

And there's the ultimate test of the veracity of the DBT and *Post* lists: The attorney general of Florida, Bob Butterworth, told me he absolutely would prosecute anyone who registered or voted illegally. A felon voting has committed a new felony—that means more jail time. The idea that 57,700 Floridians—or even 5,643—would chance years in the pokey by voting illegally was on its face incredible. If DBT and the *Post* found these criminals, why haven't they had them arrested? Butterworth was checking *six* cases when I spoke to him, and as of this writing, has not busted one single "felon voter."

The Consortium That Couldn't Count

Twisted press coverage murdered the story of ethnic cleansing of the voter rolls. But simply smothering the news wasn't good enough for the *New York Times*, CNN and the other keepers of the New Information Order. With other major news outlets, they joined

---

[8]E-mail dated June 26, 2000, from Janet Carabelli, Department of Elections, to Dee Smith, Bruder, others; obtained through Florida Open Records Act.

together as "the Consortium" and spent a wagonload of cash to hire the National Opinion Research Center (NORC), of the University of Chicago, to conduct what was wrongly called a "recount" of the ballots. For months they held back the results. Finally, more than a year after the election, they released their findings. "Bush would have won anyway," headlines reassured us. So shut up, move on, get over it: The Lion of Kabul won fair and square.

Or did he?

First, understand that NORC did not "recount" the ballots. Rather, its teams described each of the 180,000 "spoiled" ballots that Katherine Harris barred from the official total. This was the *first* count of these ballots. Also, NORC "coders" were not allowed to count these ballots either, merely provide physical descriptions of each ballot. They could note, in code, "Paper ballot, Gore circled," but could not count that ballot as a vote for Gore. The newspaper and television executives and editors, not the NORC experts, called the "winner" in this one.

Most Americans would have thought the goal of this million-dollar investigation was to find out whom Floridians wanted to vote for. That tends to be what we mean by "democracy." But the news bosses were in no mood for a democracy that threatened the legitimacy of authority, especially with the war on in Afghanistan and an economy in the toilet. So, despite the fact that NORC coders clearly found that the majority of Florida voters thought they had voted for Gore, the papers called the NORC findings for Bush. Like, huh? NORC has put its data on the Web, so the Gore majority is there for all to see (for those who bother to look). The media chiefs' trick was to say that, going by various Florida rules, which knock out ballots with stray markings, Bush would have won. Well, we already knew that: That's how Katherine Harris called it for Bush—on technicalities, not votes. Through this editorial three-card monte, the Republic was saved.

I watched the NORC operation firsthand in Miami in February 2001. There was an Alice in Wonderland weirdness in the process—"First we announce the winner, then we count the ballots."

It was not difficult to discern which candidate the voters wanted. "It screamed at you," said one counter. If someone circled "Gore," who do you think he or she wanted as president? Yet, thousands of such ballots were tossed out of the official count. Tens of thousands were disenfranchised because of a wrongly placed or stray mark—often made by the voting machine itself, as it turns out. The Consortium members did not comment on this exclusion of tens of thousands of clearly marked ballots or on its effect: the inauguration of the wrong person.

The Evidence Vanishes

And then, evidence began to disappear.

The counsel for the Civil Rights Commission told me he was most concerned about the purge of the 2,834 felons who did have a right to vote (he'd read my *Nation* article)—a willful violation of two court orders. Proof of the illegal procedure was in a September 18, 2000, letter to county supervisors.[9] The letter was read to me by two county clerks, but the sources were too nervous to fax me a copy.

So I called Janet Keels in Governor Jeb Bush's Office of Executive Clemency; I wanted a hard copy of the letter. A crew with the documentary *Unprecedented* captured the call on camera. . . .

My name is Gregory Palast and I'm calling from London.

My name is Troy Walker.

Troy, maybe you can help me. There is a letter from Janet Keels's [Governor's] Office of Executive Clemency, dated September 18, 2000. This is to Hillsborough Board of Elections dealing with registration of voters who moved to the state, committed a felony but have received executive clemency. I'm sure you have a copy of it. . . .

---

[9]The tenacious Dave Ruppe of ABC.NEWS.com discovered this document switch-a-roo independently, though his network did not broadcast the story.

We do have a letter referencing something close to that.

Okay, what date is that letter?

This letter is dated February 23, 2001.

What? He then read me a letter from Keels saying the *exact opposite* of the September 18 memo.

> September 18 (*before* the election): convicts from other states moving to Florida "would be required to make application for restoration of civil rights in the State of Florida."
>
> February 23 (*after* the election): out-of-state convicts "need *not* apply for restoration of civil rights in Florida."

The postelection letter was drafted one week after the Civil Rights Commission began to question Florida about the illegal maneuver—and now Troy was telling me there was *no record* of the first letter in Keels's files, or in the office's files, or in the state computers.

Uh, oh. There were two explanations. Maybe I had screwed up. My most serious accusation, that the governor's office barred and removed thousands of legal voters in violation of two court rulings, may have been dead wrong. After all, the cautious clerks had merely *read* me the text of the letter. What if it had never been sent? What if I'd been had by my sources? The first edition of this book had already gone to press.

The other possibility: The letter existed but had been purged faster than a Black voter from the governor's files, replaced by the February 23 letter, with opposite meaning. If so, then Jeb Bush's office was skirting close to obstruction of justice.

Did the incriminating September 18, 2000, letter exist? In 2002, I obtained the answer—from the most extraordinary source.

"Twisted"

> "Greg Palast distorts and misrepresents the events surrounding the 2000 presidential election in Florida in order to support his twisted and maniacally partisan conclusions."

Had I said something to upset the secretary of state? So began Harris's letter, a vein-popping screamer running beyond a thousand words, dated April 2002, to my editors at *Harper's*.[10] It contained, despite its gonna-beat-you-up tone, astonishing confessions. First, she does not deny the core allegation: that her list of 57,700 felons contained the names of thousands of innocent Democratic voters. You could have knocked me over with a feather when I read her acknowledgment that the debacle over which she presided as secretary of state "exposed flaws in the elections process that had festered across America for decades."

In the world according to Harris, blame flew everywhere, from the legislature to the attorney general, never landing on herself.

But what caught my eye and made me grab for the phone was her excuse for the illegal purge of out-of-state convicts. Harris wrote that the governor's Office of Executive Clemency *"issued a letter"* telling her elections divisions to carry out the deed.

> "Hello. I just received a note from Secretary Harris regarding a letter she received from Governor Bush's office regarding [here I mentioned the felon issue, leaving off the bits about "twisted"]. . . . Could you fax me a copy?"

And within the hour, the clerk had sent me, word for word as it had been read to me by my sources, the letter dated September 18. And here it is:

---

[10]See www.gregpalast.com/Harris/ for the entire text.

Fig. 1.5. Switched letters. Note that the letter dated September 18, 2000, six weeks before the presidential election, requires ex-felons to seek executive clemency from Governor Jeb Bush before they can vote. That directly violates court rulings. The letter dated February 23, 2001, written three months

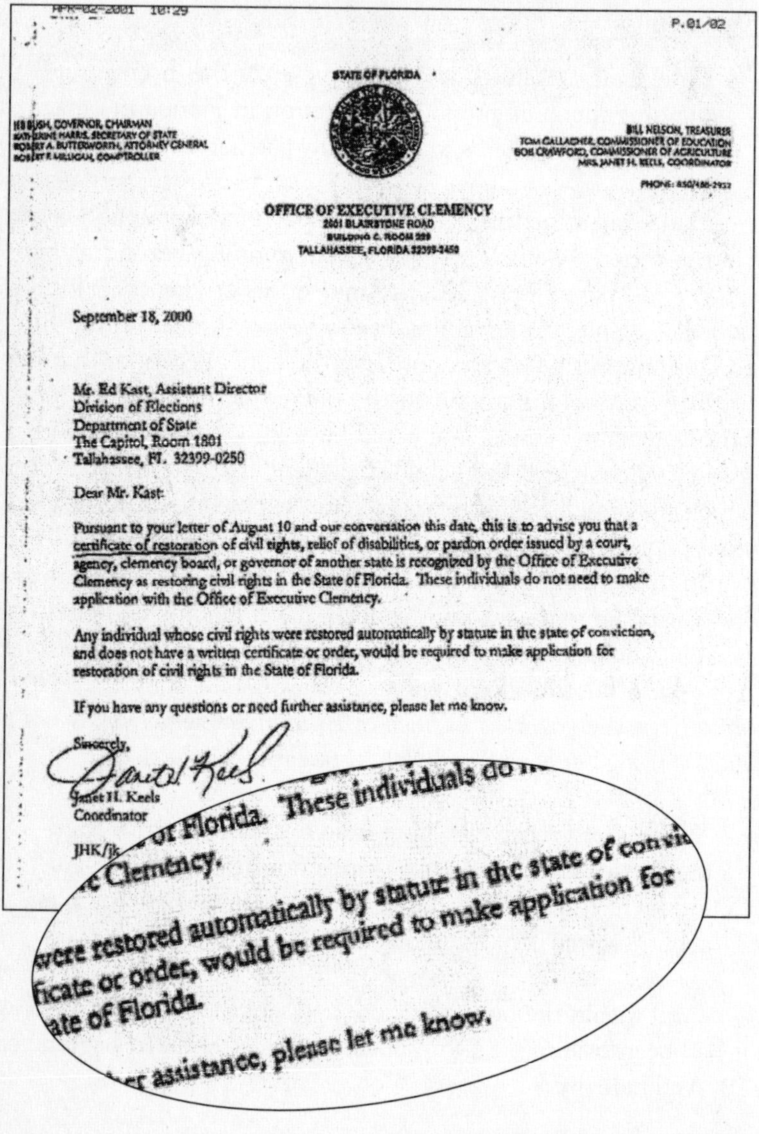

APR-02-2001 10:29   P.02/02

STATE OF FLORIDA

JEB BUSH, GOVERNOR, CHAIRMAN
KATHERINE HARRIS, SECRETARY OF STATE
ROBERT A. BUTTERWORTH, ATTORNEY GENERAL
ROBERT F MILLIGAN, COMPTROLLER

TOM GALLAGHER, TREASURER
CHARLES CRIST, COMMISSIONER OF EDUCATION
TERRY RHODES, COMMISSIONER OF AGRICULTURE
MRS. JANET H. KEELS, COORDINATOR

PHONE: 950/405-2952

OFFICE OF EXECUTIVE CLEMENCY
2601 BLAIRSTONE ROAD
BUILDING C, ROOM 229
TALLAHASSEE, FLORIDA 32399-2450

February 23, 2001

Mr. Ed Kast, Assistant Director
Division of Elections
Department of State
The Capitol, Room 1801
Tallahassee, FL 32399-0250

Dear Mr. Kast:

Some confusion has recently arisen regarding the effect of out-of-state restoration of civil rights on former felons' civil rights in Florida. To correct any misunderstanding, this letter reiterates our current policy.

If a former felon's civil rights were restored in another state, or if a person's civil rights were never lost after being convicted of a felony in another state, the individual possesses his or her civil rights in Florida and need not apply for restoration of civil rights in Florida. If a former felon attempting to register to vote in Florida claims that his or her civil rights were restored in another state or that his or her civil rights were not lost in another state, but the individual cannot produce supporting documentation, please refer that individual to my office.

My office will attempt to confirm the individual's claim by contacting the state that assertedly restored the individual's civil rights. If possession of civil rights is confirmed, the individual does not need to apply for restoration of civil rights in Florida. My office will issue a letter to that effect to the individual. Please accept that letter as proof of possession of civil rights.

I hope this clarifies any misunderstanding as to our State's policy regarding these matters. Please do not hesitate to contact my office if you have questions.

Sincerely,

Janet H. Keels
Coordinator

JHK

If a former felon's civil rights were restored in ano... being convicted of a felony in another state, the indiv... not apply for restoration of civil rights in Florida. If a... claims that his or her civil rights were restored in anothe... another state, but the individual cannot produce suppo... office.

...ce will attempt to confirm the indivi...

after the election and a week after the U.S. Civil Rights Commission began to investigate the matter, says the opposite: These voters need not apply for clemency. The voters need not seek Governor Bush's "clemency."

Part IV: THE THEFT OF THE PRESIDENTIAL ELECTION–2004

Maybe, as Ms. Harris and Florida Republicans suggest, we should just "get over it. Just move on." *They* have moved on: to 2002 and 2004. They fixed the election of November 2000—and went right to work on monkeying with the *next* election cycle. Harris and Jeb Bush weren't chastened by the exposure of their purge operation. After all, in 2000 *they got away with it*.

Burying the Loot: Keeping the Florida Voter Rolls Whiter Than White

On January 10, 2001, picking up on our Salon story, the NAACP sued ChoicePoint's DBT, Katherine Harris and Clayton "Road Runner" Roberts for violating the civil rights of thousands of Florida citizens as guaranteed by the 1965 Voting Rights Act and the U.S. Constitution.

Harris insists she did no wrong. Now she could tell it to the judge. (However, that can be a risky move for Harris. In June 2002, the last time she tried to defend herself in court, a judge reached an unusual, albeit insightful, verdict: "This lady is crazy." Lucky for Harris the judge's remarks referred to her perverse interpretations of law, not to her general state of mind; otherwise, under Florida regulations, she would have to be purged from the voter rolls.)

The bad news for defendants Harris and Roberts is that DBT would not take a dive for them in court. Once DBT shut down their Vote-Scrubs-R-Us business, the database operators had nothing to gain by defending the officials that got them in hot water. The company pleaded for mercy from the NAACP, begging for settlement, thereby avoiding class-action claims.

In July 2002, DBT signed off with People for the American Way, which acts as the NAACP's law firm, to provide a new purge list—one that comes closer to the work originally promised the state. I had estimated that the list had at best one in ten verifiable names. I was too kind. DBT indicates the new list would contain only one in twenty from the original. In other words, over 50,000 people will be removed from their hit list.

The NAACP's lawyers didn't just fall off a hayrick. They know that they can't reverse the 2000 election. Their goal: to prevent the theft of the races in 2002 and 2004. To this end, armed with DBT's admissions, the NAACP simply asked the state to return voting rights to those they acknowledge were wrongly named as felons. You'd think after DBT confessed and cut the poisonous list by 95 percent, Harris, Jeb and Clay Roberts would at least do right by those they had wronged. Not a chance. DBT has removed 50,000 names from their list . . . but not Harris. Her office refuses to return their civil rights. You can see her logic: What's the use of stealing the 2000 race if you have to give it all back in 2002? Like a confessed bank robber who hides the loot and tells his victims, "It's still mine, suckers!" the state is using every technical and legalistic trick in the book to keep illegally purged Black registrations buried for good.

But eventually, those votes must rise. How, then, can the Jeb Bush team keep the voter rolls whiter than white? The answer: new "felon" lists for 2002 and 2004. But creating new lists runs into a new obstacle: the law. Following the Salon and *Nation* stories, an embarrassed Florida legislature voted to bar the secretary of state from ever again hiring an outside firm like DBT to generate a purge list. The legislature directed Harris to turn over this work to the experts, the Florida Association of Court Clerks. The problem for Republicans is that the Clerks had done this work before and in a reasonably fair, accurate and notably unbiased way. After all, felons were removed from voter rolls long before Mortham, Harris and DBT came along.

Harris overcame the problem of the new law in a forthright

manner: She broke it. The law says her office "may not hire an outside firm . . ." The law couldn't be clearer. Yet, in December 2001, Harris cut off a series of meetings with the county Clerks—and she hired an outside firm. Her hit man Roberts told local papers the Clerks were dumped because they requested $300,000 for their costs to assess the current system. He must have had a good laugh at that one. The fee he's agreed to pay the new consultant: $1.6 million.

With DBT out, who is this new firm with whom Florida is entrusting its citizens' civil rights? Accenture—alias of Arthur Andersen Consulting.

The Harris Touch

One can't sabotage democracy with felon lists alone. Ballot-eating machines worked well in Gadsden and other Black counties, but cyberspace offers even more opportunities for fun and games. This time, it's "touch screen" voting. No paper trail, no audit path, no fights over recounts: recounts are impossible.[11]

Florida is the first state to adopt this video-game voting technology. Secretary of State Harris immediately certified the reliability of one machine, the iVotronic, from Election Systems and Software of Omaha. On their Web site, there is a neat demo of their foolproof system you can try out. I did—and successfully cast an "over-vote," a double vote for one candidate. Then the site crashed my laptop. But hey, the bugs will be worked out . . . or worked in.

The question is, who else is touching the touch screen? In the case of the iVotronics, it's Sandra Mortham. Ring a bell? She was Harris's Republican predecessor as secretary of state,

---

[11]Investigator Ronnie Dugger has warned of the dangers of computerized voting for years. See *The New Yorker*, November 7, 1988.

the one who hired DBT. Now she's iVotronics representative in Florida.

The New American Apartheid: Race and the Bush Brothers

In 2002 Harris told a campaign rally, "Before God, before my family, before my friends, before my nation, before the nation, I sleep well at night."

You're thinking, "With *whom?*" Well, shame on you. My thoughts were more sobering. Harris had, after all, effectively admitted in her note to *Harper's* that she'd moved to disenfranchise thousands of innocent Black folks. Even if she believes she wasn't at fault, how *could* she sleep at night? I suspect she—and the government and press—would have been a bit more troubled if the wrongly purged voters came from country-club membership rolls: moneyed, important and white.

Don't kid yourself: the color of the excluded voters had an awful lot to do with why this investigation was dismissed by the U.S. media for so long. The "liberal media," as Harris calls them, would never recognize their own subtle prejudices. Remember my story of Pastor Johnson of Alachua, convicted in New York and therefore entitled to vote in Florida? Publication was rejected by a U.S. outlet because of the doubts of one reporter. The preppy white Ivy Leaguer could not understand why a middle-aged Black man, an ex-con to boot, did not raise a ruckus in a county office in the rural South to demand his rights. Why didn't Pastor Johnson pound the table? After all, voters in Palm Beach had no problems complaining publicly.

Of the victims I spoke with, the only African Americans who would agree to talk on camera were the three clerics, whose collars afforded them a kind of cultural protection. Alachua County, Okeefenokee . . . this is still the Old South where, within the memory of many of these people, Black voters were hanged from trees. The deep, wounding history of Jim Crow explains the initial quiet of so many victims of the illegal purge, a caution echoed and affirmed by the silence of the Democratic Party.

At the beginning of the twenty-first century, America is back to asking the question we thought resolved by the 1965 Voting Rights Act: Should Black people be allowed the vote?

So far, we've discussed only the purge of citizens *falsely* accused of having felony records. Even if that wrong is righted, a good *half a million* Floridians will still be barred from voting. And we know their color. One-third of all Black men in Florida have lost their right to vote.

And the Bush Brothers like it that way.

Within two months of the 2000 election, President Bush convened a Bi-BURP, a Bipartisan Blue Ribbon Panel to recommend reforms to prevent "another Florida."

Our president, to ensure that we understood clearly he had no intention whatsoever of heeding his panel's findings and recommendations, put two men in charge of the Bi-BURP for whom he has the fondest disregard: Jimmy Carter and Gerald Ford. Relieved of the pressure of having to produce a plan that might be implemented, Carter and Ford got right to the heart of the matter on the faux felon purge: race. The former presidents called for an end to barring the vote to people who have served their time and gone straight. After all, only thirteen states hold on to these exclusion laws, originally passed by Deep South legislatures after Reconstruction while the Ku Klux Klan's night riders successfully cleared the voter rolls by more direct means.

Neither President Bush nor Governor Bush have bothered with even a false gesture toward implementing the Carter-Ford call to restore the rights of these (un-white) citizens. Jeb Bush's reforms are limited to multi-dollar contracts for Arthur Andersen Consulting and the Mortham-matic touch screens.

Beyond Florida

I know what you're thinking: They *all* do it. Republicans *and* Democrats both. Yes, but not on this scale, not so successfully. I remember my years in Chicago, watching Boss Daley's machine hacks carry stacks of absentee ballots into nursing homes, then carry out the same stack, all "signed," every vote for every office Democratic. But this is a new game, vote rustling of the future.

Opening night in Florida was so successful, the Republicans are taking their show on the road. Since the 2000 elections, politicians have been busy "Floridizing" state elections procedures from sea to shining sea. The race for the White House in 2004 may already be decided for you, the voting only a formality.

The Florida vote count vaudeville has been used as cover to monkey with voting systems in several states—all under the grinning disguise of "reform." These reforms suspiciously repeat the methods pioneered by Florida: centralized, computer purge lists. Who is the carrier of this ill "reform" wind? One vector is the high-sounding Voter Integrity Project, based just outside Washington, DC. The conservative, nonprofit advocacy organization has campaigned in parallel with the Republican Party against the 1993 motor voter law that resulted in a nationwide increase in voter registration of 7 million, much of it among minority voters. Its founding chairwoman? Helen Blackwell, wife of Ronald Reagan's staffer Morton Blackwell. Just before the November 2000 election, VIP presented its special Voter Integrity Award to DBT—at a VIP conference substantially paid for by . . . DBT. Noting proudly that "DBT is the company tasked with helping Florida clean up the State's voter registration records," VIP then launched into a campaign to take DBT's Florida methods to other states. VIP announced it had "entered into an agreement with DBT Online to identify small communities with demonstrated need for similar pro bono voter rolls 'scrubbing.'" Offers were extended to Pennsylvania and

Tennessee, with Florida, the states considered toss-ups in the Gore-Bush race.[12]

After the election, when the name DBT lost its marketing appeal, VIP told me their joint offer with the company was "void," like an expired coupon for detergent. But Republican senator Chris Bond, joined at a press conference by VIP's chairwoman, announced he was introducing a bill to force Florida's voting methodologies on the entire nation. Then-Senator Bob Torricelli stood with him—which proves one can always find Democrats willing to attend their own political funeral.

In June 2001, the *Washington Post* finally, and in the most cautious tones, rereported the Salon and *Nation* stories on the theft of the last election. And they granted me a platform to warn about this theft of race in 2004:

"The Wrong Way to Fix the Vote"
Washington Post, *June 10, 2001*

Lord, save us from "reform."

If you liked the way Florida handled the presidential vote in November, you'll just love the election reform laws that have passed since then in 10 states, and have been proposed in 16 others. These laws mandate a practice that was at the heart of the Florida débâcle: computer-aided purging of centralized voter files. The laudable aim is to rid registries of the names of the dead, as well as of felons and others legally barred from voting. But the likely result will be the elimination of a lot of legitimate voters and an increased potential for political mischief.

---

[12]According to the stellar research of Catherine Danielson, it looks like Al Gore won Tennessee—a less sophisticated operation than Florida's but just as odoriferous.

You would think other states would run from Florida's methods. But in their current legislative sessions, Colorado, Indiana, South Dakota, Texas, Virginia, Georgia, Kansas, Montana and Washington have passed bills that—while varying in specifics—would follow the Sunshine State's lead in centralizing, computerizing and cleansing voter rolls. Senator Christopher S. Bond (R-Mo.) has introduced a bill in which certain conditions in any state would trigger mandatory voter list purges.

To a large extent, these bills are a response to "motor voter" legislation, which has added millions of citizens, particularly minorities, to voter registries. Since minority voters tend to be Democratic, it is not surprising that "motor voter" laws are popular among Democrats, and most of the bills attempting to purge the rolls are sponsored by Republicans.

But many factors go into the ill-advised rush to reform. Take the case of Georgia. The day before the November 2000 election, the Atlanta Journal-Constitution and WSB-TV jointly reported that records indicated that deceased Georgians had voted 5,412 times over the last 20 years. They specifically cited one Alan J. Mandel, who apparently cast his ballot in three separate elections after his demise in 1997. Subsequently, a very live Alan J. Mandell (note the two L's) told the secretary of the state that local election workers had accidentally checked off the wrong name on the list. But in the midst of the chad mania that dominated the headlines in November 2000, details became less important than the newly energized drive for so-called reform.

If the reformers succeed, look out. Florida's Blackhunt purge began under the cover of the voting "reform" law passed by the state in 1998. Under a law signed April 18, 2001—an imitation of the ill Florida code—Georgia's secretary of state now controls "list maintenance" and has taken over the power of deleting the names of dead voters.

The centralization of state voter registries hands an all-too-tempting monopoly to whichever party controls the office of secretary of state. The highly technical (and, where contractors are involved, commercially confidential) nature of computer-aided purges makes bias in the cleansing of supposed felons, deceased voters and duplicate voters astonishingly easy to carry out and difficult to uncover.

Even uncovered, apparent bias is difficult to challenge.

After all, one man's overzealous purge is another man's inauguration.

Democracy and the People Who Count: A Conclusion

This story of stolen elections—the last one, the next one—is not about computers, database management or voting machinery. If the theft of the U.S. election could have been prevented by fixing our voting methods and equipment, we could solve our problems by the means suggested by the Russian Duma. The Russians voted a resolution demanding that American presidential elections, like Haiti's and Rwanda's, should be held under the auspices of the United Nations.

The solution to democracy's ills cannot be found in computer fixes or in banning butterfly ballots. All that stuff about technology and procedure is vanishingly peripheral to this fact: In 2000, the man who lost the vote grabbed the power. I reported these stories from Europe, where simple minds think that the appropriate response to the discovery that the wrong man took office would be to remove him from that office.

So where do we turn? The Democrats' employing William (son of Boss) Daley as their spokesman during the Florida vote count, and Al Gore's despicably gracious concession speech, show that both political parties share, though in different measure, a contempt for the electorate's will.

Two other presidential elections were nearly stolen in the year

2000, in Peru and in Yugoslavia. How ironic that in those nations, though not in the United States, the voters' will ultimately counted. Peruvians and Yugoslavs took to heart Martin Luther King's admonition that rights are never given, only asserted. They knew: When the unelected seize the presidential palaces, democrats must seize the streets.

$ C H A P T E R   2 $

THE BEST DEMOCRACY MONEY CAN BUY:
The Bushes and the Billionaires Who Love Them

Who owns America? How much did it cost? Was the transaction cash, check or credit card? Was it a donation to my son who's running for president? Or a consulting contract to my wife's former law partner to comfort him on his way to the federal penitentiary?

And what do you give a billionaire who has everything? That gold mine in Nevada they so covet? Immunity from prosecution?

Then there's the practical difficulty of gift wrapping the U.S. Congress.

George W. Bush may have lost at the ballot box but he won where it counts, at the piggy bank. The Fortunate Son rode right into the White House on a snorting porker stuffed with nearly half a billion dollars: My calculation of the suffocating plurality of cash from Corporate America ("hard" money, "soft" money, "parallel" spending and other forms of easy squeezy) that smothered Al Gore runs to $447 million. They called it an election but it looked more like an auction.

What did all this loot buy? In May 2001, I flew to Texas to find out.

Ya Dance with Them What Brung Ya

Ah, the smell of Houston in the morning.

According to LaNell Anderson, real estate agent, what I'm smelling is a combination of hydrogen sulphide and some other unidentifiable toxic gunk. With the crew from BBC's *Newsnight*, we've pulled up across from a pond on the Houston Ship Channel, home of the biggest refinery and chemical complex in America, owned by ExxonMobil.

The pond is filled with benzene residues, a churning, burbling goop. Though there's a little park nearby, this is not a bucolic swimming hole. Rather, imagine your toilet backed up, loaded and ripe—assuming your toilet is a half mile in circumference.

Once LaNell picked up the scent of airborne poisons, she hopped from her Lexus, pulled out a big white bucket and opened a valve, sucking in a three-minute sample of air. She'll send the bucket off to the U.S. Environmental Protection Agency, in the hopes that they will trace, and then fine, the polluter.

Hunting killer fumes is a heck of a hobby. LaNell began after learning she had a rare immune system disease associated with chemical pollution. Her mom and dad died young of lung disease and cancer. She grew up and lives near the Ship Channel.

I didn't have the heart to tell her that she might as well chuck away her buckets. Quietly tucked into President Bush's first budget was a big fat *zero* for the key EPA civil enforcement team. This has no connection whatsoever to the petrochemical industry dumping $48 million into the Republican campaign.

LaNell stopped to chat with some Chicano sub-teens playing soccer with an old bowling ball. They live in what ExxonMobil calls its "vulnerability zone." The refinery released 1.68 million pounds of toxic chemicals into the air and water here in 2000 by accident. According to ExxonMobil records, if the pentane on site vaporized and ignited, it would burn human skin within 1.8 miles: 7,300 people live in that zone.

Bush is addressing the problem. He's closing down public access to these reports on the killing zones.

The president need not worry. He lives safely within Exxon's *in*vulnerability zone: The Republicans collected $1.2 million from company personnel during Bush's campaigns, generosity bested in their industry only by Enron.

A giant flare suddenly lit up the other side of the channel—and LaNell sped off to investigate. When she reached the gate of the chemical plant spitting out the flames, she was told the refinery blew a hydrogen line. The operators, rather than store the ruined batch of ethylene, chose to ignite it. The toxic fireball, big as the White House, burned from the stack for several hours, exhaling a black cloud over Houston.

LaNell said this sickening "sky dumping" procedure is okey-dokey with Texas state regulators. As soon as Bush got into the White House, he proposed moving air quality enforcement away from the tougher Feds to these laid-back state agencies. And the Bush energy plan loosens EPA rules on the chemical industry.

That was May 2001, days before President Bush issued his proposals to end the energy crisis in California. The Golden State was suffering rolling blackouts. The state's monthly electricity bill shot up by 1,000 percent. But as soon as I got a whiff of the president's proposals, I knew his plan had nothing to do with helping out the Gore-voting surfers on the Left Coast. Bush's "energy crisis" plan reeks of pure *eau de Texas*, that sulfurous combination of pollution, payola and political power unique to the Lone Star State.

Bush put Vice President Dick Cheney in charge of the committee to save California consumers. Recommendation number one: Build some nuclear plants. Not much of an offer to earthquake-prone California, but a darn good deal for the biggest builder of nuclear plants based in Texas, the Brown and Root subsidiary of Halliburton Corporation. Recent CEO of Halliburton: Dick the Veep.

Suggestion number two: Drill for oil in Alaska's Arctic Wildlife Refuge. California does not burn oil in its power plants, but hey, committee member Commerce Secretary Don Evans gave the Arctic escapade a thumbs-up. Evans's most recent employment: CEO of Tom Brown Inc., a billion-dollar oil and gas corporation.

And so on. Former Texas Agriculture Commissioner Jim Hightower told me, "They've eliminated the middleman. The corporations don't have to lobby the government anymore. They *are* the government." Hightower used to complain about Monsanto's lobbying the secretary of agriculture. Today, Monsanto executive Ann Venamin *is* the secretary of agriculture.

Bili Clinton, before his final bow, issued an order on December 14, halting uncontrolled speculation in the California electricity market. You could hear the yowls all the way to Texas, where the big winners in the power game—TXU, Reliant, Dynegy, El Paso corporation, and the erstwhile Enron—have their headquarters.

These five energy operators, through their executives and employees, ponied up $4.1 million for the Republican presidential campaign cycle, according to the Center for Responsive Politics in Washington. They didn't have long to wait before their investment—excuse me, *donation*—paid off big time. Just three days after his inauguration, Bush swept away Clinton's orders directing controlled power sales to California.

On my way to Dallas, I flew over a vicious scar on the Texas landscape. Alcoa Aluminum's lignite strip mine, a 250-foot hole on the range, feeds their plant at the end of the ditch. Lignite's the filthiest fuel you can burn, if the government will let you. My little plane set down at Wayne Brinkley's ranch. An odd homestead: Everything's covered with this sticky goo—Wayne's pickup, Wayne's trees, and presumably, Wayne's lungs.

In 1997, the heat was on from regulators to force Alcoa to switch to clean natural gas. Exxon was facing compulsory cuts of up to 50 percent in its emissions on the Houston Ship Channel. Governor Bush set up a committee with Alcoa, headed by Exxon, which met in secret to push a law to replace hard rules with voluntary standards. Texas state anticorruption law made it illegal to donate money to Bush as governor while such legislation was under consideration, but within a month of Bush's shepherding the bill through the state legislature, he declared his run for the presidency, making the $150,000 in donations from committee representatives completely legal. Alcoa bragged that it saved $100 million, and its law firm dropped $170,000 into the Republican presidential campaign. (Bush clearly admired Alcoa executives' way with numbers. He appointed the aluminum company's chairman, Paul O'Neill, as his secretary of the treasury.)

On to Dallas, where I met with Phyllis Glazer, founder of a group of bereaved mothers in Winona, Texas. They lost their children to rare diseases that they believe are related to a local hazardous waste "injection well," a big underground chemical dump. Phyllis wore one of those fancy Western dance shirts with the metal bangles and cowhide fringe, so I brilliantly asked her if she enjoys Texas two-stepping. "Actually, I don't do a lot of dancing these days. My bones are deteriorating."

Phyllis and the moms took a bus to Washington, DC. But official doors slammed in their faces. "They say someone who's given $200,000 or a couple million, their call goes straight through."

One Texan who made his way through the doors to power was Ken Lay, former chairman of Enron, the electricity speculating outfit that made out so well in Bush's energy program. Once upon a time Lay was what they call a Pioneer—not the kind that lives in a little house on the prairie, busting the soil, but one of the big buckaroos who each pledged to raise $100,000 for Mr. Bush's campaign. Four hundred Pioneers—that's $40 million in booty.

Lay wouldn't talk to me, but his fellow Pioneer, Senator Teel Bivins, Texas Panhandle rancher, was right friendly. His office walls in the Capitol in Austin sported a pair of riding chaps, his Pioneer medallion and the head of a deceased longhorn. I was assured the back half of the beast ended up on the senator's barbecue.

Getting the hundred grand for Bush was no problem for this cowboy politician. Easiest money he ever raised ("Eezist monuh ah eva rayzed"). And Bush never forgets his friends. One unheralded milestone of Bush's first one hundred days was his allowing beef packers to zap meat with radiation to kill salmonella, a disinfectant cheaper than nonnuclear methods. (Bush's proposal to permit a bit of salmonella in school lunch meats was withdrawn after the public reacted with loud gagging and retching noises.)

Teel could have added that for a hundred grand, the president will fluff up your pillow. Two years after Clinton was caught running the White House as a Motel 6 for big donors, Bush invited his own Pioneers, including Bivins, to rough it in the Lincoln Bedroom.

I told the senator about Phyllis Glazer, the cancer victim and pollution fighter, and her complaint that Washington access required big-bucks donations.

"Well," said Pioneer Teel, "it's easy for the press to take some victim and make her a poster girl. The reality is individuals in a country with three hundred million people have very little opportunity to speak to the president of the United States." But what about Pioneer Lay of Enron Corp? His company, America's number-one power speculator, was also Dubya's number-one political career donor ($1.8 million to Republicans during the 2000 presidential campaign). Lay was personal adviser to Bush during the postelection "transition." And his company held secret meetings with the energy plan's drafters. Bush's protecting electricity deregulation meant a big payday for Enron—subsequent bankruptcy notwithstanding—sending profits up $87 million in the first quarter of Bush's reign, thanks to his reversal of Clinton orders.

The senator is nothing if not candid. "So you *wouldn't* have access if you had spent two years of your life working hard to get this guy elected president *raising hundreds of thousands of dollars?*"

In case I didn't understand, he translated it into Texan. "*Ya dance with them what brung ya!*"

I couldn't argue with that. If President Bush chose to two-step with Lay of Enron instead of Phyllis Glazer, well, let's be honest, Phyllis ain't much on the dance floor these days.

Poppy Strikes Gold

George W. could not have amassed this pile if his surname were Jones or Smith. While other candidates begged, pleaded and wheedled for donations, the Bushes added a creative, lucrative new twist to the money chase that contenders couldn't imitate: "Poppy" Bush's post–White House work. It laid the foundation for Dubya's campaign kitty corpulence and, not incidentally, raised the family's net worth by several hundred percent.

In 1998, for example, the former president and famed Desert Stormtrooper-in-Chief wrote to the oil minister of Kuwait on behalf of Chevron Oil Corporation. Bush says, honestly, that he "had no stake in the Chevron operation." True, but following this selfless use of his influence, the oil company put $657,000 into the Republican Party coffers.

That year Bush *père* created a storm in Argentina when he lobbied his close political ally, President Carlos Menem, to grant a gambling license to Mirage Casino Corporation. Once again, the senior Bush wrote that he had no personal interest in the deal. However, Bush *fils* made out quite nicely: After the casino flap, Mirage dropped $449,000 into the Republican Party war chest.

Much of Bush's loot, reports the Center for Responsive Politics, came in the form of "bundled" and "soft" money. That's the squishy stuff corporations use to ooze around U.S. law, which prohibits any direct donations from corporations.

Not all of the elder Bush's work is voluntary. His single talk to the board of Global Crossing, the telecom start-up, earned him stock worth $13 million when the company went public. Global Crossing's employees also kicked in another million for the younger Bush's run. (We'll meet Global Crossing again in Chapter 3.)

And while the Bush family steadfastly believes that ex-felons should not have the right to vote for president, they have no objection to ex-cons putting presidents on their payroll. In 1996, despite pleas by U.S. church leaders, Poppy Bush gave several speeches (he charges $100,000 per talk) sponsored by organizations run by Rev. Sun Myung Moon, cult leader, tax cheat—and formerly the guest of the U.S. federal prison system.

Some of the loot for the Republican effort in the 1997–2000 election cycles came from an outfit called Barrick Corporation. The sum, while over $100,000, is comparatively small change for the GOP, yet it seemed quite a gesture for a corporation based in *Canada*. Technically, the funds came from those associated with the Canadian's U.S. unit, Barrick Gold Strike.

They could well afford it. In the final days of the Bush (Senior) administration, the Interior Department made an extraordinary but little noticed change in procedures under the 1872 Mining Law, the gold rush–era act that permitted those whiskered small-time prospectors with their tin pans and mules to stake claims on their tiny plots. The department initiated an expedited procedure for mining companies that allowed Barrick to swiftly lay claim to the largest gold find in America. In the terminology of the law, Barrick could "perfect its patent" on the estimated $10 *billion* in ore—for which Barrick paid the U.S. Treasury a little under $10,000. Eureka!

Barrick, of course, had to put up cash for the initial property rights and the cost of digging out the booty (and the cost of donations, in smaller amounts, to support Nevada's Democratic senator, Harry Reid). Still, the shift in rules paid off big time: According to experts at the Mineral Policy Center of Washington, DC, Barrick saved—and the U.S. taxpayer lost—a cool billion or so.

Upon taking office, Bill Clinton's new interior secretary, Bruce Babbitt, called Barrick's claim the "biggest gold heist since the days of Butch Cassidy." Nevertheless, because the company followed the fast-track process laid out for them under Bush, this corporate Goldfinger had Babbitt by the legal nuggets. Clinton had no choice but to give them the gold mine while the public got the shaft.

Barrick says it had no contact whatsoever with the president at the time of the rules change.[1] There was always a place in Barrick's heart for the older Bush—and a place on its payroll. In 1995, Barrick hired the former president as Honorary Senior Advisor to the Toronto company's International Advisory Board. Bush joined at the suggestion of former Canadian prime minister Brian Mulroney, who, like Bush, had been ignominiously booted from office. I was a bit surprised that the president had signed on. When Bush was voted out of the White House, he vowed never to lobby or join a corporate board. The chairman of Barrick openly boasts that granting the title "Senior Advisor" was a sly maneuver to help Bush tiptoe around this promise.

I was curious: What does one *do* with a used president? Barrick vehemently denies that it appointed Bush "in order to procure him to make contact with other world leaders whom he knows, or who could be of considerable assistance" to the company. Yet, in September 1996, Bush wrote a letter to help convince Indonesian dictator Suharto to give Barrick a new, hot gold-mining concession.

Bush's letter seemed to do the trick. Suharto took away 68 percent of the world's largest goldfield from the finder of the ore and handed it to Barrick. However, Bush's lobbying magic isn't invincible. Jim Bob Moffett, a tough old Louisiana swamp dog who heads Freeport-McMoRan, Barrick's American rival, met privately with Suharto. When Suharto emerged from their meeting, the kleptocrat announced that Freeport would replace Bush's Canadians. (Barrick lucked out: The huge ore deposit turned out to be a hoax. When the con was uncovered, Jim Bob's associates invited geologist Mike de Guzman, who "discovered" the gold, to talk

---

[1]Barrick has responded to every allegation reported in my first report on the company in a manner certain to get my attention: The company and its chairman sued my papers, *Guardian* and the *Observer*. While I have a distaste for retort by tort, I have incorporated their legitimate concerns to ensure their views are acknowledged. More on the suit in Chapter 8.

about the error of his ways. Unfortunately, on the way to the meeting, de Guzman fell out of a helicopter.)

Who is this "Barrick" to whom our former president would lease out the reflected prestige of the Oval Office? I could not find a Joe Barrick in the Canadian phone book. Rather, the company as it operates today was founded by one Peter Munk. The entrepreneur first came to public notice in Canada in the 1960s as a central figure in an insider trading scandal. Munk had dumped his stock in a stereo-making factory he controlled just before it went belly up, leaving other investors and government holding the bag. He was never charged, but, notes Canada's *Maclean's* magazine, the venture and stock sale "cost Munk his business and his reputation." Yet today, Munk's net worth is estimated at $350 million, including homes on two continents and his own island.

How did he go from busted stereo maker to demi-billionaire goldbug? The answer: Adnan Khashoggi, the Saudi arms dealer, the "bag man" in the Iran-Contra arms-for-hostage scandals. The man who sent guns to the ayatolla teamed up with Munk on hotel ventures and, ultimately, put up the cash to buy Barrick in 1983, then a tiny company with an "unperfected" claim on the Nevada mine. You may recall that Bush pardoned the coconspirators who helped Khashoggi arm the Axis of Evil, making charges against the sheik all but impossible. (Bush pardoned the conspirators not as a favor to Khashoggi, but to himself.)

Khashoggi got out of Barrick just after the Iran-Contra scandal broke, long before 1995, when Bush was invited in. By that time, Munk's reputation was restored, at least in his own mind, in part by massive donations to the University of Toronto. Following this act of philanthropy, the university awarded Munk–adviser Bush an honorary degree. Several students were arrested protesting what appeared to them as a cash-for-honors deal.

Mr. Munk's president-for-hire did not pay the cost of his rental in Indonesia. The return on Barrick's investment in politicians would have to come from Africa.

Mobutu Sese Seko, the late dictator of the Congo (Zaire), was one of the undisputed master criminals of the last century having looted hundreds of millions of dollars from his national treasury— and a golfing buddy of the senior Bush. That old link from the links probably did not hurt Barrick in successfully seeking an eighty-thousand-acre gold-mining concession from the Congolese cutthroat. Bush himself did not lobby the deal for Barrick. It wasn't that the former president was squeamish about using the authority of his former posts to cut deals with a despot. Rather, at the time Bush was reportedly helping Adolf Lundin, Barrick's sometime industry rival. Africa specialist Patrick Smith of London disclosed that Bush called Mobutu in 1996 to help cinch a deal for Lundin for a mine distant from Barrick's.

Rebellion against Mobutu made the mine site unusable, though not for the company's lack of trying. In testimony in hearings convened by the minority leader of the House Foreign Affairs Subcommittee on Human Rights, expert Wayne Madsen alleged that Barrick, to curry favor with both sides, indirectly funded both and thereby inadvertently helped continue the bloody conflict. The allegation, by respected journalist Wayne Madsen, has not been substantiated: The truth is lost somewhere in the jungle, where congressional investigators will never tread.

Though Barrick struck out in Indonesia and the Congo, the big payoff came from the other side of the continent. The company's president bragged to shareholders that the prestige of the Mulroney-Bush advisory board was instrumental in obtaining one of the biggest goldfields in East Africa at Bulyanhulu, Tanzania. Barrick, according to its president, had hungered for that concession—holding an estimated $3 billion in bullion—since the mid-1990s, when it first developed its contacts with managers at Sutton Resources, another Canadian company, which held digging rights from the government. (See footnote 1.) Enriched by the Nevada venture, Barrick could, and eventually would, buy up Sutton. But in 1996, there was a problem with any takeover of Sutton: Tens of thousands of small-time prospectors, "jewelry miners," so called because of their minuscule finds, already lived and worked on the land. These poor African diggers held legal claim stakes to their tiny mine shafts on the property. If they stayed, the concession was worthless.

In August 1996, Sutton's bulldozers, backed by military police firing weapons, rolled across the goldfield, smashing down worker housing, crushing their mining equipment and filling in their pits. Several thousand miners and their families were chased off the property. But not all of them. About fifty miners were still in their mine shafts, buried alive.

Buried alive. It's not on Bush's resume, nor on Barrick's Web site. You wouldn't expect it to be. But then, you haven't found it in America's newspapers either.

There are two plausible explanations for this silence. First, it never happened; the tale of the live burials is a complete fabrication of a bunch of greedy, lying Black Africans trying to shake down Sutton Resources (since 1999, a Barrick subsidiary). That's what Barrick says after conducting its own diligence investigation and relying on local and national investigations by the Tanzanian government. And the company's view is backed by the World Bank. See Chapter 8 for more on this.[2]

There's another explanation: Barrick threatens and sues newspapers and human rights organizations that dare to breathe a word of the allegations—even if Barrick's denials are expressed. I know: They sued my papers, the *Observer* and *Guardian* (for more on that, see Chapter 8). Barrick even sent a letter to the internationally respected human rights lawyer Tundu Lissu, a fellow at the World Resources Institute in Washington, DC, outlining its suit against the *Observer* and warning that it would take "all necessary

---

[2]A bit of confusion here: Barrick swore to my paper that the alleged killings "related to a time years before [Barrick] had any connection whatsoever with the company to which the report referred." Yet Barrick's president and CEO, Randall Oliphant, told Barrick's shareholders that prior to their acquisition of Sutton, "we followed the progress at Bully (i.e., Bulyanhulu) for five years, remaining in close contact with the senior management team." That would connect them to the mine in 1994. The mining company wants me to report their version of events. Okay, here's both of them.

steps" to protect its reputation should the Institute repeat any of the allegations. Barrick's threats are the least of Lissu's problems. For supplying me with evidence—photos of a corpse of a man allegedly killed by police during the clearance of the mine site, notarized witness statements, even a police video of workers seeking bodies from the mine pits—and for Lissu's demanding investigation of the killings, his law partners in Dar es Salaam have been arrested and Lissu charged by the Tanzanian government with sedition.

In 1997, while Bush was on the board (he quit in 1999), *Mother Jones* magazine named Barrick's chairman Munk one of America's "10 Little Piggies"—quite an honor for a Canadian—for allegedly poisoning the West's water supply with the tons of cyanide Barrick uses to melt mountains of ore.

Notably, one of the first acts of the junior Bush's Interior Department in 2001 was to indicate it would reverse Clinton administration rules requiring gold extractors to limit the size of waste dumps and to permit new mines even if they were likely to cause "substantial, irreparable harm." The *New York Times* ran a long, front-page story on this rule-relaxing windfall for Nevada gold-mining companies, but nowhere did the *Times* mention the name of the owner of the largest gold mine in Nevada, Barrick, nor its recent payroller, the president's father.

Did Our President Spike the Investigation of bin Laden?

On my BBC television show, *Newsnight*, an American journalist confessed that, since the September 11, 2002, attack, U.S. reporters are simply too afraid to ask the uncomfortable questions that could kill careers: "It's an obscene comparison, but there was a time in South Africa when people would put flaming tires around people's necks if they dissented. In some ways, the fear is that you will be neck-laced here, you will have a flaming tire of lack of patriotism put around your neck," Dan Rather said. Without his makeup, Rather looked drawn, old and defeated in confessing that he too had given in. "It's that fear that keeps journalists from asking the toughest of the tough questions and to continue to bore-in on the tough questions so often."

Silence as patriotism? My producers at *Newsnight* and editors at the *Guardian* were not so constrained. So I was assigned to fly home to Ground Zero and ask the necessary question that could not, in the early days after the attack, leave the lips of American reporters: How did it happen that the CIA, FBI, Defense Intelligence Agency and our other extravagantly funded spooks could neither prevent nor learn in advance about the most deadly attack on America since Pearl Harbor? The answer was as unpleasant as the question.

If U.S. intelligence agencies did not see the attack coming it was because they were told *not to look*. Why? From inside the agencies were obtained statements and documents indicating that the Bush administration blocked key investigations into allegations that top Saudi Arabian royals and some members of the bin Laden family, not just Osama, funded and supported Al-Quaeda and other terrorist organizations.

The reports I did based on this information won the California State University School of Journalism's Project Censored Award in 2002. It's not the kind of prize you want to win—it's given to crucial stories that were effectively banned from U.S. airwaves and papers.[3]

I don't want any misunderstanding here, so I must emphasize what we did *not* find: we uncovered no information, none whatsoever, that George W. Bush had any advance knowledge of the plan

---

[3]Not surprisingly, our story led the news in Europe. Our team was directed by BBC *Newsnight* producer Meirion Jones. We were joined by *Guardian* investigator David Pallister and editor David Leigh with invaluable assistance provided by the National Security News Service of Washington under the direction of spy-tracker Joe Trento.

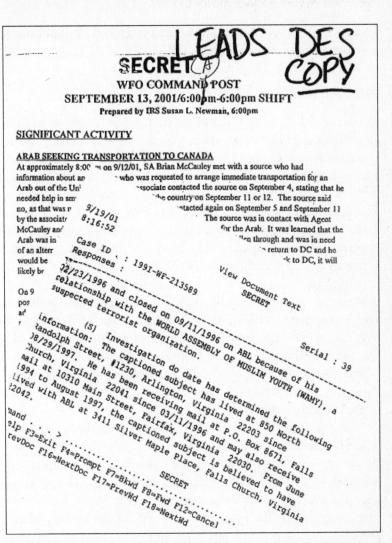

Fig. 2.1. FBI documents: "Secret." The designation "199" means "national security matter." This is the first of over thirty pages of documentation obtained by BBC and the National Security News Service (Washington) indicating that the FBI was pulled off the trail of "ABL" (Abdullah bin Laden)—until September 13, 2001. Abdullah is reportedly Osama's cousin, and should not be confused with another Abdullah, Osama's brother, a businessman in Boston.

to attack the World Trade Center on September 11, nor, heaven forbid, any involvement in the attack.

FBI Document 1991

What we *did* discover was serious enough. To begin with, from less-than-happy FBI agents we obtained an interesting document, some thirty pages long, marked "SECRET." I've reproduced a couple of pages here (figure 2.1). Note the designation "1991"—that's FBI-speak for "national security matter." According to insiders, FBI agents had wanted to check into two members of the bin Laden family, Abdullah and Omar, but were told to stay away by superiors—until September 13, 2001. By then, Abdullah and Omar were long gone from the USA.

Why no investigation of the brothers bin Laden? The Bush administration's line is the Binladdins (a more common spelling of the Arabic name) are good folk. Osama's the Black Sheep, supposedly cut off from his Saudi kin. But the official line notwithstanding, some FBI agents believed the family had some gray sheep worth questioning—especially these two working with the World Assembly of Muslim Youth (WAMY), which the file labels "a suspected terrorist organization."

Let's be careful here: WAMY may be completely innocent. The FBI targets lots of innocents, *too* many in fact, but there were plenty of signs that the WAMY crew deserved the organization's scrutiny. WAMY, funded from Riyadh by royal charities, sponsors soccer teams and educational seminars. But in their Florida summer camp, besides the usual arts and crafts for the kiddies, youngsters received a pep talk on what were presented as the good Islamic practices of hostage-taking and suicide killings. (We at BBC obtained a video tape of one of these rap sessions.) WAMY literature was found in the apartment of one of the 1993 World Trade Center bombers, praising "heroes" who killed unarmed Jews at worship.

No matter how vile WAMY's indoctrination chats, they are

none of the FBI's business. Recruitment for terror, however, is. Before September 11, the governments of India and the Philippines tied WAMY to groups staging murderous attacks on civilians. Following our broadcast on BBC, the Dutch secret service stated that WAMY, "support(ed) violent activity." In 2002, the *Wall Street Journal*'s Glenn Simpson made public a report by Bosnia's government that a charity with Abdullah bin Laden on its board had channeled money to Chechen guerrillas. Two of the September 11 hijackers used an address on the same street as WAMY's office in Falls Church, Virginia.

The "Back-Off" Directive and the Islamic Bomb

Despite these tantalizing facts, Abdullah and his operations were A-OK with the FBI chiefs, if not their working agents. Just a dumb SNAFU? Not according to a top-level CIA operative who spoke with us on condition of strictest anonymity. After Bush took office, he said, "there was a major policy shift" at the National Security Agency. Investigators were ordered to "back off" from any inquiries into Saudi Arabian financing of terror networks, especially if they touched on Saudi royals and their retainers. That put the bin Ladens, a family worth a reported $12 billion and a virtual arm of the Saudi royal household, off limits for investigation. Osama was the exception; he remained a wanted man, but agents could not look too closely at how he filled his piggy bank. The key rule of any investigation, "follow the money," was now violated, and investigations—at least before September 11—began to die.

And there was a lot to investigate—or in the case of the CIA and FBI under Bush—a lot to ignore. Through well-known international arms dealers (I'm sorry, but in this business, sinners are better sources than saints) our team was tipped off to a meeting of Saudi billionaires at the Hotel Royale Monceau in Paris in May 1996 with the financial representative of Osama bin Laden's network. The Saudis, including a key Saudi prince joined by Muslim and non-Muslim gun traffickers, met to determine who would pay how much to Osama. This was not so much an act of support but of protection—a pay off to keep the mad bomber away from Saudi Arabia.

The crucial question here is that, if I could learn about this meeting, how did the CIA miss it? In fact, since the first edition of this book, other sources have disclosed that the meeting was monitored by French intelligence. Since U.S. intelligence was thus likely informed, the question becomes why didn't the government immediately move against the Saudis?

I probed our CIA contact for specifics of investigations that were hampered by orders to back off of the Saudis. He told us that far bigger fish got away than WAMY. The Khan Laboratories investigation had been effectively put on hold.

You may never have heard of Khan Laboratories, but if this planet blows to pieces this year, it will likely be thanks to Kahn Labs' creating nuclear warheads for Pakistan's military. Because investigators had been tracking the funding for this so-called "Islamic Bomb" back to Saudi Arabia, under Bush security restrictions, the inquiry was stymied. (The restrictions were lifted, the agent told me without a hint of dark humor, on September 11.)[4]

---

[4]Dr. A. Q. Kahn is the Dr. Strangelove of Pakistan, the "father" of their bomb and, says a former associate, a crusader for its testing . . . on humans. On April 25, 1998, Kahn met at the Kushab Research Center with General Jehangir Karamat, then army chief of staff, to plan a possible preemptive nuclear strike on New Delhi, India. The Saudis lit a fuse under this demented scheme by telling Pakistan intelligence that Israel had shipped India warplanes in preparation for a conventional attack on Pakistan. We only know these details because a young researcher who claims he was at the meeting wrote a horrified letter threatening to make the plan to bomb India public, a threat which appears to have halted the scheme. After writing down his objections, the whistle-blower, Iftikhar Khan-Chaudhry, ran for his life to London, then the USA, seeking asylum. Khan-Chaudhry, when questioned, seemed to know too little to be the top nuclear physicist he claimed, and far too much about A. Q. Khan's bomb factory to be the tile company accountant Pakistan claims. Pakistan police, failing to arrest him, jailed, beat and raped his wife, suggesting they wanted him to keep secret something more interesting than bookkeeping methods. Whether his story was real or bogus, I can't possibly tell. The point is that intelligence agencies under Clinton, based on many other leads as well, were following up on the Saudi connection until the Bush team interfered.

Clinton Closed an Eye

True-blue Democrats may want to skip the next paragraphs. If President Bush put the kibosh on investigations of Saudi funding of terror and nuclear bomb programs, this was merely taking a policy of Bill Clinton one step further.

Following the 1996 Khobar Towers bombing in Saudi Arabia, Clinton hunted Osama with a passion—but a passion circumscribed by the desire to protect the sheikdom sitting atop our oil lifeline. In 1994, a Saudi diplomat defected to the United States with 14,000 pages of documents from the kingdom's sealed file cabinets. This mother lode of intelligence included evidence of plans for the assassination of Saudi opponents living in the West and, tantalizingly, details of the $7 billion the Saudis gave to Saddam Hussein for his nuclear program—the first attempt to build an Islamic Bomb. The Saudi government, according to the defector, Mohammed Al Khilewi, slipped Saddam the nuclear loot during the Reagan and Bush Sr. years when our own government still thought Saddam too marvelous for words. The thought was that he would only use the bomb to vaporize Iranians.

Clinton granted the Saudi defector asylum, but barred the FBI from *looking* at the documents. Al Khilewi's New York lawyer, Michael Wildes, told me he was stunned. Wildes handles some of America's most security-sensitive asylum cases. "We said [to the FBI], 'Here, take the documents! Go get some bad guys with them! We'll even pay for the photocopying!'" But the agents who came to his office had been ordered not to accept evidence of Saudi criminal activity, even on U.S. soil.

In 1997, the Canadians caught and extradited to America one of the Khobar Towers attackers. In 1999, Vernon Jordan's law firm stepped in and—poof!—the killer was shipped back to Saudi Arabia before he could reveal all he knew about Al-Quaeda (valuable) and the Saudis (embarrassing). I reviewed, but was not permitted to take notes on, the alleged terrorist's debriefing by the FBI. To my admittedly inexpert eyes, there was enough on Al-Quaeda to make him a source on terrorists worth holding on to. Not that he was set free—he's in one of the kingdom's dungeons—but his info is sealed up with him. The terrorist's extradition was "Clinton's." "Clinton's parting kiss to the Saudis," as one insider put it.

This make-a-sheik-happy policy of Clinton's may seem similar to Bush's, but the difference is significant. Where Clinton said, "Go slow," Bush policymakers said, "No go." The difference is between closing one eye and closing them both.

Blow-Back and Bush Sr.

Still, we are left with the question of why both Bush Jr. and Clinton would hold back disclosure of Saudi funding of terror. I got the first glimpse of an answer from Michael Springmann, who headed up the U.S. State Department's visa bureau in Jeddah, Saudi Arabia, during the Reagan–Bush Sr. years. "In Saudi Arabia I was repeatedly ordered by high-level State Department officials to issue visas to unqualified applicants. These were, essentially, people who had no ties either to Saudi Arabia or to their own country. I complained bitterly at the time there." That was Springmann's mistake. He was one of those conscientious midlevel bureaucrats who did not realize that when he filed reports about rules violations he was jeopardizing the cover for a huge multicontinental intelligence operation aimed at the Soviets. Springmann assumed petty thievery: someone was taking bribes, selling visas; so he couldn't understand why his complaints about rule-breakers were "met with silence" at the Bureau of Diplomatic Security.

Springmann complained himself right out of a job. Now a lawyer, he has obtained more information on the questionable "engineers" with no engineering knowledge whom he was ordered to permit into the United States. "What I was protesting was, in reality, an effort to bring recruits, rounded up by Osama bin Laden, to the United States for terrorist training by the CIA. They would then be returned to Afghanistan to fight against the then-Soviets."

But then they turned their talents against the post-Soviet power: us. In the parlance of spook-world, this is called "blow-back." Bin Laden and his bloody brethren were created in America's own Frankenstein factory. It would not do for the current president nor agency officials to dig back to find that some of the terrorists we are hunting today were trained and armed by the Reagan–Bush administration. And that's one of the problems for agents seeking to investigate groups like WAMY, or Abdullah bin Laden. WAMY literature that talks about that "compassionate young man Osama bin Laden," is likely to have been disseminated, if not written, by our very own government. If Abdullah's Bosnian-operated "charity" was funding Chechnyan guerrillas, it is only possible because the Clinton CIA gave the wink and nod to WAMY and other groups who were aiding Bosnian guerrillas when they were fighting Serbia, a U.S.-approved enemy. "What we're talking about," says national security expert Joe Trento, "is embarrassing, career-destroying blow-back for intelligence officials." And, he could add, for the presidential father.

The Family Business

I still didn't have an answer to all my questions. We knew that Clinton and the Bushes were reluctant to discomfort the Saudis by unearthing their connections to terrorists—but what made this new president take particular care to protect the Saudis, even to the point of stymying his own intelligence agencies?

The answers kept coming back: "Carlyle" and "Arbusto."

While some people have guardian angels, our president seems to have guardian sheiks. George W. was born with a silver oil well in his mouth; yet, despite the age of his family's money, his share was not anywhere near the pile it is now. This is a Texas oilman who seemed to drill nothing but dry holes. Yet he made the big time, not by striking oil, but by locating a gusher in the pockets of investors tied to Arabia who always seemed to appear to catch him as another one of his goofed-up business ventures was about to keel over.

Dubya's Arbusto [Spanish for "shrub"] Oil was funded in 1977 by James R. Bath, among others, whose own money came from representing Sheikhs Salim bin Laden and Khalid bin Mahfouz. When Bush's exploration firm was about to give up the ghost in 1981, he was bought out at a suspiciously high premium by Philip Uzielli, a college roommate of James Baker III, who would become Bush Sr.'s secretary of state, as well as a business associate in a firm called Carlyle. In 1986, the Uzielli operation, Spectrum Oil, with Bush on board, was saved on surprisingly good terms by Harken Oil—which would, within a year, receive a rich cash injection from Saudi Sheik Abdullah Bakhsh. When in 1990 Harken itself started to head south financially, Bahrain's government chose this Texas dry-land driller over Amoco to drill in the Persian Gulf. This surprising coup had nothing to do, we are told, with Dubya's daddy being, at the time, the president of the Free World.

Behind Carlyle is a private, invitation-only investment group whose holdings in the war industry make it effectively one of America's biggest defense contractors. For example, Carlyle owned United Technologies, the maker of our fighter jets. Carlyle has the distinction of claiming both of the presidents Bush as paid retainers. Dubya served on the board of Carlyle's Caterair airplane food company until it went bust. The senior Bush traveled to Saudi Arabia for Carlyle in 1999. The bin Ladens were among Carlyle's select backers until just after the September 11 attacks, when the connection became impolitic. The company's chairman is Frank Carlucci, Bush Sr.'s former defense secretary. The average Carlyle partner has gained about $25 million in equity. Notably, Saudi Prince Al Waleed bin Talal bin Abdul Aziz employed Carlyle as his advisor in buying up 10 percent of Citicorp's preferred stock. The choice of Carlyle for the high-fee work was odd, as the group is not an investment bank. One would almost think the Saudi potentate wanted to enrich Carlyle's members.

Dan Rather, still in his confessional mode, told BBC, "One finds oneself saying, 'I know the right question, but you know what, this is not exactly the right time to ask it.'"

But I'll ask anyway. "Where does the Bush family business end and policy begin?"

In my opinion, much too much has been made of the bin Ladens's Carlyle connection to the Bushes. It would be absurd to say that President Bush spiked the investigation of the bin Laden family and Saudi funding of terrorists in return for packets of cash. The system is not so crude. Gentlemen of the club do not act that way. Rather, what's created is a prejudice, call it a *disposition*, to conclude that these smiling Gulf billionaires, whose associates made you and your family wealthy, are unlikely to have funded mass murder of Americans, despite the evidence.

Who Lost the War on Terror?

So who lost the War on Terror? Osama? From his point of view, he's made the celebrity cutthroats' Hall of Fame. Where is he? Don't ask Bush; our leader just changes the subject to Iraq. So we have the 82nd Airborne looking for Osama bin Laden among the camels in Afghanistan when, in all likelihood, the billionaire butcher—now likely beardless—is chillin' by the pool at the Ritz Carlton, knocking back a brewsky and laughing at us while two blonde Barbies massage his feet.

Bush failed to get Osama. But we did successfully eliminate the threat of Congresswoman McKinney—you remember, the one who dared question ChoicePoint, the company that helped Katherine Harris eliminate Black voters.

Following our BBC broadcast and *Guardian* report in November 2001, McKinney cited our stories on the floor of Congress, calling for an investigation of the intelligence failures and policy prejudices you've just read here. She was labeled a traitor, a freak, a conspiracy nut and "a looney"—the latter by her state's Democratic Senator, who led the mob in the political lynching of the uppity Black woman. The *New York Times* wrote, "She angered some Black voters by suggesting that President Bush might have known in advance about the September 11 attacks but had done nothing so his supporters could make money in war." The fact that she said no such thing doesn't matter; the *Times* is always more influential than the truth. Dan Rather had warned her, shut up, don't ask questions, and you can avoid the neck-lacing. She didn't and it cost her her seat in Congress.

McKinney's electoral corpse in the road silenced politicians, the media was mum, but some Americans still would not get in line. For them we have new laws to permit investigating citizens without warrants, and the label of terrorist fellow-traveler attached to groups from civil rights organizations to trade treaty protestors. Yet not one FBI or CIA agent told us, "If only we didn't have that pesky Bill of Rights, we would have nailed bin Laden." Not one said, "What we need is a new bureaucracy for Fatherland Security." Not one said we needed to jail everyone in the Midwest named "Ahmed." They had a single request: for George W. Bush's security henchmen to get their boot heels off agents' necks and remove the shield of immunity from the Saudis.

That leaves one final, impertinent question. Who won? "The war on terror hasn't been decided yet, but a few winners are emerging," business magazine *Forbes* says cheerily. "Background checking services . . . are high up on the list of businesses that will benefit from [the] government proposal to beef up security in the world's largest economy . . . services provided by companies like . . . ChoicePoint Inc., would increase further when the U.S. Immigration and Naturalization Service steps up immigrant tracking."

On May 30, 2002, Attorney General John Ashcroft released new Guidelines on General Crimes, Racketeering and Terrorism. Ashcroft authorizes the mining of private information from commercial databases on citizens even, says the Electronic Privacy Information Center with alarm, "where there is no suspicion of criminal conduct." And who is one of the biggest commercial database firms? ChoicePoint. Forget that FBI agents say this is a big waste and a distraction to their work—ChoicePoint, having chosen our president for us, certainly knows what's best. They also want your blood: The administration is pushing for a national repository of DNA tags for each of us, a job already begun by Bode Technologies, a division of ChoicePoint. And if you have any complaints about this, just remember, *they know where you live*.

George Wins the Lotteries

The Bush family daisy chain of favors, friendship and finance goes way back to Dubya's "War Years." Junior Bush was a fighter pilot during the war in Vietnam; not in the United States Air Force, where one could get seriously hurt, mind you, but in the Texas air force, known as the Air Guard. Texas's toy army, an artifact of Civil War days, is a favorite club for warmongers a bit squeamish about actual combat. Membership excused these weekend warriors from the military draft and the real shoot-em-up in 'Nam.

During the war, Senator Prescott Bush and his son, Congress-man George Bush Sr., were more than happy to send other men's sons and grandsons to Southeast Asia. However, there were not enough volunteers for this suspect enterprise, so Congress created a kind of death lottery: If your birth date was picked out of a hat, off to the army you went. But the Air Guard flyboys were ex-empted form this macabre draft lotto.

When tested for the coveted Air Guard get-out, young George W. tested at twenty-five out of one hundred, one point above "too-dumb-to-fly" status, yet leaped ahead of hundreds of applicants to get the Guard slot.

Now, how could that happen? Only recently could I get a glimmer of the truth, a by-product of an *Observer* investigation of a New Jersey company called GTech. This firm holds the contract for a far less deadly and far more lucrative lottery operation than the one for the military draft: the Texas State Lottery.

Follow the money. It's 1997. Top-gun George Jr. is governor and GTech is in deep doo-doo with Texas lottery regulators. Texas is the nation's biggest, most lucrative lottery and GTech was about to lose its contract, worth hundreds of millions of dollars. The state's lottery director was sacked following revelations that GTech had put the director's boyfriend on the company payroll while he was under indictment for bribery. A new clean-hands director, Lawrence Littwin, ordered an audit, terminated GTech's contract and put it out for rebid. Littwin also launched an investigation into GTech's political donations.

Then a funny thing happened. The Texas Lottery Commission fired Littwin.

Almost immediately thereafter, the Bush-appointed commissioners canceled the bidding for a new operator, though the low bidder had already been announced to replace GTech. The commissioners also halted the financial audit, ended the political payola investigation, and gave the contract back to GTech.

Why did the Texas government work so hard at saving GTech's license? A letter to the U.S. Justice Department—I have obtained a copy—provides some fascinating details. The writer points to one Ben Barnes, a lobbyist to whom GTech paid fees of $23 *million*. Way back in 1968, according to the whistleblower, an aide to Barnes—then lieutenant governor of the Lone Star State—quietly suggested to Air Guard chief Brig. Gen. James Rose that he find a safe spot in the Guard for Congressman George Bush's son.

Whether the Bushes used their influence to get young George out of serving in Vietnam was a big issue during George Jr.'s neck-and-neck race for governor against Ann Richards in 1994. Bush's opponents, however, did not know of Barnes's office's contact with General Rose, so the story died.

The letter ties Barnes's knowledge of Governor Bush's draft-dodging to GTech's exclusive deal with the state.

> "Governor Bush . . . made a deal with Ben Barnes not to rebid (the GTech lottery contract) because Barnes could confirm that Bush had lied during the '94 campaign. During that campaign, Bush was asked if his father, then a member of Congress, had helped him get in the National Guard. Bush said no . . . George Bush was placed ahead of thou-

sands of young men, some of whom died in Viet Nam. . . .
Barnes agreed never to confirm the story and the governor
talked to the chair of the lottery two days later and she
then agreed to support letting GTech keep the contract
without a bid."

The whistleblower remained anonymous, but offered to come
forward later to authorities. Fingering Barnes, a Democrat, as the
man who put in the fix for the Bushes with the Air Guard seemed
wildly implausible. The letter remained sealed and buried. No investigation followed, neither Barnes nor the letter writer were
called by the Feds.

But then in 1998, Littwin—the discharged reform lottery
director—filed a suit charging that the millions GTech paid for lobbyists bought them contract protection. He subpoenaed Barnes. In
1999, facing a grilling under oath Barnes admitted, in a sworn statement to the court, that it was indeed him who got George W. into
the Air Guard.

Amazingly, though, he claimed to have done this nice thing
for Young George without any contact, direct or indirect, from the
Bushes. How Barnes knew he should make the fix without a request from the powerful Bush family remains a mystery, one of
those combinations of telepathy and coincidence common to
Texas politics.

Littwin asserted that other witnesses can verify that the cash
bought the governor's influence to save GTech's license. GTech
responds, irrefutably, that it terminated the contract with Barnes
before the 1997 dismissals of the lottery directors—but not before
the blackmailing alleged in the anonymous letter. And, although
the company denies it maintained the financial connection to
Barnes, GTech's chairman, Guy Snowden, was a partner in a big
real estate venture with Barnes's wife. (In 1995, Snowden was
forced to resign as chairman of GTech when a jury found he tried
to bribe British billionaire Richard Branson.)

What did GTech get for their $23 million to Barnes, the man

who saved Dubya from the war? Can't say. In November 1999 GTech paid a reported $300,000 to Littwin; in return, Littwin agreed to seal forever Barnes's five-hour deposition transcript about the Bush family influence on the lottery and the Air Guard.

I'm not complaining, mind you. After all, the Bush family has given us the best democracy money can buy.

Republicans and Democrats, Hand in Hand, to Save the Billionaire Boys' Club

A thoughtful reader found my Texas tales about President Bush a wee harsh:

> *"G'day, asshole! Smelled any good ones lately? That's generally where guys like you have their noses. By the way, it's PRESI-DENT Bush to you, numbnuts. Now, have a g'day and may Ireland be free!"*

So I resolved to be a bit fairer—and take a look at the strange financial history of the Arkansas Hillary-Billies. I thought it proper to check Special Prosecutor Ken Starr's evidence. He had nothing. Starr, whose mind is as small as it is vicious, spent $40 million investigating the Clintons and turned up little more than a bucket of dirty "Whitewater," a stained dress and some overwritten soft porn ("So then I pulled down the President's . . ."). How could they find nothing? Part of the problem was that Starr and staff were no Sam Spades, just a bunch of right-wing preppy snots from white-shoe law firms who thought they could replace investigative know-how with unlimited meanness.

But if Starr was lost in a nutty cavort with Clinton's slick willy, the Senate Governmental Affairs Committee was looking into the serious stuff: six-figure payments to Hillary's former law partners by the Riady family of Indonesia and Entergy International of Little Rock, Arkansas, Hillary's former client. (We'll get to those guys in the next chapter.) Then, in 1998, just as the Republicans on the Senate committee were closing in on the evidence that could, if borne out, pull down the Clintons . . . the committee closed its investigation.

Why? The answer is: Triad.

Clinton was saved from the truly threatening inquiry about his Indonesian money, an impeachable offense, by two of America's wealthiest oil and gas barons, Charles and David Koch. They had not set out to rescue Clinton. The Koch brothers despise Clinton with a passion.

Koch Industries is the biggest company you've never heard of—and their owners like it that way. Estimates of its annual turnover, at $35 billion a year, make it bigger than Microsoft or Boeing Aircraft. We can only estimate because Koch (pronounced "coke," like the cola) is a private corporation, the second largest in the United States. David and Charles Koch, who own nearly all of it, are reported to have a combined net worth of $4 billion. If you've never head of the Kochs, the politicians have. Among the Big Oil that funded the Republican party during George W. Bush's run for the White House, Koch Industries pumped in more than any corporation except Enron and Exxon-Mobil.

The Koch clan's fortune originated in Russia, where daddy Fred Koch built oil refineries for Stalin's regime. In 1946, Koch returned from the Soviet Union to Wichita, Kansas, and founded the ultra-right John Birch Society. David and Charles have rejected their father's politics, preferring to back ultra-*ultra* right-wing causes. In 1980, as a Libertarian Party candidate, David campaigned against Ronald Reagan.

Secrecy is the Kochs' trademark. From headquarters in Wichita, they operate the nation's only private, secure telephone network outside the CIA to control their core business as America's largest purchaser of oil and gas from small farmers and Indian reservations.

As owners of a private company, the Kochs answer to no one

about their expenditures. No little old ladies query them at stockholder meetings. Unconstrained, the Koch brothers can indulge their singular dream. Where other U.S. corporations throw a few million dollars into the political arena in the hopes of obtaining a few special favors, the Kochs have spent close to $100 million to change the entire tone of political discourse in America.

And they succeeded. With $21 million spent to establish the Cato Institute in Washington, DC, $30 million to start the Citizens for a Sound Economy and tens of millions more for think tanks, political action committees and the like, they constructed a nonpareil policy apparatus that reinvigorated the antigovernment movement with a new intellectual legitimacy backed by fearsome political clout. From Cato and the Koch machine came Newt Gingrich's "Contract for America" and the funds to put Gingrich in power in the 1994 elections.

Not that the Kochs don't call in special favors. In 1989, the U.S. Senate Special Committee on Investigations concluded that "Koch Oil, a subsidiary of Koch Industries, is the most dramatic example of an oil company stealing by deliberate mismeasurement and fraudulent reporting." FBI agents had watched Koch Industries truckers appearing to take, but not fully paying for, oil from small gathering tanks on Indian reservations. An expert for Indian tribes calculates that $1.5 billion of Koch Industries' wealth comes from pilfered oil. Koch denies it.

Action against Koch for stealing from the Indians stalled until 1995 when an FBI agent on the Senate investigation, Richard Elroy, charged in a letter to the Justice Department that criminal prosecution had been declined "for political reasons" during the first Bush presidency. So Clinton's Justice Department followed up on the FBI's evidence, concentrating on environmental crimes, and filed civil lawsuits charging Koch Industries with 315 willful acts of pollution. Clinton also impaneled two grand juries to consider criminal indictments.

Newt Gingrich raced to the Kochs' rescue. If one clause of

Newt Gingrich's "Contract for America," the Regulatory Reform Act, had become law, the Justice Department case against the Kochs—which sought big money and portended jail time—would have been doomed. Proposed changes in law included eliminating some environmental controls and decriminalizing violations.

Passage of the Koch-saving legislation depended upon the Republicans holding their majority in Congress. In the 1996 election cycle, Republican control was in jeopardy. Crucial to their ultimate narrow victory in that campaign was a multimillion-dollar television advertising blitz in key districts paid for by the Coalition for Our Children's Future, a registered charity. The action was extraordinary for a child protection society—as was their choice of candidates to assist. Only weeks before CCF purchased the adverts, every one of the incumbent congressmen they helped, all Republicans, voted to abolish food stamps for children of the poor.

The politicians supported by the "Children's" fund had something in common besides an antipathy to free meals for youngsters. Their districts contained Koch operations.

It may surprise you to learn that U.S. law prohibits corporate payments in aid of political campaigns. Officially, donations must come through individuals or political action committees.

Investigators with the Senate Governmental Affairs Committee located bank records linking the children's "charity" and other political front groups to Triad Management, an operation funded by the Kochs. Democratic senators threatened to subpoena Koch Industries' chiefs to question whether they funded Triad and manipulated its related groups. Democrats could drag the tycoons before the same public tribunal on campaign finances skewering Clinton.

A key Senate insider, who must remain anonymous, says Republicans then offered a straightforward trade: "A truce—you don't do Triad, we don't do Clinton." Other sources inside the committee confirm that the Republicans, under the direction of

Senators Trent Lott and Don Nickles, rather than risk exposure of the Kochs' web of mega-dollar funding operations, agreed to shut down the money probe and let Clinton off the hook.

The true, unreported reason for the collapse of the inquiry most threatening to Clinton—the Indonesia money chain, which could have knocked him out of office—reveals the ultimate measure of Koch influence: that Republicans sacrificed their case against the president to keep their secret benefactors under wraps.

Both parties were content with their mutual protection agreement. Each party's billionaires were safe. With this sub-rosa deal in place, important fund-raising allegations became off-limits. And that's how we ended up with Republican investigators with nothing left to do—except rummage through Monica Lewinsky's dirty laundry and sniff at the president's zipper.

What Every Billionaire Wants

I discovered the billionaire-donor deal not because I was on some kind of hunt for the goods on Clinton or on Newt Gingrich, but because, in my old day job as an investigator and government adviser, I'd been tracking the Koch brothers, the Riadys and their partner, Entergy International of Little Rock (we'll get to these guys in the next chapter). That Entergy and Koch, both master deal makers, popped up in the middle of a Senate inquiry that suddenly stopped dead gave off the smell of a bit too much bipartisan cooperation.

The Kochs, by the way, are a real piece of work. These are the owners of the company the FBI agent says skimmed oil out of the gathering tanks of poor Indians in Oklahoma. In 1999, Koch Industries paid $25 million to settle claims after a civil jury found the company liable for underpayments. Maybe the top guys at Koch Industries, the billionaire brothers themselves, didn't know about the skimming game; maybe there was a good explanation. But not according to Roger Williams, former executive in their oil-gathering operation.

Williams kept records of the filching—a couple of dollars' worth of oil here, a couple there—hardly the kind of petty cash that billionaires would seem to bother with. But Williams (on tape I've obtained) was asked how Charles Koch reacted to a paper that "showed how much 'overage' they had and how many dollars." Of billionaire Koch and another executive with him at the time, Williams said: "They would just giggle and nudge each other, you know, it's kind of a fun time."

Williams, who did not know he was being recorded, could have repeated Koch's words wrongly, or heard Koch wrong. But what Williams reportedly heard was a phrase that explains the success of some of America's wealthiest corporate chiefs. Williams was surprised at the billionaire's concern over these small-change scams, but Williams said Charles Koch told him, *"I want my fair share and that's all of it."*

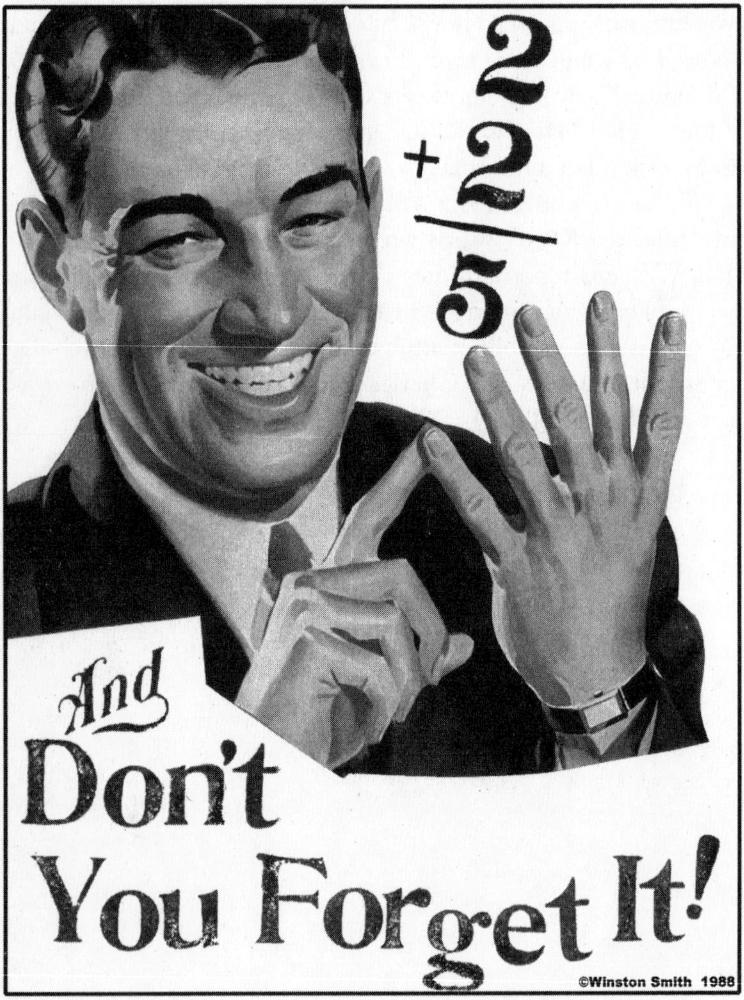

2
+2
5
And
Don't
You Forget It!
©Winston Smith 1988

CALIFORNIA REAMIN':
Deregulation and the Power Pirates

On April 10, 1989, Jacob "Jake" Horton, senior vice president of Southern Company's Gulf Power unit, boarded the company plane to confront his board of directors over the company's accounting games and illegal payments to local politicians. Minutes after take-off, the plane exploded. Later that day, police received an anonymous call: "You can stop investigating Gulf Power now."

Fast-forward to December 2000. The lights in San Francisco blinker out. Wholesale electricity prices in California rise on some days by 7,000 percent, and San Francisco's power company declares bankruptcy. Dick Cheney, just selected vice president by the U.S. Supreme Court, begins a series of secret meetings with power company executives. On their advice, within three days of Bush's inaugural, his Energy Department wipes away regulations against price gouging and profiteering ordered that December by outgoing President Clinton.

Out of Cheney's off-the-record meetings came the energy plan released by the president in May 2001. Billed as the response to the California electricity crisis, the president told us the plan contained the magic potion to end the power shortage. Then, after the horrors of September 11, 2001, the plan was remarketed as a weapon against Middle East terrorists. Nasty-minded readers may believe the Bush energy program, still rolling around Congress, is just some pea-brained scheme to pay off the president's oil company buddies, fry the planet and smother Mother Earth in coal ash, petroleum pollutants and nuclear waste. In truth, it's more devious than that.

There is a link running from Jake's exploding plane to blackouts on the Golden Gate Bridge to the polluters' wet dream of an energy plan offered by Cheney and Bush. They are connected through the mystical economics of electricity deregulation. Beneath the murky surface of this odd backwater of market theory is a multicontinental war over the ownership and control of $4 trillion in public utility infrastructure—gas, water, telephone and electricity lines—a story that began a decade earlier with Jake Horton and continued through a coup d'état in Pakistan and the bankruptcy of a company called Enron.[1]

Andersen's Magic Show

In 1989, I was brought into an investigation of Horton's employer, Southern Company of Atlanta, by Georgia civic groups suspicious that Southern had overcharged its several million electricity customers in Georgia, Alabama, Mississippi and Florida. I focused on transcripts of tape recordings made a year earlier by accountant Gary Gilman. Wearing a hidden microphone, Gilman recorded his fellow executives detailing the method by which Southern charged customers $61 million for spare parts which, in fact, had not been used. Like all good accountants, Southern's kept a careful record of the phantom parts in electronic ledgers—found in the

---

[1]This chapter is based on, and updated from, a series of commentaries for the *Guardian* and *Observer*, *Washington Post*, *New York Times*, *La Republica* (Peru) and *Financial Times*, and a series of lectures at Cambridge University School of Applied Economics and the University of São Paolo. An expanded discussion is contained in *Democracy and Regulation*, a policy guide written for the United Nations, which I coauthored with Theo MacGregor and Jerrold Oppenheim.

trunk of one executive's car. I obtained copies of the documents, spending months decoding the accounts, gaining an insight into what would, a decade later, lead to blackouts and bankruptcies from California to Argentina.

Take a look at a bit of what I saw (figure 3.1).

There's two sets of numbers—one for government and one for the boys at the top of the company structure to keep track of reality. Here's where it turns a little technical. The parts held in inventory should have been "capitalized," that is, listed as an investment in "Account 154." In fact, they were "expensed"—to use the accounting lingo—and charged as if they were used. The difference between capitalizing and expensing is the difference between having your cake (investing) and eating it (using it up). Moving numbers from one account to the other cheated the IRS and bill payers out of millions.

Shortly after Horton's death, a grand jury in Atlanta was prepared to indict Southern Company's Georgia unit for the spare-parts accounting manipulations. But, invoking a rarely used procedure under the federal racketeering statute, Bush Sr.'s Justice Department overruled local prosecutors to quash the request for indictment. The reason? Keeping hidden accounts in secret files and booking costs into the wrong accounts may be a bit unusual,

GEORGIA POWER COMPANY
POWER GENERATION MATERIALS
ESTIMATED VALUE AS OF DECEMBER 1985

PLANT	INCIDENTAL MATERIAL	MAINTENANCE SPARES	EMERGENCY SPARES	TOTAL	CONVERTED TO 154
OWEN	(SEE NOTE 1)	15,405,163.97	17,682,000.00	33,087,163.97	15,405,163.97
HAMMOND	969,811.13	5,971,752.79	3,211,581.68	10,153,145.60	6,941,563.92
CHERER	(SEE NOTE 2)	0.00	0.00	0.00	0.00
ANSLEY	(SEE NOTE 3)	3,402,868.62	3,822,999.23	7,225,867.85	0.00
ATCH	5,149,097.21	3,012,574.43	9,327,527.26	17,489,198.91	0.00
ATES	1,074,050.41	7,825,819.06	7,182,598.02	16,082,467.49	0.00
RANCH	695,063.47	6,846,779.41	11,290,207.68	18,832,050.56	0.00
MCDONOUGH	1,665,480.20	6,489,757.67	1,572,948.35	9,728,186.22	0.00
MITCHELL	323,972.42	1,781,848.30	1,133,903.46	3,239,724.18	0.00
ARKWRIGHT	103,091.29	567,002.08	360,819.51	1,030,912.87	567,002.08
MCMANUS	30,604.67	168,325.71	107,116.36	306,046.75	168,325.71
WILSON	24,147.09	132,808.99	84,514.81	241,470.89	132,808.99
HYDRO'S	48,677.93	267,728.61	170,372.75	486,779.29	267,728.61
TOTALS	10,083,995.82	61,872,429.64	55,946,589.12	117,903,014.58	23,482,593.28

Fig. 3.1. Spare parts. The secret set of accounts.

and may have cost the public a bundle, but it was approved at each step by that upstanding auditing firm, Arthur Andersen.

Indeed they had. I found one letter from Andersen coaching the power company executives on how to wave a bookkeeping magic wand over the spare-parts records to make the problem disappear.

I suggested at the time, "Why not indict Andersen?" and proposed a civil racketeering claim against the accounting giant, naming them as Southern's coconspirator. My suggestion, not surprisingly, was dismissed with a chuckle by lawyers who understood that politics trumps law. The signal from the Bush administration was clear enough: Hire Andersen, knead your account books like cookie dough, and get a "Get Out of Jail Free" card.

The New World Business Order

What about poor Jake? "Looks like he saw no other way out," says former Southern chairman A. W. "Bill" Dahlberg of the airplane explosion. A suicide? Jake's brother doubts it: He says Horton had planned to meet with the U.S. attorney in Atlanta. Jake apparently had a lot to say about Southern's charging consumers for loads of coal bought from an affiliated mining company. At times the train cars were filled with rock instead of coal.

Jake's death and the failure to indict Southern and Andersen in 1989 marked the radical turning point, albeit unseen at the time, in the way corporate America would do business—or, as it turned out, *fail* to do business.

This new world business order would be lead by power, water, and natural gas corporations and telecommunications (what we used to call phone companies). Until the 1990s, U.S. state governments kept a tight lid on these monopolies' profits. America's old regulatory system, based on public hearings and open records, was uniquely democratic, found nowhere else in the world. This was a legacy of the Populists, an armed and angry farmers' movement whose struggles from 1900 through 1930 bequeathed to Americans just about the lowest priced, most reliable electricity services in the world—which is, of course, anathema to power company shareholders.

In 1933, President Franklin Roosevelt caged the man he believed to be the last of the power pirates, Samuel Insull, a wheeler-dealer whose electricity trust companies were cesspools of rigged prices, cooked books, watered stock and suffocating monopoly. Roosevelt hit Insull and his ilk with the Public Utility Holding Company Act, the Federal Power Act and the Federal Communications Act which, combined with state laws, told electricity, gas, telephone and water companies when to sit, stand and salute. Prices and profits were capped; the tiniest asset had to be accounted for; issuing stock and bonds required government approval; sales between affiliated companies were controlled; "offshore" and "off-books" subsidiaries were prohibited and lights kept on by force of law: no blackout blackmail to hike prices. Furthermore, FDR made political donations from these companies illegal—no soft money, no hard money, no money *period*.

Roosevelt's rules held for half a century. And utilities hated it, for good reason. Southern Company was typical: In the 1980s, it was an unremarkable regional electricity company dying the death of a thousand financial cuts. Consumer groups used the old regulatory hearings to force Southern to eat the company's dumb investments on overpriced nuclear plants. As a result, Southern showed nothing but cash losses for years.

Then CEO Dahlberg, who took over after Horton's death, conceived an unorthodox way out for Southern from its regulatory and financial troubles. The company had tried breaking the law without much to show for it (it pled guilty to political donations, a felony crime, and suffered penalties, though not criminal charges, for its accounting games). Now it would go straight, not by adhering to the law but by changing the law to adhere to Dahlberg's plan. That plan was not small stuff: The near-bankrupt local company would take over the entire planet's electricity system and, at the same time, completely eliminate from the face of the earth those pesky utility regulations that had crushed his company's fortunes. California blackouts were just a hiccup on the road to the astonishing success of this astonishing program. Today, in 2003, Southern is by far the biggest power company in America (that is, since the collapse of Enron).

In early 2001, America's papers were filled with tales of the woes of the two California electric companies bleeding from $12 billion in payments for electricity supplies. Yet, at the time, virtually nothing was said of the companies collecting their serum: Southern and a half dozen of its corporate fellow travelers—Entergy International of Little Rock, Duke Power of North Carolina, and Texas operators Reliant, TXU, Dynegy, El Paso Corp and Enron. Until November 2001, when America discovered a hole in Houston where Enron used to be, the U.S. press could not be bothered with the who, how and why of these companies. True, there were some profiles of Enron's chairman, Ken Lay, but these were drooling hagiographies portraying Enron's chairman as a cross between Einstein and Elvis.

There have been some changes since the first edition of this book. America's media have finally taken note of the Harry Potter accounting methods of many U.S. corporations. But I have yet to read the *whole* truth: that this ledger-demain began with the senior Bush's crusade to eliminate Roosevelt's pesky rules, and crucially, the utility accountants' rule book, the Uniform System of Accounts. Electricity deregulation, voted into law in 1992, the last big gimme for Bush donors before the elder Bush left the White House, tore the heart out of FDR's Holding Company Act. At the same time, Bush's Federal Communications Commission castrated its own oversight system.

As a result, the Uniform System of Accounts became a museum curiosity. Without it, power and telecommunications companies could outfit their balance sheets with antigravity shoes. It is no accident that ten of the twenty mega-bankruptcies of the last two years involved the utility industry. Two companies in particular—WorldCom and Global Crossing—became virtuosi at

Enron and their Texas followers for world power conquest (or, if you prefer, "vision for globalization of energy supplies") hinged on Britain. As the economist J. M. Keynes said, "The mad rantings of men in authority often have their origins in the jottings of some forgotten professor of economics." The professor in question here is Dr. Stephen Littlechild. In the 1970s, young Stephen, a Briton who studied at the University of Texas, cooked up a scheme to re-place British government ownership of utilities with something al-most every economist before him said simply violated all accepted theorems and plain common sense: a free market in electricity.

The fact that a truly free market didn't exist and cannot possi-bly work did not stop Britain's woman in authority, Prime Minister Margaret Thatcher, from adopting it. It was more than free market theories that convinced her. Whispering in her ear was one Lord Wakeham, then merely "John" Wakeham, Thatcher's energy min-ister. Wakeham approved the first "merchant" power station. It was owned by a company created only in 1985—Enron. Lord Wakeham's decision meant that, for the first time in any nation, an electricity plant owner, namely Enron, could charge whatever the market could bear . . . or, more accurately, could *not* bear.

It was this act in 1990 that launched Enron as the deregulated international power trader. Shortly thereafter, Enron named Wakeham to its board of directors and placed him on Enron's Audit and Compliance Committee, charged with keeping an eye on the company's accounting methods. In addition to his board fee ($10,000 a month), the company paid him for consulting ser-vices. If that strikes you as a conflict of interest, conflict is Wake-ham's forte. His lordship took the Enron posts while remaining a voting member of Parliament. In Britain, that's quite legal.

Following the Enron deal, Wakeham pushed the British gov-ernment to sell off every power plant in the nation along with all the wires from plant to home. Thatcher then launched the England-Wales Power Pool, Professor Littlechild's dream: an auc-tion house for kilowatts that would set electricity prices for the na-tion based on free market principles. On paper, the Power Pool was an academic beauty to behold. The new, privately owned power plant owners would bid against each other every day, ruthlessly undercutting each other's prices for the right to sell to England's consumers, who would, as a result of this market competition, benefit from lower bills.

That was the theory. I can't say whether the market scheme failed in minutes or days, but the Power Pool quickly became a playground for what the industry called "gaming"—bid manipulation techniques that allowed the deregulated companies to expertly vacuum the pockets of consumers. Electricity prices jumped and the owners of the power plants saw their investments grow in value by 300 percent and 400 percent virtually overnight.

Thatcher put the nutty professor Littlechild in charge of regulating the power industry mess. When his term ended in 1998, he left behind a "free market" that worked like a fixed casino and stank of collusion. Littlechild then landed on the board of one of Enron's strange little affiliate companies.

There was no way that Southern was going to let Enron and the Brits have all the loot to themselves. In 1995, the Atlanta company, besieged at home by consumers and regulators, bought up England's South Western Electricity Board. In England, Southern could charge double what they charged in Georgia and earn *five times* the profit allowed by U.S. regulators. This was the first purchase ever by an American power company outside the United States. The takeover was new, bold—and illegal.

Or, at least the law said so. Bush Sr. had mangled and beaten FDR's regulations, but many still stood, including the prohibition, written in clear no-nonsense language, that barred U.S. electric companies from gambling on foreign operations (or even operating outside their home states). But as Enron showed, rules were made to be broken—or "reformed." Despite a formal complaint by elderly "New Deal" Democratic congressmen, the Securities and Exchange Commission blessed the Southern Company purchase after the fact. Getting the SEC to bend over wasn't easy, but then, Southern had political insurance: Entergy International of Little Rock, Arkansas. Bill Clinton was president, and Entergy, his wife's former client, also wanted a piece of the English action.

Entergy, the near-bankrupt owner of some badly built nuclear plants and lines running across Louisiana and Arkansas, soon became the proud owner of giant London Electricity. In just eighteen months, Entergy would "flip" London to the French government for a gain of over $1 billion. The return on investment was infinite; Entergy bought London without putting up one dime in equity cash.

Behind Southern and Entergy came TXU of Dallas and other Americans, which within three years owned 70 percent of the British power distribution market, no money down. Southern nearly grabbed Britain's biggest power seller, but reports of Horton's demise and unsavory stories of accounting trickery forced the Tory government, then fighting a losing election battle, to ban the takeover.

The new government of Tony Blair was outwardly hostile to the American colonizers. But in 1998, while working undercover for the *Observer* newspaper, I secretly recorded the details of a backroom deal between government ministers and a power company executive to let Reliant of Houston take over the second-largest company in England. I also learned that Blair had personally overruled his regulators to allow Enron and Entergy to build new deregulated power plants—the special request of the Clinton White House.[2]

Texas Gets Lay'd

By 1998, after boarding and capturing England, U.S. power buccaneers, led by Southern, Enron, TXU, Reliant and Entergy had

---

[2]See "Tony Blair and the Sale of Britain" in Chapter 6.

grabbed generating stations and wires on every continent save Antarctica.

But not in the United States, not at first. Americans believe in free enterprise, but we prefer cheap electricity and nearly free water, the product of a combination of our tight regulations and government ownership. Almost alone on the planet, the USA stubbornly exempted itself from what the World Bank calls "neoliberal reform"—and this rankled the new international players who hungered to work the free market con in the USA. The industry lobbyists landed on two beachheads, Texas and California, the only two states with electric systems big enough, and governments Republican enough, to convert to "free" markets.

California was the first to fall over the electricity deregulation cliff, but Texas was the first to leap—with a push from its young new governor, George W. Bush. With Texas companies raking it in worldwide, it's not surprising that the rush to deregulate started in the Lone Star State.

But there was a technical problem that delayed the ripping down of regulation in Texas. To understand why requires a little lesson in engineering. The power stations of Texas produce three things: electricity, pollution and political donations. And, as always, Texas is biggest in all three. Take, for example, the giant power plant named, with admirable candor, Big Brown, owned by TXU. When it comes to filth, Big Brown is champ. A strip mine near Waco stuffs Big Brown's furnaces with lignite, a kind of flammable dirt. TXU dumps 389,000 tons of contaminants into the air each year, making it the number-one polluter in the number-one polluting state in the USA.

Bush made Dallas residents gasp (literally) when he signed a "grandfather" statute exempting some TXU plants from laws requiring scrubbers for these fossil-burning dinosaurs. The other beneficiary: polluter number two, Reliant. TXU and Reliant popped over half a million dollars into Bush's second gubernatorial race.

In 1995, the Clinton Justice Department opened an investigation into evidence of conspiracy by TXU and Reliant to monopolize the Texas power lines. The promised "competition" created by deregulation could placate the Feds and make Enron's Ken Lay a very happy man at the same time. Problem was, TXU and Reliant were stuck with Big Brown and plants so costly, inefficient, dangerous and contaminated the companies would lose billions in a true competitive market.

Governor Bush was always cautious to avoid conflicts of interest—in this case, the conflict between the interests of his top donors, Enron, El Paso Corporation and Dynegy (power traders) and TXU and Reliant (power producers). Former Enron lobbyist Terry Thorn told me straight up this quandary for the governor kept Texas deregulation stalled for two legislative sessions until Bush found a third party to pick up the tab: Texas electricity customers.

In 1999, the governor, the power traders and power producers shook hands on a deal to add a $9 *billion* "stranded cost" surcharge to Texans' electric bills.

Ken Lay had another concern. Bush's stranded cost surcharge would let the games begin, but if the deregulation house of cards ever folded, there would be hell to pay because one set of rules remained: tort law, the unique right of Americans to sue the bastards who rip us off. In 1994, the year Bush ran for governor, Lay founded Texans for Lawsuit Reform. Lay doesn't fool around: TLR's PAC pays out a million dollars a year to Lone Star politicians. In 1995, Bush's first big move as governor was to call an *emergency* session of the legislature to act on TLR's agenda. "Tort reform" in the hands of Bush and Lay became tort *deformed*. The governor pushed through the legislature new restrictions on the right of stockholders, workers and pensioners to sue rogue executives. It looks like Ken Lay thought of everything.

The Texans Grab California by the Bulbs

While Texas companies delayed deregulation to haggle over the spoils, their lobbyists, and the industry's, bored ahead in California.

Lincoln said you can't fool all the people all the time—but, then, you don't have to. To turn a quick buck, a slick line of academic hoodoo and some well-aimed campaign contributions will do the trick. Like Columbus bringing Indians back to the Old World for display, the power industry lobbyists brought Margaret Thatcher's professors and their wheezing free market contraptions to California. In 1996, armed with the suspect calculations of well-compensated academics and inebriated with long droughts of utility political donations, the California legislature tossed out a regulatory system which, until then, had provided reasonably cheap, clean, reliable energy to the state.

Despite knowledge of the British disaster, the sun-addled legislators wrote into the preamble of the enabling legislation the lobbyists' line that a deregulated market would cut consumer prices by 20 percent.

In 1999, my parents sent me their bill from San Diego. Instead of the 20 percent savings promised by the law, in the first year of full deregulation, their energy charges rose 379 percent over the previous year. But before the big bills hit San Diego, the new planetary power merchants, using a combination of money, muscle and Americans' penchant to follow the Hula Hoop state, suckered twenty-three other states into adopting deregulation laws.

Not every economist was for sale. Dr. Eugene Coyle, an incorruptible expert, calculated that his fellow Californians were in for a multibillion-dollar fleecing. In 1998, in an extraordinary uprising of the lambs on the slaughterhouse ramp, Dr. Coyle and a band of community activists were able to get a referendum on the California ballot to overturn the legislature's deregulation vote. The power merchants didn't have to wait for the ballots to be counted to know the outcome: They had bought it. In what is unarguably the highest price ever paid to buy an election, Southern California Edison, Pacific Gas and Electric and their allies spent *$53 million* to defeat professor Coyle's proposal to slow deregulation.

From the get-go, California's new computer-controlled electricity auction system was a mess. The flow chart looked like a bowl of linguini thrown against the wall. In confusion is profit, in complexity more profit. I smelled Texans. Commissioner Carl Wood, appointed after the blackout disasters began, told me that Enron had little to do with the initial lobbying for deregulation, but much to do with writing these weird, knotted details.

In 2000, Beth Emory told me something quite astonishing. Emory had been vice president and general counsel to the agency that oversees California's auction house for kilowatts. It struck me that if Coyle and I knew the English-style system would lead to a price explosion and blackouts, certainly the ·Republican utility commissioners blessing the system knew it too. Politicians expressed po'-faced shock when in 2002 they discovered an Enron memo that describes tricks used to manipulate the market—with filmic names like *Get Shorty, Death Star* and *Ricochet*. Yet every one of these tricks the power gang used on California had been well rehearsed in England. Even the players were the same: Enron, TXU, Duke, Southern California Edison (which owns England's dams) and Southern of Atlanta. Over there, market hucksters used "stacking," "cramming," and "false scheduling," Get Shorty's crude progenitors.

So, I asked Emory, did the state go ahead with their deregulation plan knowing it would blow up? "Oh yes, we *knew* it," Emory told me in 2000. Now an industry lawyer in Washington, she added, "What happened [the blackouts and price explosion] was predictable. We knew *last year* we'd have serious problems." There was, she said, discussion of stalling deregulation but the political push was on, despite foreknowledge of disaster.

Insider Emory says the state was not surprised that on the first hot summer day after deregulation, when California needed every bit of juice it could find, the small coterie of plant owners held California's power system hostage. They could name their price for electricity and they did: $9,999 per unit of power—*30,000 percent* above the old regulated price of about $30. Californians were lucky, says Emory: The power pirates thought that the state's computer could only accept four-digit bids in the automated auction.

In fact, the computers would have accepted seven digits, bankrupting half the families in Los Angeles in a day.

But one man's disaster is another man's windfall. And if that other man is someone like Ken Lay or Steve Letbetter of Reliant, one might expect some of the windfall to end up in the Republican Party pokey. The Typhoid Mary of deregulation was California Utility Commission chairman Daniel Fessler who, after an industry-sponsored junket to England, carried back this economic virus to California. Fessler didn't know a darn thing about electricity when Governor Wilson put him in charge of the state's power agency, but as a Republican functionary, he certainly knew how to get the party's bread buttered.

How They Did It

Markets for electricity don't work and can't work. Electricity is not a bagel—that is, unlike your morning muffin, you can't do without it when it gets too pricey.

Enron knew that too. Shortly after the California market opened for business, for example, an Enron trader sold the state about 5,000 megawatts of power to go over a 15 megawatt line. That's like trying to pour a gallon of gasoline into a thimble—it can't be done. This forced the system operator, the agency that actually keeps our lights on, to make costly emergency purchases, blowing market prices through the roof. Enron, knowing in advance of the panic it would create, could earn a super-profit.

The slightest shortage on a hot or cold day and—whammo!—the tight little wolfpack of electricity sellers can extract a limitless ransom. When the weather would not create a shortage, a monkey wrench could. Repairs were scheduled at peak times. Reliant employees say the company was running plants at odd hours, "ramping" them up and down, which whistleblowers at the company considered deliberate sabotage. Duke Power of North Carolina was less subtle. Its managers, say employees, simply threw away spare parts needed to keep the plants running. And San Diego's power distribution company told me that Duke Power of North Carolina ordered them to shut down a plant during a shortage period—an order the California firm refused.

Merely by holding back the power from a single generator, the power merchants could make the electricity from their other plants worth more than gold. In a report for California's purchasing agency, Dr. Anjali Sheffrin had evidence that California power companies used "physical withholding" and "economic withholding" to create false shortages in California 98 *percent of the time* between May and November 2000. Three giant companies (for which I have, frustratingly, only code names A1, A4 and A5) didn't put in a single honest bid in those months. Add in "false congestion," "false scheduling" and "megawatt laundering," and the overcharges add up, conservatively, to $6.2 billion in a single year.

In addition to the $39 million they paid to defeat Dr. Coyle's antideregulation referendum in 1998, the three big California power companies, PG&E, Edison and Sempra, spent another $34.8 million that year on lobbying and campaign contributions. It was a big payout, but the payback in billions proved again that investing in politicians has a consistently higher rate of return than investing in plants or products.

"Hello. I Am the Son of the Vice President."

While America hesitated over deregulation, the rest of the planet dove headfirst into the "power pool." Although the idea of allowing for-profit electricity companies to run free of regulation was a poor idea proved worse in practice, virtually every nation adopted England's goofy Thatcherite system. In California, deregulation's victory, though greased by political donations, was won chiefly through an expensive campaign of lobbying and propaganda. In poorer nations of the Southern Hemisphere, privatization and deregulation spread the old-fashioned way: threats, coercion and cash in offshore bank accounts.

Resistance was futile. The IMF and World Bank made the sale of electricity, water, telephone and gas systems a condition of loans to every developing nation. Since a loan cutoff meant economic death, it was sell or die.

The World Bank's former chief economist told me the Bank-dictated sell-off program wasn't privatization, it was "briberization." Virtually every bid was bent. (I must grant, however, that the World Bank has its limits. The Bank forced the African nation of Ghana to cancel a deal with Enron in which the evidence of corruption became embarrassingly public.) The baksheesh flowed and power systems were sold off from Brazil to Pakistan.

The spoils are enormous: $4 *trillion* in public assets up for sale. More than electric systems were put on the block. Gas companies, phone companies and, with the most tragic consequences, water companies were handed over to American, French and British corporate buccaneers.

While there was a killing to be had in the "free" market in electricity, grabbing water systems was a sure bet: Governments had already paid for the pipes and the market is captive, customers underserved and thirsty. Again, Thatcher's England led the way with the first privatizations. In Britain, water bills shot up to 250 percent of the U.S. price, water company stock prices quintupled, and in 1995, the system fell to pieces: In some parts of England, you could get arrested for watering your lawn. A big winner (and big political donor) was Wessex Water, 100 percent owned by Enron.

Argentina was first to offer up booty, beginning with the 1988 sale of a trans-Andean gas pipeline. The minister for public works at the time, now Senator Rodolfo Terragno, told me that in the fall of 1988 he received a strange telephone call in Buenos Aires from America from someone who identified himself as the "son of the vice president." But *which* Bush? Terragno knew it wasn't Neil Bush, an acquaintance and big-time investor in Argentina; it had to be George W. (Terragno's assumption), or, my industry sources tell me, Brother Jeb. Whichever, the son of a Bush told the minister that giving the project to a newly formed company called Enron would "strengthen ties between the U.S. and Argentina."

Coming from a son of the man about to enter the White House, this was not a light-handed pitch.

At that time, the Bush brothers were private businessmen, so using their father's name may have smelled a bit, but it was all quite legal. Therefore, I could not understand why the Bush brothers would not fess up to the call to Terragno. George W.'s spokesman denied he met with Terragno, and Jeb, who usually has a lot to say, inscrutably refuses comment.[3]

In 2002, when I met with the Argentine, Terragno provided me a clue to the motive for the Bush boys' tongue-tied response. Enron, he said, wanted a giveaway—the Texans would pay only one-fifth the world price for Argentina's natural gas, ridiculously below other bids. Enron's local lobbyist, said Terragno, indicated that if the Argentine minister greased the lowball Enron bid, the company would have shown its gratitude. "I have no doubts that if I said yes at least part of that money would have ended up in my pockets. They didn't *say* that, but it was implicit." Terragno turned down Enron with a laugh—but then called for investigation two years later when a close friend of the Bush family, Argentina's President Carlos Menem, stepped in to give Enron another natural gas pipeline on sweetheart terms. (A government inquiry was launched, then died when Menem fired the chief investigator.)

Enron culminated its Argentine shopping spree with the purchase of the water system of Buenos Aires province. It got the full Enron treatment: Workers were fired en masse, allowing Enron to pocket their pay, in violation of the company's solemn promises to invest. Without maintenance workers, water mains were left bro-

---

[3]George Bush's spokesman and business partner Karl Rove denied Dubya met Terragno and provided reporter Louis Dubose with pages from the president's personal diary to prove Bush was in Texas, not Argentina. But Terragno talked of a call, not a visit. Jeb's office in Florida has not responded to requests for information made by BBC television's *Newsnight*, for whom I interviewed Senator Terragno.

ken. Enron's profitable neglect of the system left water contaminated.

But despite an economy flat on its back, Argentines had had enough from Enron, and they weren't going to take it anymore. In October 2001, the province forced Enron to clear out of town, dropping their thirty-year contract. While you may enjoy hearing of Enron's comeuppance, the Houstonians weren't playing with their own cash, but with yours. The majority of Enron's acquisitions flings abroad were subsidized by the U.S. taxpayer, in this case by the Inter-American Development Bank, a World Bank subsidiary half owned by the U.S. Treasury.[4]

A Good Responsible Dictator

Before their assault on the California beachheads, the power pirates landed in Rio de Janeiro, South America's City of Light. In 1999, I received a postcard from Rio, which was completely black. "Cariocis" (Rio residents) mailed them in protest against Light, Rio's electricity company, now nicknamed "Dark."

Brazil's government privatized Rio Light, selling it to Electricité de France and Reliant, the Houston company befriended by Governor Bush. Reliant and partners promised improved service for Rio—then axed 40 percent of the company's workforce. Unfortunately, Rio's electricity system is not fully mapped. Rio Light's electricity workers had kept track of the location of wires and transformers in their heads. When they were booted out by the new Franco-Texan owners, the workers took their mental maps with them. Nearly every day, a new neighborhood went dark. The foreign owners blamed El Niño, the weather in the Pacific Ocean. Rio is on the Atlantic.

But for Reliant and the Parisians, not all was darkness. The

---

[4]See Daphne Wysham's "Enron's Pawns: How Public Institutions Bankrolled Enron's Globalization Game" (Institute for Policy Studies, 2002).

windfall from reduced wages and price increases allowed the foreign owners to hike dividends by 1,000 percent. Rio Light's share price jumped from $300 to $400.

And to whom had the World Bank turned over South America's energy future? Governor Gray Davis of California named Reliant price gouger number one. And our federal government, in the 1980s, had ruled the company morally unfit to manage a nuclear power plant.

In its preglobalization incarnation as Houston Power & Light, the company managed construction of the South Texas nuclear station—or, more accurately, mismanaged the plant's construction. To reduce the number of negative safety reports, workers who wrote up safety violations were fired: John Rex for blowing the whistle on forged safety inspection documents; Thomas Saporito for exposing security violations; Ron Goldstein for flagging faked welding records. To hunt down the disloyal workers for Houston Power, the company's contractor, Brown and Root, now a Halliburton company, drilled tiny holes in the ceiling of the workers' locker room and placed three-inch espionage-style cameras to identify workers who ratted to the federal inspectors.[5]

Let me not leave the wrong impression: Reliant can be honest when the need arises. In the fall of 2002, after the implosion of Enron, Global Crossing and WorldCom, the Securities Exchange Commission required big firms' CEOs to sign an oath that their company's books were accurate. Odd that: One liked to assume they already believed their reports. In the last days before signing, Reliant erased $2 billion in revenues from its "pre-honesty" books. They called it a "restatement."

---

[5] I should be careful what I say about Reliant. The company maintained a file on me, including a phantasmic profile of my sex life far spicier than the mundane reality. In 1999, Reliant concocted this filth file to hand "confidentially" to Dutch reporters who had dared to quote me. Nice guys.

* * *

Another one of the big multicontinental players was Entergy International, once a division of a struggling regional electricity company, which grabbed London Electricity and other huge foreign assets following the election of their hometown boy, Bill Clinton, to the White House. Entergy used their Clinton connections to sign deals in China, whose totalitarian regime must have held a particular attraction for the company's chairman, Ed Lupberger. In hunting for assets in Peru, Lupberger said, "They've got a good stable situation there, sort of a benevolent dictator, which means good, responsible leadership."

Pakistan looked like another Entergy jackpot when, in 1992, the government of Benazir Bhutto, in a manner most strange, agreed to increase the amount Pakistan's power agency would pay for electricity from plants part-owned by Entergy (10 percent) and Britain's National Power (40 percent). But in 1998, Bhutto lost the election and the new Pakistani government discovered her secret ownership of posh properties in London. Putting her unexplained riches together with the crazy generous deal with the U.K.-U.S. power companies, Pakistani prosecutors in October 1988 charged her and the Western consortium with bribery. Pakistan's new government then ended the high payments to the British-American consortium on the internationally accepted rule of law that contracts allegedly obtained by bribery are unenforceable.

Officially, the IMF and World Bank condemn bribery. Nevertheless, within days of Pakistan's filing corruption charges and cutting payments to the accused power combine, the IMF Bank, at the request of Bill Clinton and Tony Blair, threatened to cut off Pakistan's access to international finance.

Panicked by the threat of economic blockade, Pakistan prepared to collect the cash to pay off the U.K.-U.S. consortium. On December 22, 1998, Pakistan's military, under the direction of General Pervez Musharraf, sent thirty thousand troops into the nation's power stations. Peter Windsor, National Power's director of International Operations, told me, "A lot changed since the army moved in. Now we have a situation where we can be paid, they've found a way to collect from the man in the street." Yes, *at gunpoint,* trade union lawyer Abdul Latif Nizamani told me after his arrest and release following mass demonstrations. (Windsor vehemently denied the bribery charges.)

With Pakistan's army in control of the nation's infrastructure, and acting as guarantor of payment to the multinationals, General Musharraf's final takeover nine months later—a "surprise coup" to the Western press—was, in fact, a forgone conclusion to the power plant dispute.

In the months before he left office, President Clinton flew to Pakistan. Shocked U.S. congressmen could not understand why Clinton would place the American Eagle seal of approval on a notoriously unbalanced dictator with a Strangelovian affection for nuclear weapons and, at the time, a fondness for the Taliban. The answer was the real item on the agenda: higher electricity prices to pay the questionable contracts with the British-American power group.

Meanwhile, on the other side of the border in India, police were beating the daylights out of protestors marching against Enron's power plant project at Dabhol, a deal so costly to India that in 1998 the Maharashtra State government voided the contract on grounds of bribery. Clinton felt India's pain . . . and sent in the collection agents: Secretary of State Madeleine Albright, and former power industry exec, Clinton's energy secretary Hazel O'Leary. The ladies beat the daylights out of Indian officials in their diplomatic way, threatening the nation with economic strangulation if Enron didn't get its pound of flesh. The more chivalrous Bush would never send a woman to do a man's job: In 2001, the threats were repeated to the Indian government by Vice President Dick Cheney.[6]

---

[6] I often knock U.S. television for missing the story, but *60 Minutes* did run a terrific show on Enron and India—in 2002, after Enron was already exposed and in bankruptcy. Five years of dust had already gathered on the India story. Once again, American media proved it has the courage to shoot the wounded.

Bringing It All Back Home

Following Enron's declaration of bankruptcy in November 2001, its employees, creditors and bilked customers went on a hunt to secure any assets of the company and its sticky-fingered executives it could find. The Bushes also joined the Enron asset scavenger hunt, in their own way. Two months after the bankruptcy, Governor Jeb Bush of Florida traveled to the Texas home of Enron's ex-president, Rich Kinder, to collect a stack of checks totaling $2 million at the power pillager's $500-per-plate fund-raising dinner. There are a lot of workers in Florida who will wish they had a chance to lick those plates, because that's all that's left of the *one-third of a billion dollars* Florida's state pension fund invested in Enron—three times as much as any other of the fifty states.

After the December 2000 blackouts and Enron charges of half a billion dollars bankrupted Pacific Gas & Electric, not many officials wanted to be seen getting up close and personal with Enron's Ken Lay. But not Jeb. The Florida governor sent a personal message that he'd "love" to meet with Lay. Despite this statement of affection, Jeb says he doesn't remember speaking to Ken Lay, but his diary does: a half-hour phone call between the governor and Enron chief on April 17, 2001, to discuss deregulation.

Like his presidential father and brother, Jeb remains a fan of Lay's deregulation nostrums. But the Florida governor has more urgent issues that would have interested Lay. Sugar plantations leach phosphorus into the Everglades causing, with the help of other agribusiness polluters, $867 million in damage a year. Simple-minded souls may think the solution is easy: Tell the planters to stop crapping in the 'Glades. But while dumping phosphorus in the water, plantation owners also dumped big money into political party coffers, nearly $1 million coming from the Fanjul family alone. Sugar magnate Pepe Fanjul was a member of Bush Sr.'s "Team 100." Team players raised $100,000 each for the elder president.

Rather than demand that his sugar daddies stop polluting the Everglades, Governor Bush encouraged a scheme by a company called Azurix to repipe the entire Southern Florida water system with new reservoirs that would pump fresh water into the swamps. From the view of expert hydrologists, such a mega-project is a crackbrained and useless waste of gobs of money. As part of the deal, Azurix would be handed the right to sell the reservoirs' water to six million Florida customers. Azurix was the wholly owned subsidiary of Enron that had recently been kicked out of Buenos Aires.

Money for Nuthin'

The media wants us to shed tears for the po' widdle stockholders blown to pieces by Enron's bankruptcy. Count me out. Enron did not survive on watered stock and magic bookkeeping alone. The company's stock flew high, fueled by cash filched from consumers and workers on five continents.

Enron was the Rosemary's Baby of the frightening coupling of deregulation and campaign cash. But Enron wasn't the devil's only child. I looked into the December 2000 blackouts in Southern California. The wholesale price of electricity there jumped 1,000 percent over the previous year and the price of natural gas, fuel for the power plants, rose 1,000 percent *in one week*. Power shortage? Nope. Take a look at figure 3.2, "Natural Gas Prices." Note that at the Henry Hub gas pipeline switching center in Texas, you could buy plentiful gas for $1 a therm. Yet, down the pipe at the California border, the price was $10.

It turns out the Texas merchant who controlled the biggest pipeline into California, El Paso Corporation, simply blocked access to part of the tube. Result: panic, price spikes, blackouts. Market speculators made an estimated half a billion dollars on that cute little maneuver. In other words, California didn't run out of *energy*, it ran out of *government*.

There are glimmers of justice. Pacific Gas & Electric, the company that crushed Dr. Coyle's referendum, wrote a price freeze into that deregulation law. The sly codicil permitted the San Francisco outfit and its L.A. counterpart, Edison, to stuff their pockets

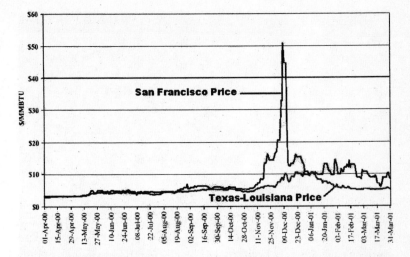

Fig. 3.2. Natural gas prices. The big spike—over $50 per unit for natural gas—was charged to Californians. At the same time, Texas paid less than $10 from the "Henry Hub." (Source: California Independent System Operator.)

with a $20 billion windfall as oil prices fell. They earned even more selling off their power plants to the out-of-state power merchants—who then used all those English tricks to beat the two California companies financially senseless. Their $20 billion windfall soon became a $12 billion loss—and PG&E declared bankruptcy at the end of 2000.

But we didn't have long to enjoy PG&E's comeuppance. California's governor Gray Davis moved to bail out the companies. Davis signed off on long-term contracts to buy electricity for PG&E and Edison, some of it priced at $500 per megawatt hour, more than ten times the old regulated tariff. The state is paying for these pricey contracts by issuing several billion dollars in government bonds. As Sam Wyly said, the Bushes' hard work has paid off—and now, California will pay back at the rate of $2 billion a year for thirty years.

CHAPTER 4

SELL THE LEXUS, BURN THE OLIVE TREE:
Globalization and Its Discontents

I was getting myself measured for a straitjacket when I received an urgent message from Bolivia.

The jacket was Thomas Friedman's idea. He's the *New York Times* columnist and amateur economist who wrote *The Lexus and the Olive Tree*, which is kind of a long, deep kiss to globalization. I was in Cleveland to debate Friedman at the Council on World Affairs meeting in May 2001. Globalization, he told the council, is all about the communications revolution. It's about the Internet. It's about how you can sit in your bedroom, buy shares in Amazon.com and send e-mails to Eskimos all at the same time, *wearing your pajamas*.

According to Friedman, we are *"connected"* and *"empowered"* and *"enabled."* And if that isn't cool enough by itself, globalization makes economies grow. Any nation on the planet that takes the pledge and follows the map can open the hidden gold mine. Poverty will end, as will the tyrannies of government. And every Bolivian will get their own e-mail address.

The end of world poverty! Eskimos! E-mail! I wanted this brave new future and I wanted it *now!* All I had to do, said Friedman, is change into something a little more form-fitting. "The

Golden Straitjacket is the defining political economic garment of globalization," Friedman says. And, he explains, the tighter you wear it, "the more gold it produces."

Friedman is talking—figuratively, of course—about the latest *economic* fashion, "tailored by Margaret Thatcher." Ronald Reagan, he adds, "sewed on the buttons." There are about a dozen specific steps, but the key ones are: cut government, cut the budgets and bureaucracies and the rules they make; privatize just about everything; deregulate currency and capital markets, free the banks to speculate in currency and shift capital across borders. But don't stop there. Open every nation's industry to foreign trade, eliminate those stodgy old tariffs and welcome foreign ownership without limit; wipe away national border barriers to commerce; let the market set prices on everything from electricity to water; and let the arbitrageurs direct our investments. Then haul those old government bureaucracies to the guillotine: cut public pensions, cut welfare, cut subsidies; let politics shrink and let the marketplace guide us.

Selling these rules is easy work, he said and grinned, as *there is no dissent.* Yes, there were tree-hugging troublemakers demonstrating in Seattle. But as Britain's prime minister Tony Blair said, "People who indulge in the protests are completely misguided. World trade is good for people's jobs and people's living standards. These protests are a complete outrage."

But let's forgive youth its lack of sophistication. What the kids in the street didn't know is that history's over with, done, *kaput!* Friedman tells us: "The historical debate is over. The answer is free-market capitalism." And whether Republicans or Democrats, Tories or New Labour, Socialists or Christian Democrats, we're all signed on, we're all laced up in our straitjackets, merely quibbling about the sleeve length.

I was about to say, "Strap me in." But then I received this note—an e-mail—from Cochabamba, Bolivia. It was about Oscar Olivera, a community leader I knew through my work with Latin American labor unions. It said: *Close to 1,000 heavily armed mem-*

bers of the Bolivian security forces dispersed peaceful marchers with tear gas, beating them and confiscating their personal possessions.

What was the problem? Maybe the Internet was down and the Bolivians were protesting that they couldn't unload their Amazon.com shares.

The message ended: *"Oscar is missing. His whereabouts are unknown."* Didn't Oscar know that he was "connected and enabled"?

This reminded me that a large cache of documents had recently fallen into my hands. They came from the deepest files of the World Bank and International Monetary Fund, from the desk drawers of officials at the European Commission and the World Trade Organization: Country Assistance Strategies, an Article 133 diplomatic letter, memos from the secretariats—the real stuff of globalization—from inside the organizations that dream up, then dictate, the terms of the new international economics.

There was nothing here about Eskimos on cell phones, but I did find an awful lot about cutting Argentine pensions by 13 percent, breaking up unions in Brazil . . . and raising water prices in Bolivia, all laid out in chilling techno-speak and stamped "for official use only."

The spiky-haired protesters in the streets of Seattle believe there's some kind of grand conspiracy between the corporate powers, the IMF, the World Bank and an alphabet soup of agencies that work to suck the blood of Bolivians and steal gold from Tanzania. But the tree huggers are wrong; the details are far more stomach-churning than they even imagine. In March 2001, when Ecuador's government raised the price of cooking gas and hungry Indians burned the capital, I was reading the World Bank's confidential plan issued months before. The bank, with the IMF, had *directed* this 80 percent increase in the price of domestic fuel, knowing this could set the nation ablaze. It's as if the riots were scheduled right into the plan.

And they were. That's according to one of the only inside sources I can name—Joseph Stiglitz, former chief economist of the World Bank. "We called them the IMF riots." The riots as well as the response were programmed, the latter referred to euphemistically as "resolve"—the police, the tanks, the crackdown.

I threw off my straitjacket and began to write. And that's what you'll find in this chapter: my reports explicating lists of "conditionalities" (167 for Ecuador) required by the World Bank and IMF for their loans; unpublished proposed terms for implementing article VI.4 of the GATS treaty under the World Trade Organization; intellectual property rules under something called the "TRIPS" agreement, which determines everything from breast cancer treatment to Dr. Dre's control of rap music: all the dirty little facts of globalization as it is actually practiced. And you can read it in your pajamas.

You'll also find out why Oscar was missing; he was seized, in fact, by Bolivia's own globalization enforcement army.

Friedman ended his talk—it turns out he won't debate face-to-face, so we had to speak on separate days—by quoting with joyous approval the wisdom of Andy Grove, the chairman of Intel Corporation: "The purpose of the new capitalism is to shoot the wounded."

That day, for Oscar's sake, I was hoping Friedman was wrong.

Dr. Bankenstein's Monsters: The World Bank, the IMF and the Aliens Who Ate Ecuador

Get this: I was standing in front of the New York Hilton Hotel during the big G7 confab in 2000, the meeting of presidents, prime ministers and their financiers, when the limousine carrying International Monetary Fund director Horst Köhler zoomed by and hit a bump. Out of the window flew a report titled "Ecuador Interim Country Assistance Strategy." It was marked "Confidential. Not for distribution." You may suspect that's not how I got this document, but you can trust me that it contains the answer to a very puzzling question.

Inside the Hilton, Professor Anthony Giddens explained to an earnest crowd of London School of Economics alumni that "Globalization is a *fact*, and it is driven by the communications revolution."

Wow. That was an eye-opener! The screeching green-haired freakers outside the hotel demonstrating against the International Monetary Fund had it all wrong. Globalization, Giddens seemed to say, is all about giving every villager in the Andes a Nokia Internet-enabled mobile phone. (The man had obviously memorized his Thomas Friedman.) Why on earth would anyone protest against this happy march into the globalized future?

So I thumbed through my purloined IMF "Strategy for Ecuador" searching for a chapter on connecting Ecuador's schools to the World Wide Web. Instead, I found a secret schedule. Ecuador's government was *ordered* to raise the price of cooking gas by 80 percent by November 1, 2000.[1] Also, the government had to eliminate twenty-six thousand jobs and cut real wages for the remaining workers by 50 percent in four steps and on a timetable specified by the IMF. By July 2000, Ecuador had to transfer ownership of its biggest water system to foreign operators, then grant British Petroleum rights to build and own an oil pipeline over the Andes.

That was for starters. In all, the IMF's 167 detailed loan conditions looked less like an "Assistance Plan" and more like a blueprint for a financial coup d'état.

The IMF would counter that it had no choice. After all, Ecuador was flat busted, thanks to the implosion of the nation's commercial banks. But how did Ecuador, once an OPEC member with resources to spare, end up in such a pickle?

For that, we have to turn back to 1983, when the IMF forced

---

[1] It annoys me something fierce when I expose some institution and they don't respond with a complaint, comment or a lawsuit. But from the IMF and World Bank honchos—nothing. Turns out I hadn't looked on the right continent: in fact, the World Bank wrote a long response to this exposé and published it in an African newspaper. That was odd. Odder still, in defense of their wacko, destructive plans for Ecuador, they simply denied the documents existed. Figure 4.1 shows a page from one of the documents that doesn't exist.

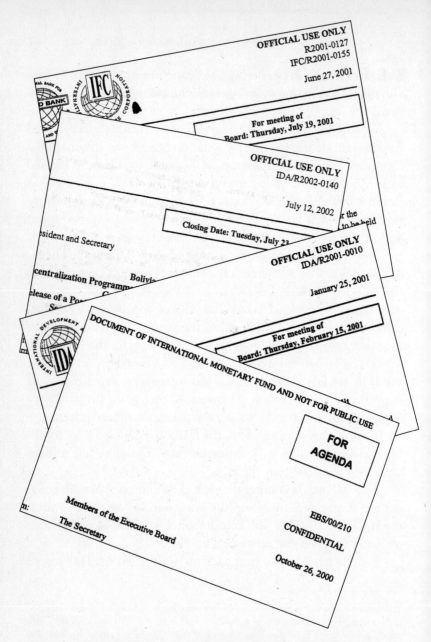

OFFICIAL USE ONLY
R2001-0127
IFC/R2001-0155

June 27, 2001

For meeting of
Board: Thursday, July 19, 2001

OFFICIAL USE ONLY
IDA/R2002-0140

July 12, 2002

Closing Date: Tuesday, July 23

OFFICIAL USE ONLY
IDA/R2001-0010

January 25, 2001

For meeting of
Board: Thursday, February 15, 2001

DOCUMENT OF INTERNATIONAL MONETARY FUND AND NOT FOR PUBLIC USE

FOR
AGENDA

...sident and Secretary

...centralization Programm...   Bolivi...

...lease of a Po...

Members of the Executive Board
The Secretary

EBS/00/210
CONFIDENTIAL

October 26, 2000

Fig. 4.1. IMF and World Bank documents. Several stacks of documents walked out of the IMF and World Bank that dictate everything from the price of cooking oil in Ecuador to a $40 cut in the monthly pay of Argentines on a public works program.

the nation's government to take over the soured private debts Ecuador's elite owed to foreign banks. For this bailout of U.S. and local financiers, Ecuador's government borrowed $1.5 billion from the IMF.

For Ecuador to pay back this loan, the IMF dictated price hikes in electricity and other necessities. And when that didn't drain off enough cash, yet another "Assistance Plan" required the state to eliminate 120,000 workers.

Furthermore, while trying to pay down the mountain of IMF obligations, Ecuador foolishly "liberalized" its tiny financial market, cutting local banks loose from government controls and letting private debt and interest rates explode. Who pushed Ecuador into this nutty romp with free market banking?

Hint: The initials are *I-M-F*—which made liberalization of the nation's banking sector a condition of another berserker assistance plan. The facts of this nasty little history come from yet another internal IMF report that flew my way marked "Please do not cite." Pretend I didn't.

How the IMF Cured AIDS

The IMF and its sidekick, the World Bank, have lent a sticky helping hand to scores of nations. Take Tanzania. Today, in that African state, 1.3 million people are getting ready to die of AIDS. The IMF and World Bank have come to the rescue with a brilliant neoliberal solution: require Tanzania to charge for what were previously free hospital appointments. Since the Bank imposed this requirement, the number of patients treated in Dar es Salaam's three big public hospitals has dropped by 53 percent. The Bank's cure is working!

The IMF World Bank helpers also ordered Tanzania to charge fees for school attendance, then expressed surprise that school enrollment dropped from 80 percent to 66 percent.

Altogether the Bank and IMF had 157 helpful suggestions for Tanzania. In April 2000, the Tanzanian government secretly agreed to adopt them all. It was sign or starve. No developing nation can borrow hard currency from any commercial bank without IMF blessing (except China, whose output grows at 5 percent per year by studiously following the *reverse* of IMF policies).

The IMF and World Bank have effectively controlled Tanzania's economy since 1985. Admittedly, when they took charge they found a socialist nation mired in poverty, disease and debt. The IMF's love-the-market experts wasted no time in cutting trade barriers, limiting government subsidies and selling off state industries. The World Bank's shadow governors worked wonders. According to World Bank watcher Nancy Alexander of Citizens' Network on Essential Services (Maryland), in just fifteen years Tanzania's GDP *dropped* from $309 to $210 per capita, literacy *fell* and the rate of abject poverty *jumped* to 51 percent of the population. Yet, the World Bank did not understand why it failed to win the hearts and minds of Tanzanians for its free market game plan. In June 2000, the Bank reported in frustration, "One legacy of socialism is that most people continue to believe the State has a fundamental role in promoting development and providing social services."

When Larry Landed

It wasn't always thus, this affection for pricing, not people. The World Bank and IMF were born in 1944 with simple, laudable mandates—to fund postwar reconstruction and development projects (the World Bank) and lend hard currency to nations with temporary balance-of-payments deficits (the IMF).

Then, beginning in 1980, the Banks seem to take on an alien form. In the early 1980s, Third World nations, hemorrhaging after the fivefold increases in oil prices and a like jump in dollar interest payments, brought their begging bowls to the IMF and World Bank. But instead of debt relief, they received Structural Assistance Plans listing an average of 114 "conditionalities" in return for loans. While the particulars varied from nation to nation, in every case the rollover of debts dangled from edicts to remove trade barriers, sell national assets to foreign investors, slash social spending and make labor "flexible" (read "crush your unions").

Some say the radical and vicious change in the Banks' policies after 1980 resulted from Ronald Reagan's election that year as president, the quickening of Mrs. Thatcher's powers in England and the ascendancy of "neoliberal" (free market) policy. My own theory is that the IMF and World Bank were taken over by a space alien named Larry. It's obvious that "Larry" Summers, once World Bank chief economist, later U.S. treasury secretary, is in reality a platoon of extraterrestrials sent here to turn much of the human race into a source of cheap protein.

So what have the aliens accomplished with their structural assistance free market prescriptions? Samuel Brittan, the *Financial Times'* globalization knight errant, declares that new world capital markets and free trade have "brought about an unprecedented increase in world living standards." Brittan cites the huge growth in GDP per capita, life expectancy and literacy in the less-developed world from 1950 to 1995.

Now hold on a minute. Before 1980, virtually every nation in his Third World survey was either socialist or welfare statist. They were developing on the "Import Substitution Model" by which locally owned industry was built through government investment and high tariffs, anathema to the free marketeers. In those Dark Ages (1960–80) of increasing national government control and new welfare schemes, per capita income grew 73 percent in Latin America and 34 percent in Africa. By comparison, since 1980, the Reagan/Thatcher model has seen Latin American growth come to a virtual halt—growth of less than 6 percent over twenty years—and African incomes decline *by 23 percent.*

Now let's count the corpses: From 1950 to 1980, socialist and welfare statist policies added more than a decade of life expectancy to virtually every nation on the planet. From 1980 to today, life under structural assistance has gotten brutish and decidedly shorter. Since 1985, in fifteen African nations the total number of illiterate people has risen and life expectancy fallen—which Brittan attributes to "bad luck, [not] the international economic system." In the former Soviet states, where IMF and World Bank shock plans hold sway, life expectancy has fallen off a cliff—adding 1.4 million a year to the death rate in Russia alone. Tough luck, Russia!

Admittedly, the World Bank and IMF are reforming. No longer do they issue the dreaded "Structural Assistance Plans." No, they now call them "Poverty Reduction Strategies." Doesn't that make you feel better?

In April 2000, the IMF reviewed the fruits of globalization. In its "World Outlook" report, the Fund admitted that "in the recent decades, nearly one-fifth of the world population has regressed. This is arguably," the IMF concedes, "one of the greatest economic failures of the 20th Century." And that, Professor Giddens, is a fact.

The Globalizer Who Came in from the Cold: The IMF's Four Steps to Economic Damnation

"It has condemned people to death," the former apparatchik told me in a scene out of a Le Carré novel. The brilliant old agent comes in from the cold, crosses to our side and, in hours of debriefing, empties his memory of horrors committed in the name of a political ideology he now realizes has gone rotten. Here before me was a catch far bigger than some used Cold War spy. Joseph Stiglitz was chief economist of the World Bank. To a great extent, the new world economic order was his theory come to life.

I "debriefed" Stiglitz over several days—at Cambridge University, in a London hotel and finally in Washington during a big confab of the World Bank and the International Monetary Fund in April 2001. Instead of chairing the meetings of ministers and central bankers as he used to, Stiglitz was kept safely exiled behind the blue police cordons, the same as the nuns carrying a large wooden cross, the Bolivian union leaders, the parents of AIDS victims and the other "antiglobalization" protesters. The ultimate insider was now on the outside.

In 1999 the World Bank fired Stiglitz. He was not allowed a discreet "retirement"; U.S. Treasury Secretary Larry Summers, I'm told, demanded a public excommunication for Stiglitz's having expressed his first mild dissent from globalization World Bank–style.

In Washington we talked about the real, often hidden, workings of the IMF, World Bank and the bank's 51 percent owner, the U.S. Treasury.[2]

In addition to the Ecuador document, I had by 2001 obtained a huge new cache of documents, from sources unnamable, from inside the offices of his old employer, marked "confidential," "restricted" and "not otherwise [to be] disclosed without World Bank authorization." Stiglitz helped translate these secret "Country Assistance Strategies" from bureaucratese.[3]

There is an Assistance Strategy specially designed for each nation, says the World Bank, following careful in-country investigations. But according to insider Stiglitz, the Bank's staff "investigation" consists of close inspection of a nation's five-star hotels. It concludes with the Bank staff meeting some begging, busted finance minister who is handed a "restructuring agreement," predrafted for his "voluntary" signature (I have a selection of these).

Each nation's economy is individually analyzed; then, according to Stiglitz, the Bank hands every minister the exact same four-step program.

---

[2]The interviews were for the London *Observer* and BBC Television's *Newsnight*. See a tape of a segment of the interview and read a long excerpt from the interview with the Dangerous Dissenter at *www.GregPalast.com/Stiglitz/*.

[3]The documents did *not* come from Dr. Stiglitz. I'm not kidding. He never, ever gave me a confidential document. He didn't have to: So many people in the IMF and World Bank are sick to death of what their bosses make them do, I'm never short of inside info.

Step 1

Step 1 is Privatization—which Stiglitz says could more accurately be called "Briberization." Rather than object to the sell-offs of state industries, he says national leaders—using the World Bank's demands to silence local critics—happily flog their electricity and water companies. "You could see their eyes widen" at the prospect of 10 percent commissions paid to Swiss bank accounts for simply shaving a few billion off the sale price of national assets.

And the U.S. government knows it, charges Stiglitz—at least in the case of the biggest "briberization" of all, the 1995 Russian sell-off. "The U.S. Treasury view was *this was great* as we wanted Yeltsin reelected. We *don't care* if it's a corrupt election. We *want* the money to go to Yeltsin" via kickbacks for his campaign.

I have to interject that Stiglitz is no conspiracy nutter ranting about Black Helicopters. The man was *inside* the game, a member of Bill Clinton's cabinet as chairman of the president's Council of Economic Advisers.

Most heinous for Stiglitz is that the U.S.-backed oligarchs' corruption stripped Russia's industrial assets, cutting national output nearly in half, causing economic depression and starvation.

Step 2

After briberization, Step 2 of the IMF/World Bank's one-size-fits-all rescue-your-economy plan is Capital Market Liberalization. This means repealing any nation's law that slows down or taxes money jumping over the borders. In theory, capital market deregulation allows foreign banks' and multinational corporations' investment capital to flow in and out. Unfortunately, in countries like Indonesia and Brazil, the money simply flowed out and out. Stiglitz calls this the "hot money" cycle. Cash comes in for speculation in real estate and currency, then flees at the first whiff of trouble. A nation's reserves can drain in days, hours. And when that happens, to seduce speculators into returning a nation's own capital funds, the IMF demands these nations raise interest rates to 30 percent, 50 percent and 80 percent.

"The result was predictable," said Stiglitz of the hot money tidal waves in Asia and Latin America. Higher interest rates demolished property values, savaged industrial production and drained national treasuries.

Step 3

At this point, the IMF drags the gasping nation to Step 3: Market-Based Pricing, a fancy term for raising prices on food, water and domestic gas. This leads, predictably, to Step $3^1/2$: what Stiglitz calls "the IMF riot." The IMF riot is painfully predictable. When a nation is "down and out, [the IMF] takes advantage and squeezes the last pound of blood out of them. They turn up the heat until, finally, the whole cauldron blows up"—as when the IMF eliminated food and fuel subsidies for the poor in Indonesia in 1998 and the nation exploded into riots. There are other examples—the Bolivian riots over water price hikes pushed by the World Bank in April 2000 and, in early 2001, the riots in Ecuador over the rise in domestic gas prices that we found in the secret Ecuador "Assistance" program. You'd almost get the impression that the riot is written into the plan.

And it is. For example, we need only look at the confidential "Interim Country Assistance Strategy" for Ecuador. In it the Bank states—with cold accuracy—that they expected their plans to spark "social unrest," their bureaucratic term for a nation in flames.

Given the implosion of the economy, that's not surprising. The secret report notes that the plan to make the U.S. dollar Ecuador's currency has pushed 51 percent of the population below the poverty line, what Stiglitz called their squeeze-until-they-explode plan. And when the nation explodes, the World Bank "Assistance" plan is ready, telling the authorities to prepare for civil strife and suffering with "political resolve." In these busted nations, "resolve" means tanks in the street.

Each new riot (and by "riot" I mean "peaceful demonstration dispersed by batons or bullets") causes panicked flights of capital and government bankruptcies. Such economic arson has its bright side, of course—foreign corporations can then pick off a nation's remaining assets, such as the odd mining concession or port, at fire-sale prices.

Stiglitz notes that the IMF and World Bank are not heartless adherents to market economics. At the same time the IMF stopped Indonesia "subsidizing" food purchases, "when the banks need a bail-out, intervention [in the market] is welcome." The IMF scrounged up tens of billions of dollars to save the country's financiers and, by extension, the U.S. and European banks from which they had borrowed.

A pattern emerges. There are lots of losers in this system, but two clear winners: the Western banks and U.S. Treasury. They alone make the big bucks from this crazy new international capital churn. For example, Stiglitz told me about an unhappy meeting, early in his World Bank tenure, with the president who had just been elected in Ethiopia's first democratic election. The World Bank and IMF had ordered Ethiopia to divert European aid money to its reserve account at the U.S. Treasury, which pays a pitiful 4 percent return, while the nation borrowed U.S. dollars at 12 percent to feed its population. The new president begged Stiglitz to let him use the aid money to rebuild the nation. But no, the loot went straight off to the U.S. Treasury's vault in Washington.

Step 4

Now we arrive at Step 4 of what the IMF and World Bank call their "poverty reduction strategy": Free Trade. This is free trade by the rules of the World Trade Organization and World Bank. Stiglitz the insider likens free trade WTO-style to the Opium Wars. "That too was about opening markets," he said. As in the nineteenth century, Europeans and Americans today are kicking down the barriers to sales in Asia, Latin America and Africa, while barricading their own markets against Third World agriculture.

In the Opium Wars, the West used military blockades to force markets open for their unbalanced trade. Today, the World Bank can order a financial blockade that's just as effective—and sometimes just as deadly.

Stiglitz is particularly emotional over the WTO's intellectual property rights treaty (it goes by the acronym TRIPS, of which we have more to say later in this chapter). It is here, says the economist, that the new global order has "condemned people to death" by imposing impossible tariffs and tributes to pay to pharmaceutical companies for branded medicines. "They don't care," said the professor of the corporations and bank ideologues he worked with, "if people live or die."

By the way, don't be confused by the mix in this discussion of the IMF, World Bank and WTO. They are interchangeable masks of a single governance system. They have locked themselves together by what they unpleasantly call "triggers." Taking a World Bank loan for a school "triggers" a requirement to accept every "conditionality"—they average 114 per nation—laid down by both the World Trade Organization and IMF. In fact, said Stiglitz, the IMF requires nations to accept trade policies more punitive than the official WTO rules.

Stiglitz's greatest concern is that World Bank plans, devised in secrecy and driven by an absolutist ideology, are never open for discourse or dissent. Despite the West's push for elections throughout the developing world, the so-called Poverty Reduction Programs are never instituted democratically, and thereby, says Stiglitz, "undermine democracy." And they don't work. Black Africa's productivity under the guiding hand of IMF structural "assistance" has gone to hell in a handbag.

Did any nation avoid this fate? Yes, said Stiglitz, identifying Botswana. Their trick? "They told the IMF to go packing."

So then I turned on Stiglitz. Okay, Mr. Smart-Guy Professor, how would *you* help developing nations? Stiglitz proposed radical land reform, an attack at the heart of what he calls "landlordism," on the usurious rents charged by propertied oligarchies worldwide, typically 50 percent of a tenant's crops. I had to ask the professor: As you were top economist at the World Bank, why didn't the Bank follow your advice?

"If you challenge [land ownership], that would be a change in the power of the elites. That's not high on [the Bank's] agenda." Apparently not.

Ultimately, what drove Stiglitz to put his job on the line was the failure of the Bank and U.S. Treasury to change course when confronted with the crises—failures and suffering perpetrated by their four-step monetarist mambo. Every time their free market solutions failed, the IMF demanded more free market policies.

"It's a little like the Middle Ages," the insider told me. "When the patient died they would say, 'Well, he stopped the bloodletting too soon; he still had a little blood in him.'" I took away from my talks with the professor that the solution to world poverty and crisis is simple: Remove the bloodsuckers.

Equal Time for Briberizers

Let's be fair. There's two sides to every story, so I sought the World Bank's and the IMF's. A version of this story was first published in *The Big Issue*—a magazine the homeless flog outside London tube stations. *The Big Issue* offered equal space to the IMF, whose "deputy chief media officer" wrote: ". . . I find it impossible to respond given the depth and breadth of hearsay and misinformation in [Palast's] report." At first, they denied the existence of quoted documents . . . such as the one whose cover is reproduced here as figure 4.1.

Denial is no longer an option for the IMF, but their attacks continue, most cruelly, against Professor Stiglitz. As to the World Bank, I had the opportunity to debate these matters with the Big Kahuna himself, James Wolfensohn, the World Bank's president. After the initial publication of this book, on February 15, 2002, CNN Television asked me to appear in response to a Wolfensohn interview praising his own work at the World Bank. I thought, maybe he'd like to discuss some of these "assistance" plans; after all, they had his signature on them. But then I was called by an assistant producer. "If Greg Palast is allowed on," she said, the World Bank would not let the Wolf appear, nor could they even use his *prerecorded* words. "They [the World Bank] really *hate* you." Heavens! In the end, CNN did the courageous thing and barred me from the studio.[4]

Trying to get a defense of "briberization" was even more difficult. Not many executives fess up to payments of easy squeezy. There was a Mobil Oil executive who told a court that it was "the normal course of things" for the oil company (now a division of ExxonMobil) to "buy off" (Mobil's term) British members of parliament with consulting fees in return for support on legislation. (Because bribing a member of Parliament was not against the law until recently, Britain remains one of the few places where purchasing a politician remains a bargain.) But ExxonMobil won't give me the list of their "consultants."

But then I had a stroke of luck. A big-name London corporate lawyer told me that he'd met the chairman of international construction giant Balfour Beatty Corporation, which builds everything from Amtrak lines in the USA to giant hydroelectric dams, like the one at Pergau in Malaysia. The lawyer told me that in 1997, at a cocktail party, he and the corporate chief, ". . . were talking about corruption. He announced with enormous pride that he personally had handed over the check to the government minister for the Pergau Dam bribe." My source then regretted his statement.

---

[4]Like I say, every story has two sides—the truth and the spin. After the young CNN producer told me I was spiked, I said, "That will make a fun story." I then received a parade of messages and calls from CNN network operatives with various conflicting stories of what happened, though none denied that the World Bank demanded I be silenced.

But it just so happened I had my tape recorder on. Yet, I recognized that, despite the stature of my source, it was still hearsay. So I sent Balfour Beatty a letter: "Did Balfour Beatty pay bribes in Malaysia—yes or no?" Receiving no response, I printed the accusation against Balfour Beatty among a list of several other grease jobs.

Now I was in Trouble. Balfour Beatty's spokesman, Mr. Tim Sharp, called my paper in London to demand a retraction. There's no religious doctrine of journalistic infallibility, so I was happy to withdraw the accusation if Mr. Sharp could answer this question in the negative:

QUESTION: Was a payment made to a government official by Balfour Beatty, its chairman or an agent for its chairman regarding the Pergau Dam project, yes or no?

BALFOUR B: *I tell you I've worked with some journalists in my time!*

QUESTION: Did you pay a bribe?

BALFOUR B: *I like your approach.*

QUESTION: I just want to know if you bribed the Malaysians.

BALFOUR B: *We could spend the rest of the afternoon!* [We nearly did. This continued for almost an hour.]

QUESTION: I'm worried about the issue of bribery and corruption.

BALFOUR B: *Aren't we all? . . .*

QUESTION: I'm happy to print "Balfour Beatty states unequivocally that no payment was made to a Malaysian official."

BALFOUR B: *I suggested to you that you might have misled people. The thing you wrote has been denied flatly by your alleged source!*

Really? I had a tape recording. After another half-hour joust, the company man read the letter from my source.

BALFOUR B: [reading from the letter] "I do not deny the accuracy of the words attributed to me in the article."

Oh. For their helpful clarification, Balfour Beatty won my annual Golden Vulture Award, which I offered to deposit in a numbered Swiss account. And the Observer printed the following correction: We hereby retract the statements made regarding Balfour Beatty's alleged boasting of corrupt practices on the grounds that our article was wholly accurate.

And Joe Stiglitz? He survived his sacking from the World Bank and IMF complaints about his bad attitude. In September 2001, he was awarded the Nobel Prize in economics. Stiglitz, remember, had been fired merely for seeking to study why IMF policies failed so often. He conceded to me, however, the globalizers could point to one big success: Argentina. Then, five months after we spoke, I received the sad news that Argentina had died.

Who Shot Argentina?
The Fingerprints on the Smoking Gun Read "IMF"

It was a warm night in August 2001 when I got the call: Argentina's economy was found dead.

This was an easy case to crack. Next to the still-warm corpse, the killer left a smoking gun with fingerprints all over it. The murder weapon: "Technical Memorandum of Understanding," dated September 5, 2000. It was signed by Pedro Pou, president of the Central Bank of Argentina, for transmission to Horst Köhler, managing director of the International Monetary Fund.

I received a complete copy of the "Understanding," along with confidential attachments and a companion letter from the

Argentine Economics Ministry to the IMF, sent from . . . well, let's just say the envelope had no return address.

The Understanding required Argentina to cut the government budget deficit from $5.3 billion in 2000 to $4.1 billion in 2001. Think about that. That September, when the Understanding was drafted, Argentina was already on the cliff edge of a deep recession. One in five workers was unemployed. Even the half-baked economists at the IMF should have known that holding back government spending in a contracting economy would be like turning off the engines of an airplane in stall. Cut the deficit at a time like this? As my four-year-old daughter would say, "Stooopid."

Later, as the economy's wings were falling off, the IMF brain trust ordered the *elimination* of the deficit, causing the economy to implode.

Officially, unemployment hit a grim 16 percent—unofficially another quarter of the workforce was either unpaid, locked out or getting too little to survive. Industrial production—already down 25 percent halfway through the year—fell into a coma induced by interest rates which, by one measure, have jumped to over 90 percent on dollar-denominated borrowings.

The IMF is never wrong without being cruel as well. And so we read, under the boldface heading "Improving the Conditions of the Poor," an agreement to drop salaries under the government's emergency employment program by 20 percent—from $200 a month to $160. But you can't save much by taking $40 a month from the poor. For further savings, the Understanding also promised "a 12–15 percent cut in salaries" for civil servants and the "rationalization of certain privileged pension benefits." In case you haven't a clue what the IMF means by "rationalization," it means cutting payments to the aged by 13 percent under both public and private plans. Cut, cut, cut in the midst of a recession. Stooopid.

Salted in the IMF's mean-spirited plans for pensioners and the poor were economic forecasts bordering on the delusional. In the Understanding, the globalization geniuses projected that once Argentina carried out the IMF plan to snuff consumer spending, somehow the nation's economic production would leap by 3.7 percent and unemployment would fall. In fact, by the end of March 2001, the nation's GDP had already dropped 2.1 percent below the previous year's mark, and has nose-dived since.

Then, *another* envelope walked onto my desk. It contained the World Bank's "Country Assistance Plan" for the four years through 2005. Dated June 5, 2001, it was signed by World Bank president Wolfensohn. On the cover: a warning that recipients may use it "only in the performance of their official duties."

My official duty as a reporter is to tell you what's in it: a breathtaking mix of cruelty and *Titanic*-sized self-deception. "Despite the setbacks," Wolfensohn wrote, "the goals set out in the last [year's] report remain valid and the strategy appropriate." The IMF plan, cooked up with the World Bank, would "greatly improve the outlook for the remainder of 2001 and for 2002, with growth expected to recover in the later half of 2001."

Argentina swallowed the World Bank's fiscal medicine. But the nation did not appreciate the "greatly improved outlook." In December, the middle class, unused to hunting the streets for garbage to eat, began to burn down Buenos Aires.

In this strange, official-eyes-only document, the World Bank president expressed particular pride that Argentina's government had made "a $3 billion cut in primary expenditures accommodating the increase in interest obligations." In other words, the government gouged spending on domestic needs to pay interest to creditors, mostly foreign banks.

Crisis has its bright side, Wolfensohn crowed to his elite readership. "A major advance was made to eliminate outdated labor contracts," he wrote. Wages ("labor costs," as he calls them) had fallen, due to "labor market flexibility induced by the *de facto* liberalization of the market via increased informality." Translation: Workers lost unionized industrial jobs and turned to selling trinkets in the street.

What on Earth would lure Argentina into embracing this goofy program? The bait was a $20 billion emergency loan package and "stand-by" credit from the IMF, the World Bank and their commercial bank partners. But there is less to this generosity than meets the eye. The Understanding assumed Argentina would continue its "Convertibility Plan," instituted in 1991, which pegged the peso, the nation's currency, to the Yankee dollar at an exchange rate of one to one. The currency peg hadn't come cheap. Foreign banks working with the IMF had demanded that Argentina pay a whopping 16 percent risk premium above U.S. Treasury lending rates for the dollars needed to back the scheme.

Now do the arithmetic. When Wolfensohn wrote his memo, Argentina owed $128 billion in debt. Normal interest plus the premium amounted to $27 billion a year. In other words, Argentina's people didn't net one penny from the $20 billion in "bailout" loans. The debt grew, but none of the money escaped New York, where it lingered to pay interest to U.S. creditors holding the bonds, big fish like Citibank and little biters like Steve Hanke.

I spoke with Hanke, president of Toronto Trust Argentina, an "emerging market" fund that loaded up 100 percent on Argentine bonds during a 1995 currency panic. Don't cry for Steve, Argentina. His 79.25 percent profit that year put his outfit at the top of the speculators' league.

Hanke profits by betting on the failure of the IMF policies. This junk-bond speculation—the players call it "vulture investing"—is merely his lucrative avocation. By day he is a Johns Hopkins University economics professor. Despite the fact that his advice would put him out of business, Hanke offers a simple cure for Argentina's woes; "Abolish the IMF." And, Hanke advised last year, abolish the peg.

But the importance of this one-for-one dollar exchange rate has been far overstated. When the Argentine government finally devalued the peso in January, it wiped out the value of local savings accounts. But it was not the peg itself that skewered Argentina rather IMF policies. The currency peg is best understood as the meat hook on which the IMF hung Argentina's finances. It forced Argentina to beg and borrow a steady supply of dollars to back each peso, and this became the rationale for the IMF and World Bank to let loose in the pampas their Four Horsemen of neo-liberal policy. Described by Stiglitz, they are liberalized financial markets, reduced government, mass privatization and free trade.

"Liberalizing" financial markets meant allowing capital to flow freely across a nation's borders. And indeed, after liberalization the capital flowed with a vengeance. Argentina's panicked rich dumped their pesos for dollars and sent the hard loot to investment havens abroad. In June 2001 alone, Argentines withdrew 6 percent of all bank deposits, a devastating loss of assets.

Once upon a time, Argentina's government-owned national and provincial banks supported the nation's debts. But in the mid-1990s, the government of Carlos Menem sold these off to foreign operators, including Citibank of New York and Fleet Bank of Boston. Former World Bank advisor Charles Calomiris told me these bank privatizations were a "really wonderful story." Wonderful for whom? With the foreign-owned banks unwilling to repay Argentine depositors, the government froze savings accounts, effectively seizing money from regular Argentines to pay off the foreign creditors.

To keep the foreign creditors smiling, the Understanding also required "reform of the revenue sharing system." This is the IMF's kinder, gentler way of stating that the U.S. banks would be paid by siphoning off tax receipts that the provinces had earmarked for education and other public services. The Understanding also found cash in "reforming" the nation's health insurance system.

But when *cut cut cut* isn't enough to pay the debt holders, one can always sell *"las joyas de mi abuela"*—grandma's jewels, as journalist Mario del Cavril described his nation's privatization scheme to me. French multinationals picked up a big hunk of the water system and promptly raised charges in some towns by 400 percent. In his confidential memo, the World Bank's Wolfensohn sighs,

"Almost all major utilities have been privatized," so now there's really nothing left to sell.[5]

The coup de grâce, the final bullet loaded into the Understanding, was imposition of "an open trade policy." This forced Argentina's exporters (with their products priced via the peg in U.S. dollars) into a pathetic, losing competition against Brazilian goods priced in that nation's devalued currency. Stooopid.

Have the World Bank and IMF learned from the Argentina horror? They learn the way a pig learns to sing: They can't, they won't, and, if they try, the resulting noise is unbearable. On January 9, with the capital in flames, IMF Deputy Managing Director Anne Krueger ordered Argentina's latest in temporary presidents, Eduardo Duhalde, to cut still deeper into government expenditures. (President Bush backed the IMF budget-cutting advice—the same week he demanded that the U.S. Congress adopt a $50 billion scheme to spend the United States out of recession.)

In the midst of disaster, Wolfensohn's memo insisted that the World Bank–IMF scheme could still work: All Argentina needed to do was "reduce the cost of production," a step that required only a "flexible workforce." Translation: even lower pensions and wages, or no wages at all. To the dismay of Argentina's elite, however, the worker bees proved inflexibly obstinate in agreeing to their impoverishment.

One inflexible worker, Anibal Verón, a thirty-seven-year-old father of five, lost his job as a bus driver from a company that owed him nine months' pay. Verón joined angry unemployed Argentines, known as *"piqueteros,"* who block roads in protest. In a November 2000 blockade clearing, the nation's military police killed him with a bullet to the head.

Globalization boosters portray resistance to the New World Order as a lark of pampered, naïve Western youths curing their

---

[5]And as in every country, the sell-off (the privatization) quickly became "briberization."—with a little help, says a top government official, from the Bush family. See Chapter 3, "Power Pirates."

ennui by, as British prime minister Tony Blair puts it, "indulging in protest." The U.S. and European media play to this theme, focusing on demonstrations in Seattle and Genoa, while burying news of a June 2000 general strike honored by 7 million Argentine workers.

The death in Genoa of demonstrator Carlo Giuliani was front-page news, but Verón's death went unreported. Nor did U.S. media record the June 17 deaths of protesters Carlos Santillán, twenty-seven, and Oscar Barrios, seventeen, gunned down by police in a churchyard in Salta Province, north of Buenos Aires. Only in December, when Argentina failed to make an interest payment on foreign-held debt, did the Euro-American press suddenly report a "crisis," feeding us the images we expect from Latin America: tear gas, burning cars and a parade of new *presidentes* taking oaths of office.

Who done it? Who killed Argentina's economy? The Understandings and memoranda are evidence that the World Bank and IMF pulled the triggers, acting as hit men for foreign creditors and asset snatchers. But did they have accomplices?

I called Adolfo Pérez Esquivel, leader of Buenos Aires–based Peace and Justice Service (SERPAJ), a church-based human rights organization. He had investigated police torture of protesters in Salta Province, where Santillán and Barrios died. Pérez Esquivel, who won the Nobel Peace Prize in 1980, told me repression and economic "liberalization" are handmaidens. SERPAJ has filed a formal complaint charging police with recruiting children as young as five years old as informers for paramilitary squads, an operation he compares to the Hitler Youth.

Pérez Esquivel, who last year led protests against the proposed Free Trade Agreement of the Americas, doesn't agree with my verdict against the IMF in Argentina's death. He notes that the IMF's fatal "reforms" were embraced with enthusiasm by Finance Minister Domingo Cavallo, a World Bank favorite. Cavallo, fired in December after the mass protests, is best known by Argentines for heading the nation's Central Bank during the nation's 1976–1983 military dictatorship. For Pérez Esquivel, Cavallo's enthusiastic collaboration with the IMF and World Bank suggests that the untimely demise of the nation's economy wasn't murder, but suicide.

GATS, the Invisibles and the Free Trade Jihad

On September 11, I remember listening to our president, when he emerged from hiding, tell the nation, "America is open for business!" Not in my neighborhood, Mr. President. Mostly, we were shaken and worried sick waiting for word of missing friends.

But some people caught the spirit. Within days, some enterprising souls tried to sell little bags to victims' families, supposedly full of the ashes of their deceased kin. George Bush's globalization czar, Trade Representative Robert Zoellick, made the most of the mass murder too. Within days, he proclaimed that President Bush could defeat Osama bin Laden if only the wusses in Congress would grant our president extra-Constitutional powers—not to wage war, but to bargain new *trade treaties*. Now before you jump to the conclusion that Ambassador Zoellick is some kind of heartless crackpot jackal, consider his sound reasoning. "Terrorists hate the ideas America has championed around the world," he told a meeting of CEOs. "It is inevitable that people will wonder if there are intellectual connections with others who have turned to violence to attack international finance, globalization and the United States." Got it? You're either for free trade—or for Al-Quaeda.

The weapon meant to make Osama shake and quake is called "Fast-Track Trade Authority." It's a kind of blank check for globalization. With fast-track powers, the president can sign any agreement with the World Trade Organization and any treaty involving trade, and Congress cannot challenge a single specific provision of these pacts. The details would be left to Zoellick.

Zoellick, who arrived in Bush's cabinet after representing Enron Corporation, spoke out while preparing for a meeting of the World Trade Organization. What did Zoellick and the WTO trade lords have in their little bag of political ashes too important for mere congressmen to scrutinize? I glimpsed part of the answer in a memorandum that came through my fax machine. It was dated March 19, 2001, and marked. "Confidential."

The "Necessity Test" Better Than Democracy

When Churchill said "democracy is the worst form of government except all the others," he simply lacked the vision to see that, in March 2001, the WTO would design a system to replace democracy with something much better—Article VI.4 of General Agreement on Trade in Services, better known as GATS. And I had it in my hand: The unassuming six-page memo the WTO modestly hid away in secrecy may one day be seen as the post-democratic Magna Carta. At its heart was a bold plan to create an international agency with veto power over individual nations' parliamentary and regulatory decisions.

The memo begins by considering the difficult matter of how to punish nations that violate "a balance between two potentially conflicting priorities: promoting trade expansion versus protecting the regulatory rights of governments."

Think about that. A few centuries after America set the standard, almost all nations now rely on elected congresses, parliaments, prime ministers and presidents to make the rules. It is these ungainly deliberative bodies that "balance" the interests of citizens and businesses.

Now kiss that obsolete system good-bye. Once nations sign on to the proposed GATS Article VI.4, something called "the Necessity Test" will kick in. Per the secretariat's program outlined in the March 19 memo, national parliaments and regulatory agencies will be demoted, in effect, to advisory bodies. Final authority will rest with the GATS Disputes Panel to determine if a law or regulation is "more burdensome than necessary." And the GATS panel, not any parliament or congress, will tell us what is "necessary."

GATS is one of the half dozen treaties that together constitute and empower the World Trade Organization. I would have dismissed the March 19 memo had it been just another wacko design for trade-rule totalitarianism by some WTO functionary. But the memo is the summary of the consensus of member nations' trade ministers meeting behind closed doors as the Working Party on Domestic Regulation. As a practical matter, the Necessity Test they agreed on, if signed and implemented, means nations will have to shape laws protecting the air you breathe, the trains you ride in and the food you chew by picking not the best or safest means, but the *cheapest* methods for foreign investors and merchants.

Let's get down to concrete examples. The Necessity Test had a trial run in North America via inclusion in NAFTA, the region's free trade agreement. The state of California had banned a gasoline additive, MBTE, a chemical cocktail that was found to contaminate water supplies. A Canadian seller of the "M" chemical in MBTE filed a complaint saying California's ban on the pollutant fails the Necessity Test.

The Canadians assert, quite logically, that California, rather than ban MBTE, could require all gas stations to dig up storage tanks and reseal them, and hire a swarm of inspectors to make sure it's done perfectly. The Canadian proposal might cost Californians a bundle and might be impossible to police, but that's just too bad. The Canadians assert their alternative is the *least-trade-restrictive* method for protecting the California water supply. "Least-trade-restrictive" is NAFTA's Necessity Test. If California doesn't knuckle under, the U.S. Treasury may have to fork out over $976 million to the Canadian pollutant's manufacturer.

The GATS version of the Necessity Test is NAFTA on steroids. Under GATS, as proposed in the March 19 memo, national laws and regulations will be struck down if they are "more burdensome than necessary" to business. Notice the subtle change from banning "trade restrictive" rules (NAFTA) to "burdensome rules." Suddenly the GATS treaty is not about trade at all, but a sly means to wipe away restrictions on business and industry, foreign *and* local.

What burdensome restrictions are in the corporate crosshairs? The U.S. trade representative has already floated proposals on retail distribution. Want to preserve Britain's greenbelts? Well, forget it—not if some bunch of trees are in the way of a Wal-Mart superstore. Even under the current, weaker GATS, Japan was forced to tear up its own planning rules to let in the retail monster boxes.

Officially, the WTO assures us that nothing threatens the right to enforce laws in the nation's public interest. But that's not according to their internal memo, where the WTO reports that trade ministers, in the course of secretive multilateral negotiations, agreed that, before the GATS tribunal, a defense of "safeguarding the public interest . . . was rejected." In place of a public interest standard, the secretariat proposes a deliciously Machiavellian *"efficiency principle."*

The March 19 memo suggests "It may well be politically more acceptable to countries to accept international obligations which give primacy to economic efficiency." This is an unsubtle invitation to load the GATS with requirements that rulers know their democratic parliaments could not accept. This would be supremely dangerous if, one day, the United States elected a president named Bush who wanted to shred air pollution rules. How convenient for embattled chief executives: what elected congresses and parliaments dare not do, GATS would require.

For example, as president—and previously as governor of Texas—George W. Bush has fought to tear apart the one remaining effective control over corporate miscreants: the right of victims to sue corporations and executives that poison workers, kill consumers and cook their books. As Governor, Bush guided such so-called tort reform into Texas law in 1999, a favor to a business front group headed by Enron's then-CEO Ken Lay. Because the Bush administration's campaign against victims' rights later belly flopped in the U.S. Congress, their game plan now is to take the debate over the right to sue away from U.S. courts and Congress and twist it into a "trade issue"—with all powers handed to an offshore GATS "disputes panel." The sly shift has already begun, under NAFTA. In

1996, a jury ruled that Canadian funeral parlor chain Loewen Corporation broke U.S. law when it bullied small U.S. operators so it could monopolize the market and jack up prices. Rather than appeal to a higher court, Loewen agreed to pay $150 million to its victims . . . then whipped around and demanded the U.S. government refund the entire sum and then some, $725 million, under NAFTA. The Canadian-U.S.-Mexican NAFTA panel has accepted jurisdiction in *Loewen v. Mississippi Jury,* and that's a bit scary. It means that the NAFTA panel has declared itself the ultimate legal authority for America—not the U.S. Supreme Court or our Constitution.[6]

The replacement of courts and congresses by these disputes panels has given the British Medical Association the jitters. Will England's National Health Service be sold? In its journal, *Lancet,* the BMA nervously questions European commissioner Pascal Lamy's assurances that "interpretation of the rules [must not be] settled by disputes procedures," that is, the GATS panel. One defender of GATS calls the British doctors' concern "hysterical."

But after reading the WTO's March 19 internal memo, hysteria may be the right prescription. The secretariat's memo makes no concession to sovereign interpretation of trade rules. Under the postdemocratic GATS regime, the Disputes Panel, those Grand Inquisitors of the Free Market, will decide whether a nation's law or a regulation serves what the memo calls a "legitimate objective."

While the U.S. Congress, state legislatures and our courts are constrained by old-fashioned constitutional requirements to debate the legitimacy of any law in public, with public evidence, with hearings open to citizen comment, GATS panels are far more efficient. Hearings are closed. Mere citizens—and their unions, consumer, environmental and human rights groups—are barred from participating or even knowing what is said before the panel.

In the Fantasy Island version of free trade, the GATS disputes

---

[6]Luckily, Loewen Corp. went belly up and was sold to a U.S. outfit. Now the NAFTA panel may have to give up its grandiose grab for authority on a technicality: There's no cross-border dispute. The bullet missed, but the gun's still loaded.

panels are used by our government to defend American jobs when evil foreigners lock out our products. But the biggest complaint brought by the United States under current rules was to slam Europeans over barriers to our markets in bananas. Exactly how many banana-picking jobs did our government save by this action? When Harry Belafonte sang "Day-O!" he wasn't talking about Bayonne, New Jersey. America doesn't grow bananas—so how did it get in this dispute anyway? Did it have anything to do with the fact that Carl Lindner, chief of the Chiquita Banana Company, is one of the top donors to both Democrats and Republicans?

Dare we suspect the hand of the corporate lobby in this banana appeal? And as for the March 19 WTO memo: Where did the trade ministers get these ideas?

The LOTIS Committee

There are conspiracy cranks and paranoid antiglobalizers who imagine that the blueprints for WTO supranational control are designed in secret meetings between the planet's corporate elite and government functionaries, with media leaders attending to adjust propaganda as ordered. They're right.

One of these quiet groups calls itself the LOTIS Committee. The inner group of this inner group is called the "High Level LOTIS," which sounds like a stage of Buddhist enlightenment. It isn't. LOTIS, standing for "Liberalization of Trade in Services," grew out of the less wisely named "British Invisibles." LOTIS High and Low are chaired by the Right Honorable Lord Brittan of Spennithorne, Q.C., who, as Leon Brittan, was chief of the European Union, the "Common Market." He now attends to LOTIS as vice chairman of international banking house UBS Warburg.

The minutes—how I got them is not important—are a fun read. In the meeting of February 22, 2001, Britain's chief negotiator on the GATS treaty references the European Commission's paper on industry regulation privately circulated to LOTIS members for their vetting (figure 4.2). The European memo—supposedly a

Liberalisation of Trade in Services (LOTIS) Committee

Minutes of meeting held on Thursday, 22 February 2001 at Lloyd's, One Lime Street, London EC3

Present:

Chair
Christopher Roberts, Covington and Burling

Secretary
Neil Jaggers, International Finan~

Alistair Aber~~~
John ~

...nti-GATS Counter-measures. Alistair Abercrombie introduced IFSL's paper
...t the "civil society" NGOs campaign against the GATS and what might be done
...he UK private sector to challenge the criticisms which were being made about
...Agreement. It was hoped that the question and answer part of the paper
...uld be agreed quite quickly so that the material could be posted on IFSL's
...ebsite. It was proposed that, at its meeting on 8 May, the High-Level LOTIS
...roup should discuss private sector strategy, particularly the identification of
...pportunities for business leaders to engage in the exercise.

9.2 Matthew Lownds welcomed the private sector's help in countering the anti-
GATS arguments. He noted that the campaign was leading to a broadening of concerns. If business was
Movement in particular was leading to a broadening of concerns. If business was
to help convince the public, a case was needed based on the development-related
benefits which the GATS can bring. He also pointed to the need to coordinate
business responses to the NGOs allegations. Malcolm McKinnon said that the
pro-GATS case was vulnerable when the NGOs asked for proof of where the
economic benefits of liberalisation lay. Christopher Ehrke said that his firm was
very willing to be involved in the exercise. He felt that some of the points made
in the IFSL paper needed to be more punchy and floated the idea of creating a
sub-group to take the work forward. Matthew Goodman said that the exercise
should be taken forward in close consultation with the WTO Secretariat, which
had already produced some useful material on the matter. Pete Maydon
undertook to circulate a recent Finnish paper about the economic benefits of
liberalisation, on which the LOTIS paper could draw. He felt that developing
countries should be encouraged to refute the arguments put forward by the
NGOs. In particular, if every member of the WTO could sign up to the counter-
arguments produced by the Secretariat, this would have the broadest impact.
Action Pete Maydon

...y Manisty wondered how business views could best be communicated
...respect, his company would be most willing to give them
... ~an could be involved in his capacity of Chairman
... ~ke considered that the Committee ne~
... ~oordinate a proactive

confidential government document—gave LOTIS the inside track on the GATS Necessity Test proposals. The dreams and wishes of LOTIS members were amply fulfilled in the consensus of the trade ministers, as recorded one month later in the March 19 WTO memo.

The movers and shakers of LOTIS got a look-see at several confidential documents; but the public—the moved and shaken—got the runaround. Barry Coates, director of the WTO watchdog organization World Development Movement, told me he was refused these documents by the British government. Coates was told the papers "did not exist."

You'd think that the LOTIS tribe, whose banks and insurance operations controlled several hundred billion dollars in assets, would not care a jot whether Coates and his WDM researchers had the info. But in fact, WDM had LOTIS members in a panic, according to the notes under the heading "Anti-GATS Counter-measures." It was like a herd of elephants panicked by a mouse. But the WDM is a mouse that roars. At the February LOTIS meeting, according to the minutes, much time was spent "in countering the anti-GATS arguments." In these private sessions, they worried that WDM factual presentations had raised questions about free trade that the businessmen could not counter. One member fretted, "The pro-GATS case was vulnerable when NGOs [non-governmental organizations] asked for proof of where the economic benefits of liberalisation lay."

LOTIS swung into action, with a plan to buy a friendly study from some professors they could enlist for about $75,000 to $100,000 apiece.

And in attendance, helpfully, was Henry Manisty of Reuters—the giant news service whose stories are carried by every major paper around the globe. Manisty volunteered his news agency for the propaganda effort. Just plant the material with him, he offered. "His company would be most willing to give them publicity."[7]

---

[7] To view the confidential WTO and LOTIS documents in full, visit www.gatswatch.org/LOTIS/LOTIS.html.

Revolt of the Dammed: The Bolivian Water Wars

As if on queue from the LOTIS group, a business-friendly columnist (are there any others?) for the *International Herald Tribune*
paved Ambassador Zoellick's way to the WTO meeting with this:

> Here we go again: Enemies of open markets are seek-
> ing to derail another set of trade negotiations intended
> to increase world prosperity, to the benefit of both rich
> and poor nations.[8]

My God, who are our Enemies? "Anti-globalization activists,"
warned the *Trib* writer, and anyone who opposes GATS. What
should be the punishment for those opposing world prosperity?
Should we arrest them? Shoot them? Well, that had already been
done—in Bolivia.

One of the key aims of the GATS treaty is to turn publicly
owned water services over to private enterprise. Governments
have built a trillion dollars in piping systems worldwide, with no
intention of turning a profit. The WTO, the World Bank, Azurix
(subsidiary of Enron), Vivendi (formerly Lyonnaise des Eaux) and
an outfit called International Water Limited thought this a terrible
waste. But water was cheap stuff—foolish governments seemed to
give the stuff away, just covering the cost of the pipes. Higher
prices would make markets in water possible, and lure entrepreneurs to the spigots.

Public water was first sold off to corporate operators in
England. Prices jumped 250 percent and watering English gardens
has, at times, been criminalized. The English, as they do, grum-
bled, then shrugged, then paid. Meeting no resistance, the water
privateers marched on Egypt, Indonesia, and Argentina. But when
they reached Cochabamba, Bolivia, something happened that the

---

[8]This from Reginald Dale; *International Herald Tribune*, April 3, 2001, but I could have
chosen any of the columnists from the U.S. press establishment.

water barons did not expect. The thirsty poor resisted. In the end they paid, too—in blood.

"Protests Claim Two Lives" was squeezed into a single paragraph blip in the World in Brief page of my paper, Britain's *Guardian*. In U.S. papers, the story of the Bolivian dead vanished under Monica Lewinsky's dress. It was April 2000, and I used the Internet and my *turista* Spanish to try to find out what the heck was going on there.

First, let's correct the *Guardian*'s arithmetic. Six died in Bolivia. Another 175 were injured, including two children who were blinded, after the military fired tear gas and bullets at demonstrators. The victims were opposing the 35 percent hike in water prices imposed on the city of Cochabamba by the new owners of the water system, International Waters Ltd. (IWL) of London. Following the Cochabamba killings, Hugo Banzer (once Bolivia's dictator, then the elected president) declared a nationwide state of siege, setting curfews and abolishing civil liberties. On April 12, 2000, just after the martial law declaration, World Bank president Wolfensohn took time out from his own preparations against protests in Washington to comment to reporters, "The riots in Bolivia, I'm happy to say, are now quieting down."

I contacted Oscar Olivera, leader of the Cochabamba protests, to ask him how he organized the riots. On April 6, following the first protests against the price increases, Olivera, a trade union official, with a coalition of fourteen economists, congressmen, lawyers and community leaders, accepted a government invitation to discuss the IWL price hikes. After entering the government offices in Cochabamba, Olivera and his colleagues were arrested. With Olivera in chains, the riot outside the building could only have been directed by the leader of the five hundred protesters, Cochabamba's Roman Catholic archbishop (figure 4.3).

There is, of course, the possibility that the World Bank's Wolfensohn had it wrong, and that what he calls rioters were in fact innocent victims of deadly repression. Olivera, one of five protest leaders released (the government banished the seventeen

Fig. 4.3. From February through April 2000, Bolivians, including this Quechua woman, took to the streets of Cochabamba to protest huge increases in the price of drinking water. (© Tom Kruse)

others to internal exile in the desert), flew to Washington to try to speak with Wolfensohn. But the Bank prez is a busy man and Olivera left without a meeting.

Never heard of International Water Limited (IWL)? It's just another alias for Bechtel Corporation of San Francisco, USA, once headed by Nixon's secretary of state, George Shultz. Also feeding at the Bechtel trough: Reagan secretary of defense Casper Weinberger (pardoned for his crimes by Bush Sr.) and, in years past, two former directors of the CIA, John McCone and William Casey (whose crimes are unpardonable).

From its U.S. headquarters, Bechtel issued a statement flatly denying the upheaval in Bolivia had anything to do with its water price hikes. Rather, IWL's American owner hinted darkly that the revolt was partly the work of those opposing a "crackdown on coca-leaf production." Olivera insists that neither he nor the archbishop traffics in narcotics.

The price hikes that triggered the water war were driven by IWL's need to recover the cost of the huge Misicuni Dam project. Water from the Misicuni Dam system costs roughly six times that of alternative sources. Why would IWL buy water from a ludicrously expensive source? Perhaps because IWL owns a part of the Misicuni Dam project?

The public had one other objection with IWL's charging for the dam project: There is no dam. It has not yet been built.

It is a basic tenet of accounting that investors, not customers, fund capital projects. The risk takers then recover their outlay, with profit, when the project produces a product for sale. This is the heart, soul and justification of the system called "capitalism." In theory, anyway. But when a monopoly operator gets its fist round a city's water spigots, it can pump the funds for capital projects (even ones that cost 600 percent over the market) from captive customers rather than its shareholders.

Samuel Soria, the Bolivian government's former consultant on the water projects, said he was unable to extract evidence from IWL that it had put any funds at all into the operation. Soria, chairman of Cochabamba's Council of Economists, was told the water system's purchasers had deposited $10 million into a Citibank account in New York, but Soria found no evidence of its transfer to Bolivia. Water prices, he feared, could eventually rise 150 percent under IWL management.

Luis Bredow, the editor of Cochabamba's newspaper *Gente* [*People*], told me that his investigation concluded that IWL/Bechtel grabbed the entire system for nothing. "No money was shelled out by anybody" for the water company, he said. Bredow attributes these exceptionally favorable terms to IWL's partnering with former Bolivian president Jaime Paz Zamora, leader of a political party allied to Banzer.

I contacted IWL's spokesman in London, who said little more than, "How did you find out that IWL was involved in Cochabamba?" (The company's Bolivian group is called Aguas de Tunari.) In fact, Bechtel's IWL operation, based out of London, is getting to be, to use Bredow's term, "misterioso." To quell the spreading demonstrations, President Banzer announced cancellation of the water privatization on April 5, 2000.

A day later, word leaked that IWL was back in the saddle at the water company and people took to the streets again, nationwide. On April 10, the panicked government declared that the foreign consortium had "abandoned" their franchise when its British CEO supposedly fled the country. But I was able to track down the IWL executive at a La Paz hotel where, his associates told me, they were about to open negotiations with the Banzer government.

It can't be said that Bechtel brought misery to Cochabamba; they found plenty already there. Intestinal infections leading to diarrheal illness is Bolivia's number-one disease and child killer, a result of the fact that water hookups and sanitation reach only 31 percent of rural homes.

World Bank director Wolfensohn has a solution to the lack of water: *raise its price*. So pay up, Wolfensohn demanded of the protesting Bolivian water users in his extraordinary April 12 dia-

tribe against the "rioters." Wolfensohn's shut-up-and-pay-up out-
burst contradicts the internal counsel of his own experts. In July
1997, at a meeting in Washington, the Bank's technocrats laid out
to the Bolivians the case against Misicuni and even warned about
social upheaval if prices rose. According to World Bank insiders (I
won't use their names lest I get them fired), the Bank's hydrologists and technicians devised a water plan for Cochabamba at a
fraction of Misicuni's bloated cost.

This alternative could be paid off without raising prices on
current customers. Water supply and distribution, the Bank's experts told me, would be divided between two companies to avoid
the kind of self-dealing inherent in IWL's Aguas de Tunari setup.

So why did Wolfensohn condemn the protests against a project the World Bank itself found dodgy and damaging? Long before
ministerial limousines clogged the U.S. capital for the April 2000
World Bank "Ministerial" meeting, the big policy decisions were
settled in far-flung "sectoral" meetings. In the case of water, nearly
one thousand executives and bureaucrats gathered in The Hague
in March 2000 to review and refine a program to privatize the
world's water systems.

But these private operators who carved the planet into "market segments" in March can only turn in profits if prices rise radi-
cally and rapidly. IWL secured from Bolivia a 16 percent real
guaranteed return. This profit boost itself was enough to account
for the initial 35 percent hike in rates. The ransacking of Bolivia's
water supply would not have occurred without a bit of helpful
arm-twisting by the World Bank. The IMF, World Bank and Inter-
American Development Bank have written water system sell-offs
into what they modestly term "master plans" for each Latin American nation. Consortia such as IWL were formed to capture these
cast-off public assets.

The IMF and World Bank justify the sell-offs by claiming that
privateers are committed to delivering capital for desperately
needed water system repairs and expansion. But, like a gigolo's
flowers, the promises wilted rapidly.

Cochabamba's protest organizers knew that just across the border in Buenos Aires, the region's first privatization consortium eliminated 7,500 workers, the system bled from lack of maintenance and prices jumped, repeating the story of virtually every water privatization from the Philippines to the English midlands. In Argentina, the new owners of the Buenos Aires system include, notably, the World Bank itself.

The reversal of the water system sell-off and the general boycott against higher water bills marked the first successful resistance to the globalization blitzkrieg. From Wolfensohn on down, the globalizers were not happy. The big money in the globalization racket is not in hawking video decks to Bangladeshis. The real loot is in rapid low-capital takeovers of former state assets, concentrated in infrastructure where monopoly control virtually guarantees outsized profit. From the British Gas takeover of the São Paolo gas company to United Utilities' buyout of the Manila water company, it all seemed a riskless romp—until a few thirsty, angry peasants in the Andes decided they could stop the new global order in the streets.

Bolivia Vanishes: see Style Section

You didn't read about the killings in Bolivia in your newspaper?

Come now, it was right there in the *Washington Post* . . . in paragraph ten of the story on page thirteen of the Style section. I kid you not: the *Style* section. It dangled from the bottom of a cute little story on the lifestyle of some local anti-WTO protesters.

And so one of the most extraordinary international stories of 2000 just went PFZZZT!—and disappeared from sight.

Some vital stories get buried because they fail the "sex" test of hot photos or have no domestic news hook. But Bolivia had it all. TV networks could obtain high-quality video footage of the military gunning down civilians. At the center of this story were huge American corporations, including the political players at Bechtel. Most importantly, this general strike in South America offered a dramatic and bloody parallel to protests in Washington occurring on the very same days. By any normal news measure, this was a helluva story of globalization stopped dead in its tracks.

When Wolfensohn called the massacred protesters "rioters" he was hoping to discourage the press from writing sympathetically about the Bolivians. He need not have worried. There was nothing on the tube; and aside from the mention in the *Post*'s Style section and a few news wire paragraphs in the *New York Times*, for the mainstream media the Bolivians simply vanished.

However, the little bit of coverage obtained was actually worse than none.

The *Financial Times* sent a reporter to Bolivia. The lead paragraph of his report informed us that on the wall of the protesters' headquarters hung "faded portraits of Che Guevara and Fidel Castro." There was no mention at all that six people had died.

The *FT* reporter, who should know better, picked up the line that drug traffickers were somehow behind the water protests. The fanciful accusation was put out on a Bechtel Corporation news release, but hey, a corporate press release is better than a fact.

Bolivians themselves were also denied the full story, but by more direct means. The courageous editor of the Bolivian newspaper *Gente* published an investigative series exposing the sweetheart deals between the U.S.-European investors and politically connected Bolivians. At the end of April, *Gente*'s publishers submitted to threats of financial ruin by the water system's Bolivian partners an demanded that their editor, Luis Bredow, print a retraction of his reports. Instead, Bredow printed his resignation. Dr. Soria, the government expert who spoke with me about his hunt for Bechtel's assets, faces arrest for making his findings public.

As to the Cochabamba protest leader Oscar Olivera, his release was secured by an international campaign (more than once—he has been arrested three times). That was good news I got the night after I debated Thomas Friedman. But what of "Protests Claim Two Lives," the note that sent me on this trail? Needless to say, the Western papers told me nothing, nor did the

Bolivian press; no names were given for these protesters who lost their lives. Who were they? Coca dealers, as Bechtel claimed? Provocateurs? Guerrillas? Months later, I finally obtained this from a colleague:

IN A MESSAGE DATED 9/5/00 9:29:32 AM EASTERN DAYLIGHT TIME, SENDER WRITES: SUBJECT HEADING: BOLIVIA DEAD ON THE AFTERNOON OF SATURDAY APRIL 8TH 17 YEAR OLD VICTOR HUGO DAZA WAS KILLED BY A SHOT THROUGH HIS FACE. A FRIEND OF MINE KNOWS HIS FAMILY AND SAYS HE WAS IN TOWN RUNNING AN ERRAND FOR HIS MOTHER.

Bad TRIPS at the WTO

In July 2002, the *New York Times* reported that George W. Bush had saved Africa. That bighearted lug proposed giving African and Caribbean nations half a billion dollars for AIDS drugs. Combine this with Bill Clinton's deal with the pharmaceutical companies to practically give away their AIDS drugs to Africa at 75 percent off their list price and I was ready to concede that private enterprise without regulations could, at times, perform miracles.

But just when I was ready to announce Christmas in July, I came into possession of a twelve-page document from Argentina. It appears to have originated in the Office of the United States Trade Representative in Geneva (which does not deny the document's authenticity). The confidential official missive, dated June 2000, threatens Argentina against opening its borders to the drug trade—not the fun stuff, but sales of legal, licensed medicines. If Argentina did not end its commitment to free cross-border trade in pharmaceuticals, wrote the U.S. trade rep, America would keep Argentina on the "Section 301 Watch List"—a kind of death row for trading partners.

There's more to the World Trade Organization than GATS and combat over water ownership. The WTO treaty most perti-

nent here is the psychedelically named TRIPS: Trade-Related Intellectual Property Rights.

If you read the gospels of globalization apostles, you might get
the impression that the World Trade Organization is all about
doing away with tariffs and trade barriers. *Only in your dreams.* In
the real world, the WTO is the mechanism for *privatizing* the tariff
system. Once, countries protected their workers and local industry
behind taxes at national borders. In the new world trade order,
global corporations may demand levies against nations that sell or
buy products outside the zones they have marked out by brand
names and market segments. TRIPS is the WTO's penal system for
countries caught importing or exporting in contravention of marketing plans of corporations that own ideas.

The story of TRIPS, Africa and Argentina begins with this
unfun fact: 25.3 million people in Southern Africa are going to die
of AIDS unless medicine arrives *now*. Luckily, Brazil, India and,
most aggressively, Argentina can make the necessary drugs dirt
cheap and ship them to the dying. But U.S., British and Swiss
pharmaceuticals giants howled about the proposed cross-border
shipments.

During the Clinton administration, the U.S. trade cops, led by
then–Vice President Al Gore and backed by Big Pharma, halted
the life saving plan of selling cheap Argentine drugs to South
Africans—Nelson Mandela's pleas, Nobel Prize and flowered shirts
notwithstanding.

Unfortunately for Gore, who was running for president at the
time, the let-them-eat-aspirin policies he was advocating resulted
in packs of enraged Gay-mericans protesting his every campaign
stop, hollering about his killing more Africans than Michael
Caine did in *Zulu*. This did not make good TV for Al.

In response President Bill found a few billion to quell the rest-
less natives. However, the billions came with strings attached—or,
more accurately, chains and manacles. South Africa had to buy
100 percent of the medicine from the United States and pay back
all the cash at "commercial interest rates."

On the supply side of this scheme to stop South Africa breaking the de facto embargo on free trade in pharmaceuticals was the U.S. trade rep's poison pen letter to Argentina. South Africa hoped to use a loophole in TRIPS that permits the importing of patent drugs in extreme emergencies, even without the patent holder's approval. Initially, Clinton retaliated against South Africa by taxing some of its imports to the United States—until the anti-Gore demos. The U.S. trade rep's threat against Argentina indicates that the Clinton administration re-aimed the sanctions missiles at Argentina to avoid the impolitic Mandela imagery, while still cutting off South Africa's AIDS drugs supply at the source.

If Argentina hadn't backed down, there would have been an expected WTO show trial, after which Argentina's economy would have been hung from a pole in Geneva as an example for India and Brazil, other potential exporters. As Argentina was already on its knees, it gave in quickly to Clinton's swift kicks to its economic gonads. The Africans were too wise and too poor to accept Clinton's fraudulently generous loan con. Bush promises a fourth of the Clinton sum—albeit as a grant, not a loan. But one thing did not change with the White House party turnover: The U.S. trade rep (now Zoellick) remains the knuckle-dragging enforcer of Big Pharma's withholding medicine by authority of WTO TRIPS.

Maybe I'm not being fair. After all, TRIPS seeks to protect and compensate manufacturers for their risky investments and inventiveness in creating medicines like AZT, Glaxo-Wellcome's anti-AIDS drug. Right?

Glaxo was inventive, all right, but not in discovering AZT. A Professor Jerome Horowitz synthesized the drug in 1964, under a grant from the U.S. government's National Institutes of Health (NIH). A Glaxo unit bought the formula to use on pet cats.

In 1984, an NIH lab discovered the HIV virus. The government lab urgently asked drug makers to send samples of every anti-retrovirus drug on their shelves. NIH spent millions inventing a method to test these compounds. When the tests showed AZT killed the virus, the government asked Glaxo, as the compound's owner, to conduct lab tests. Glaxo refused. You can't blame them. HIV could contaminate labs, even kill researchers. So the NIH's Dr. Hiroaki Mitsuya, combining brilliance, bravery and loads of public cash, performed the difficult proofs on live viruses. In February 1985, NIH told Glaxo the good news and asked the company to conduct human trials.

Glaxo refused again. Here's where Glaxo got inventive. Within days of the notice, the company filed a patent in Britain for its "discovery." Glaxo failed to mention the U.S. government work.

But Glaxo has a heart. In July 2000, the American-British behemoth announced it would sell South Africa an AZT-based drug for only $2 a day per patient, more than 75 percent off the price charged in America and Europe. I called Glaxo USA to say thanks but, after a few questions, it became clear that the $2 price merely matched the Brazilian/Argentine prices, still about triple the cost of production.

Think about that. If $2 is the free market price, then Americans and Europeans pay 400 percent over the odds, price discrimination explicitly protected by TRIPS. That's the funny thing about the WTO's expansion of so-called intellectual property rights. TRIPS trade barriers are sold in the West on the slick line that *those people*—the dark, unindustrious tribes of the Southern Hemisphere—are trying to steal *our* inventions. In fact, says expert Jamie Love of the Consumer Project on Technology in Washington, Western patients have as much to lose as Africans under the new regime of thought ownership.

This came to Love graphically in 1997 when Maude Jones, a thirty-year-old London woman, called him, begging help to obtain Taxol. The drug could have cured her breast cancer, but the National Health Service did not prescribe it because of its stratospheric cost.

There is no patent on Taxol. U.S. government scientists discovered it. But pharmaceutical behemoth Bristol-Myers Squibb, because it performed minor work calculating dosage levels, holds the intellectual property rights on dose-related data, even though the data were originally collected by government. Even without a patent, Britain's data protection laws give Bristol-Myers lockup control on Taxol in the United Kingdom for ten years.

Bristol-Myers takes no chances with its cancer monopoly. Taxol comes from the yew tree. While Western drug companies have long argued that Asian rain forest plants are theirs for the taking without paying royalties, Bristol-Myers obtained from Congress the exclusive right to harvest yew trees on U.S. government lands, about the only place it grows on the planet. For these public assets, B-M paid nothing.

But Maude Jones paid. Ultimately, the company was shamed into offering her the medicine for free, if she moved to America. However, doctors concluded the offer was probably too late. As her family already faced bankruptcy, Maude (not her real name) phoned Love to say she had chosen to die.

Love told me the young woman, from her deathbed, hoped South Africans, Americans and Europeans would discover "a helpful solidarity." In AIDS and breast cancer, the stricken North and South share a horrific commonality as the new landless peasantry in the apartheid of intellectual property rights.

Dr. Dre Guards Sony's Plantation House

When I asked the Doctor about the WTO TRIPS treaty, he didn't mince words: "Now shut the fuck up and get what's coming to you!" In my exchange with Endre Young, the artist known as Dr. Dre, this was the example he gave of his copyright intellectual property, which was reproduced, without compensation, by ne'er-do-wells accessing www.napster.com. Mr. Young filed suit and a California judge, to protect this gentleman beset by copyright pirates, effectively ordered Napster's closure. Mr. Young was philosophical about the ruling: "I'm in a murderous mind-state with a heart full of terror."

Yo, what's going on here? Behind the angry Black face of the rapper's assault on Napster are the grinning white faces of his coplaintiffs, Recording Industry Association of America, front for the Big Five record companies—BMG, EMI, Sony, Time-Warner, and Universal. Together, these five media megaliths distribute over 95 percent of all music CDs sold in the Western world. Behind their public tears shed for compensating their artists—and since when did *that* become a concern of the music industry?—is the deeper agenda of protecting this musical OPEC.

Now let's look at the B-side of the recording industry combine. According to consent decrees in little-noticed cases filed by the U.S. Federal Trade Commission, the Big Five have for years bullied retailers to ensure that you get whacked for $36 for that Abba tribute CD you just had to have. As Bill Gates teaches us, a well-functioning monopoly fleeces its customers at one end while simultaneously squeezing suppliers at the other. In the case of the music cartel, the suppliers of raw material—the musicians—have to get through one of five tightly guarded gateways. As a result, the only stuff that makes it out the other end of these resistant sphincters onto the airwaves and into the big stores are Spicebunnies, Eric Clapton de-plugged, prefabricated bad boys like Eminem and middle-aged moguls' talent-free trophy wives (which should not be taken as a dig at the gifted Mariah Carey).

In other words, the Big Five don't just control *how* you buy what you want, they tell you *what* you want.

It used to be that industry's inputs, the talent, railed against this closed system. That's where Dre's posse comes in. His tinker-toy "ganstas" give street cred to the moguls' assault on the Internet, the first serious alternative route for distributing music Time-Warner hasn't chosen for you. The system suits rap producer Dre just fine as the cartel allows him and Puff Daddy to jointly lock out musicians that could replace them or the artists in their stable, such as Mr. Marshall Mathers (Eminem), author of the "get what's coming to you" lyric. Dre's no fool. He knows that control of his little patch is dependent on his defending his bosses' intellectual property plantation.

Dre v. Napster is the musical sideshow of the bigger war over ownership of intellectual property, ranging from ditties to DNA. When Nelson Mandela suggested that South Africa could issue "compulsory licenses" for local manufacture of cheap AIDS drugs, Al Gore threatened him with the WTO hammer. Yet, at the same time, at the behest of the "Gore-Techs," Al's Silicon Valley billionaire buddies from AOL and Oracle, the U.S. Justice Department compelled Microsoft to divulge its proprietary codes and license Windows software to Gore's buddies at a government-capped price.

Hey, I'm all for the U.S. seizure of Gates's intellectual property, but I can't ignore the rank whiff of hypocrisy.

But then, hypocrisy is the oxygen of the new imperial order of thought ownership. Every genteel landlord of fenced-in intellectual real estate began life as a thief. Under WTO and U.S. law today, how many products built on others' ideas might never have made it to market? As Isaac Newton would say now, "If I see further than others, it is because I stand on the shoulders of giants *too dumb to patent their discoveries*."

I bet Mr. Gates, so quick to shout "piracy!" could name two products that depend heavily on the lifted intellectual discoveries of others: MS-DOS and Windows. To make sure no one could steal from him what he had so freely boosted, Gates has run an international campaign to legally lock up his monopoly on ideas. Bill's nobody's fool. He must know that if the intellectual property defenses are breached, it will come from the need to get cheap AIDS drugs to Africa. So we see Gates putting his two cents (in his case, two billion) into the Africa AIDS holocaust issue. In February 2002, Bill and wife Melinda made the cover of *Newsweek* for their bighearted philanthropy. The grinning couple's foundation has spent hundreds of millions for AIDS treatment in Africa, working paw-in-claw with Merck and other Big Pharma corporations tied to a PR campaign that drowns out the calls of doctors pleading to end TRIPS restrictions. If there's any doubt where the

Gates's hearts lie, the *Wall Street Journal* notes that their foundation has, oddly, invested over $200 million in drug company stocks. If this "charitable" operation eviscerates protest against the TRIPS thought-police and medical patents are upheld, Gates's donations could have the effect of killing more people than they save.

Not everyone is entitled to compensation. The WTO requires, on penalty of sanctions, that every nation pass laws granting patents on "life-forms," by which Americans and Europeans mean genetically modified Frankenstein seeds or drugs, often remakes of traditional genomes shoplifted from Third World forests. When Thailand mischievously registered traditional medicines as that nation's intellectual property, the U.S. trade representative wrote that turning nature's bounty into patent property could "hamper medical research" (reinforcing the notion that Americans are incapable of irony).

WTO is sold as the defender of unfettered markets. But Lori Wallach of Ralph Nader's Global Trade Watch notes that WTO's TRIPS exists to *prevent* free trade. No pharmaceutical or media magnate has to suffer the same lectures that workers who lose their jobs to uncontrolled imports do—that sales lost to open borders will benefit them in the long run.

As the Napster case shows, the new expansion of intellectual property rights has little to do with compensation for the creator and everything to do with corporate control.

Still, shouldn't originators receive remuneration? Well, Dr. Dre swears his touching soliloquies about his piteous "bitch mama" are taken from The Streets. Has he sent royalty checks to the brothers?

I confess I never interviewed Dre. He didn't return my call. But the words quoted here are, unarguably, his intellectual property, and I wish to compensate him. I want to make sure that you, Dre—and Sony and Microsoft and Glaxo-Wellcome—get what's coming to you.

The Price of Dissent:
Venezuela, Exception to the New Globalization Order, Taken Hostage

Sometimes a picture is worth a thousand lies. Take the *San Francisco Chronicles*'s front-page story of June 13, 2002. Not much of a story actually, just a big photo of angry people and a caption under the headline "100,000 March Against Venezuelan President." The caption said the angry people wanted Hugo Chavez, president of Venezuela, kicked out. The demonstrators say Chavez is a dictator. There was no story beyond the photo and caption from Reuters (Mr. Manisty's amenable service), but they ran in almost every paper in the USA.

I'd just come back from Caracas—and I have to report the photo is legit. In fact, I saw a good 200,000 march against President Hugo Chavez. But what the American papers did not report was that nearly *half a million* Venezuelans marched *for* Chavez (figure 4.4).

By the time the story reached the *New York Times*, the anti-Chavez crowd had metastasized into 600,000, a fantasy easy to print as the paper of record had no reporter in Venezuela. Pro-Chavez demonstrations of up to a million citizens had, appropriate to Latin America, "disappeared" from American papers and broadcasts.

This Stalinesque cropping of the news simply continued the yearlong disinformation campaign against the populist South American president. It hit bottom when, on April 12 and 13, 2002, every major paper in the USA—with no exception—announced that Chavez had resigned his presidency. He was "unpopular," he was "dictatorial" and so, admitting to these truths, he quit. Two things caught my eye about that story: First, every one of these factoids was dead wrong. Second, almost all papers used identical words, the ones quoted, plus "resigned" . . . which I traced back to a U.S. State Department briefing.

In fact, President Chavez had been kidnapped but had spoken to cabinet members via a cell phone handed him by a sympathetic

Fig. 4.4. The demonstration in Caracas you weren't supposed to see. (© Paul Francis)

guard. Chavez had agreed to his "arrest" by leaders of a coup d'état who, had he resisted, would have slaughtered everyone in Venezuela's White House, Miraflores. But, he told his cabinet, "I am still president." Within twenty-four hours, Chavez was back at his desk, "unresigned."

What was this all about—a president taken hostage, the bent coverage, the smears? Why was the Bush administration's maniacal hatred of Chavez fiercer, if less public, than its hatred of Saddam Hussein? In Caracas, Chavez minister Miguel Bustamante Madriz explained it to me. "America can't let us stay in power. We are the exception to the new globalization order. If we succeed, we are an example to all the Americas." Bustamante Madriz, who had first tipped me off about the false "resignation" reports, is a lucky man. He came close to a bullet in the head from the coup leaders. But he didn't feel lucky. The Bush administration still had his government in its crosshairs.

That Bush had played footsy with the coup plotters is beyond question. Chavez has videotape of a U.S. military attaché from our embassy entering the army base where Chavez was held captive—something the State Department would not deny. And there was no denying that Bush's ambassador had rushed down from his hilltop compound to have his picture taken with the grinning cutthroats who had overthrown a democratically elected president. Bush's White House is quoted as saying that Chavez's election by "a majority of voters" did not confer "legitimacy" on his government. (How appropriate from the victors of Florida.)

What "exception to the new globalization order" could instigate such fury from Washington?

Back to the demonstrations. On May Day, 200,000 blondes started out from the Hilton Hotel marching east through Caracas's shopping corridor along Casanova Avenue. At the same time, half a million brunettes converged on them from the west. It would all have seemed like a comic shampoo commercial izf sixteen people hadn't been shot dead when the two groups crossed paths two weeks earlier.

The May Day brunettes support Chavez. They funneled down from the "ranchos," pustules of crude red-brick bungalows, stacked one on the other, that erupt on the steep, unstable hillsides surrounding the capital city. The bricks in some ranchos are new, a recent improvement in these fetid, impromptu slums where many previously sheltered behind cardboard walls. "Chavez gives them bricks and milk," a local TV reporter told me, not hiding her contempt, "and so they vote for him."

Chavez's crimes go beyond giving milk and housing to the poor. His real sin was to pass two laws through Venezuela's national assembly. First was the Ley de Tierras, the new land law that promised to give unused land to the landless—but only those properties held out of production for more than two years by big plantation owners.

But Chavez's tenure would not have been threatened had he not also passed the petroleum law that doubled the royalty taxes paid by ExxonMobil and other oil operators from about 16 percent to roughly 30 percent on new finds. Chavez also moved to take control of the state oil company PDVSA—nominally owned by the government, but in fact in thrall to these foreign operators.

This was no minor matter to the United States. Few Americans realize that Venezuela has at times become the USA's number-one supplier of foreign oil. It was the South American nation that broke the back of the 1973 Arab oil embargo by increasing output from its vast reserves way beyond its OPEC quota. Chavez is not only president of Venezuela, but equally importantly, president of the Organization of Petroleum Exporting Countries (OPEC). Chavez had almost single-handedly rebuilt OPEC by committing Venezuela to adhere to OPEC sales quotas, causing world oil prices to double to over $20 per barrel. It was this oil money that paid for the "bricks and milk" program and put Chavez head to head against ExxonMobil, the number-one extractor of Venezuelan oil.

As OPEC's general secretary Ali Rodriguez says: "The dependence of the U.S. on oil is increasing progressively. Venezuela is one of the most important suppliers of the U.S., and the stability of Venezuela is very important for [them]." It is from Rodriguez that I learned the April 12, 2002, coup was enacted before the plotters were ready, and why. Iraq and Libya were trying to organize OPEC to stop exporting oil to the United States to protest American support of Israel. U.S. access to Venezuela's oil suddenly became urgent. The April 12 coup against Chavez was triggered by U.S. fears of a renewed Arab oil embargo without the Venezuela fail-safe in place. Chavez had to go, and right now.

The Ultimate in Corporate Lobbying

Chavez is dark and round as a cola nut. Like his followers, he is an "Indian." But the blondes, the "Spanish," are the owners of Venezuela. A group near me on the blonde march screamed "Out! Out!" in English, demanding the removal of the president. One edible-oils executive, in high heels, designer glasses and push-up bra had turned out, she said, "To fight for democracy." She added: "We'll try to do it institutionally," a phrase that meant nothing to me until a banker in pale pink lipstick explained that Chavez's removal "can't wait until the next election."

Like their hero George W. Bush, the anti-Chavistas don't equate democracy with voting. With 80 percent of Venezuela's population at or below the poverty level, elections are not attractive to the protesting financiers. Chavez had won the election in 1998 with a crushing 58 percent of the popular vote and that was unlikely to change except at gunpoint.

And so on April 12 the business leadership of Venezuela, backed by a few "Spanish" generals, turned their guns on the presidential palace and kidnapped Chavez. Pedro Carmona, the chief of Fedecamaras, the nation's confederation of business and industry, declared himself president. One might say this coup was the ultimate in corporate lobbying. Within hours, Carmona set about voiding the forty-nine Chavez laws that had so annoyed the captains of industry, executives of the foreign oil companies and *latifundistas*, the big plantation owners. Carmona had dressed himself in impressive ribbons and braids for the inauguration. In the Miraflores ballroom, filled with the Venezuelan elite, Ignazio Salvatierra, president of the Bankers' Association, signed his name to Carmona's self-election with a grand flourish. The two hugged emotionally as the audience applauded.

Carmona then decreed the dissolution of his nation's congress and supreme court while the business people clapped and chanted, "*Democracia! Democracia!*" I later learned the Cardinal of Caracas had led Carmona into the presidential palace, a final Genet-esque touch to this delusional drama. But this fantasy would evaporate "by the crowing of the cock," as Chavez told me in his poetic way.

OPEC director Rodriguez, now a lawyer-executive but once a leftist guerrilla in Venezuela's mountains, helped clear up a mystery for me: How Chavez saved himself from execution by the coup plotters. It turns out Rodriguez had telephoned his old buddy Chavez from OPEC headquarters in Geneva just before the coup to tip him off about the Arab embargo talk. Chavez himself told me that the call helped him prepare. According to Juan Barreto, a leader of Mr. Chavez's party in the national assembly, pro-Chavez troops were hidden in the corridors underneath the presidential palace.

On April 13, corporate coup leader Carmona, fresh from his fantasy inaugural, received a call from the head of a pro-Chavez paratroop regiment stationed in Maracay, outside the capital. Up to a million Venezuelans were marching on the presidential palace demanding Chavez's return. Carmona, surrounded, could choose his method of death: bullets from the inside, rockets from above, or dismemberment by the encircling "bricks and milk" crowd. Carmona took off his costume ribbons and surrendered.

The Anti-Argentina

While the immediate cause of America's panicked need to remove Chavez was a looming oil embargo, the heart of the Bush administration's grievance goes much deeper, to Venezuela's unique place as the "Anti-Argentina"—to globalizers, the economic equivalent of the Anti-Christ. Argentina accepted the World Bank's four-step economic medicine with fatal glee: free trade, "flexible" labor laws, privatization and reduced government budgets and regulation. Chavez rejects it all outright, beginning with the phony "free" trade agenda under the terms of the WTO and NAFTA (which the United States would expand to South America under the aegis of the Free Trade Area of the Americas). Trade under these terms is anything but free to the peoples of the Southern Hemisphere—the "Opium Wars" coercive imbalance as identified by Joe Stiglitz. Instead, Chavez calls for a change in the North-South terms of trade, increasing the value of commodities exported to Europe and America. Chavez's longer-term policies of rebuilding OPEC and higher tariffs on oil must be seen in the context of smashing imbalanced trade relations epitomized by the WTO.

We saw how the World Bank's secret June 2001 "Country Assistance Strategy" progress report ordered Argentina to pull out of its economic depression by increasing "labor force flexibility." This required cutting works programs, smashing union rules and slicing real wages. Contrast that with Chavez's first act after defeating the coup: announcing a 20 percent increase in the minimum wage. Chavez's protection of the economy by increasing the purchasing power of the lower-paid workers, rather than cutting wages, is anathema to the globalizers.

Chavez moved to renationalize oil and rejected the sale of Venezuela's water systems, while Argentina sold off everything including the kitchen-sink tap. Economist Mark Weisbrot of the Center for Economic Policy Research calculated that the loss of income from state businesses accounts for 100 percent of Argentina's cavernous fiscal deficit. Argentina followed World Bank and WTO directions and sold off the banks and water companies owned by the state or Argentines to Citibank, Enron, Bank Santander and Vivendi of the United States, Spain and France. These swiftly vacuumed up Argentina's hard currency reserves, setting the stage for the national bankruptcy at the first hint of speculator-driven currency panics. Imagine if Argentina had not sold off its oil companies on the cheap, or impoverished Ecuador had not dropped out of OPEC—they would today be wealthy, not wanting.

Chavez took the path exactly opposite to the guidance given, and ultimately imposed, on Argentina by the World Bank and IMF. To pull out of the downturn threatened by a corporate embargo of investment in his nation, Chavez taxed the oil companies and spent the money—the "bricks and milk" solution, old-style Keynesianism. This is none too revolutionary despite his rhetoric. Chavez is no Fidel—in fact, he's not a socialist of any sort. With Marx discredited as the philosophy of the "losers" of the Cold War, "Chavismo" is as radical as it gets. Chavez is an old-style social democratic reformer: increased investment in housing and infrastructure, control over commodity export prices and land to the landless—an attack on the "landlordism" that Professor Stiglitz places at the heart of world poverty. Had Chavez won office in the time of Jack Kennedy, he would have fit in nicely with the old "Alliance for Progress" development model, JFK's kinder, gentler answer to Communism. Today, Chavez's redistributionist reformism offers an operating, credible alternative to the IMF's corporate-friendly free market nostrums.

Unfortunately for Chavez, his economic plan was working. Despite the European and American media's hoo-ha over how Chavez has "ruined" Venezuela's economy, its gross domestic product grew by 2.8 percent in 2001. And it wasn't all due to improvements in oil prices; excluding crude oil, economic activity jumped by about 4 percent. Compare the "ruined" Venezuelan economy to Argentina, which the World Bank displayed as the pet student of market theory, now a financial delinquent.

The Keystone Kops–style plot against Chavez by Venezuela's military-industrial complex served Big Oil's interests. But that's an old-style shoot-'em-up coup, likely to fail. The coup d'états of the twenty-first century will follow the Argentine model, in which the international banks seize the financial lifeblood of a nation, making the official presidential titleholder merely inconsequential except as a factotum of the corporate agenda.

This is what Chavez's minister meant when he said Venezuela represented a threatening example that could not be allowed to succeed. Dissent from the new globalization order will be punished. Already, the plan I saw put in place in Chile against Allende (President Richard Nixon's order to his CIA chief to "make their economy scream") is in the offing for Venezuela: capital boycotts, sabotage, disinformation intended to cause panics and financial runs. And lastly, there is the all-important propaganda war aimed at U.S. citizens to ensure that Americans remain ignorant and quiescent when a democratically elected president is assassinated, overthrown or hounded from office.

Two Friedmans, One Pinochet and the Fairy-Tale Miracle of Chile: Questioning Globalization's Genesis Myth

I have an advantage over globalization fetishists like Thomas Friedman, Mr. Lexus-and-Olive-Tree. I was there at the beginning, at the moment of globalization's conception when the sperm of Milton Friedman's oddball economic theories entered the ovum of the fertilized mind of Ronald Reagan, who was then governor of California. I witnessed the birth of Thatcherism before Thatcher—there, at the University of Chicago, in the early 1970s, as the only American member of an elite group later known as the "Chicago Boys." Professor Friedman (no relation to Thomas) was the economic god who walked among us, soon to win the Nobel Prize for his extremist laissez-faire theories. Other academics found Friedman intriguing, but considered his free market fanaticism off the kooky edge. But the Chicago Boys believed; and, quite different from other students, were handed an entire nation to experiment on, courtesy of a coup d'état by a general in Chile. Most of the "Boys" were Latin Americans, a strange collection in white turtleneck sweaters and dark shades, right out of the movie *Missing,* who would return to Chile and make it into a Friedmanite laboratory. (. . . With a twist. Contrary to typical academic exercise, those who asked questions "disappeared.")

Like Tinkerbell and Cinderella's fairy godmother, General Augusto Pinochet is reported to have performed magical good deeds. In the case of Pinochet, he is universally credited with the Miracle of Chile, the wildly successful experiment in free markets, free trade, privatization, deregulation and union-free economic expansion designed by the Chicago Boys, whose laissez-faire seeds have spread from Santiago to Surrey, from Valparaiso to Virginia.

Some may be a bit squeamish about the blood on his chariot, but all conservative "reformers" must agree, globalization's free market revolution was born from the barrel of Pinochet's guns. Whatever the general's shortcomings, they tell us, he was Chile's economic savior and lit the world's future economic path.

Within the faith of the Reaganauts and Thatcherites, Pinochet's Chile serves a quasi-religious function. It provides the necessary genesis fable, the ersatz Eden from which the laissez-faire dogma sprang successful and shining. But what if Cinderella's pumpkin did not really turn into a coach? What if the Miracle of Chile, too, is just another fairy tale? The current measurable failure of the economics of free markets, starvation from Quito to Kyrgyzstan, is dismissed as the pain of "transition" to market economies. But unblinking study discloses that the original claim to "success"—that General Pinochet begot an economic powerhouse—is one of those utterances, like "we are winning the war on terror," whose truth rests entirely on its repetition.

Chile can claim some economic success. But that is the work of President Salvador Allende, who saved his nation, miraculously, a decade after Pinochet had him murdered.

These are the facts. In 1973, the year the general seized the government, Chile's unemployment rate was 4.3 percent. In 1983, after ten years of free market modernization, unemployment reached 22 percent. Real wages declined by 40 percent under military rule. In 1970, before Pinochet seized power, 20 percent of Chile's population lived in poverty. By the year "President" Pinochet left office, the number of destitute had doubled to 40 percent. Quite a miracle.

Pinochet did not destroy Chile's economy all alone. It took nine years of hard work by the most brilliant minds in world academia, that gaggle of Milton Friedman's trainees, the Chicago Boys. Under the spell of their theories, the general abolished the minimum wage, outlawed trade union bargaining rights, privatized the pension system, abolished all taxes on wealth and on business profits, slashed public employment, privatized 212 state industries and sixty-six banks and ran a fiscal surplus. The general goose-stepped his nation down the "neoliberal" (free market) path, and soon Thatcher, Reagan, Bush, Clinton, the IMF and the planet would follow.

But what actually happened in Chile? Freed from the dead hand of bureaucracy, taxes and union rules, the country took a giant leap forward . . . into bankruptcy. After nine years of economics Chicago-style, Chile's industry keeled over and died. In 1982 and 1983, gross domestic output dropped 19 percent. That's a *depression*. The free market experiment was *kaput*, the test tubes shattered. Blood and glass littered the laboratory floor.

Yet, with remarkable chutzpa, the mad scientists of Chicago declared success.

In the United States, President Ronald Reagan's State Department issued a report concluding: "Chile is a casebook study in sound economic management." Milton Friedman himself coined the phrase "the Miracle of Chile." Friedman's sidekick, economist Art Laffer, preened that Pinochet's Chile was "a showcase of what supply-side economics can do."

It certainly was. More exactly, Chile was a showcase of deregulation gone berserk. The Chicago Boys persuaded the junta that removing restrictions on the nation's banks would free them to attract foreign capital to fund industrial expansion. (A decade later, such capital market liberalization would become the sine qua non of globalization.) On this advice, Pinochet sold off the state banks—at a 40 percent discount from book value—and they quickly fell into the hands of two conglomerate empires controlled by speculators Javier Vial and Manuel Cruzat. From their captive banks, Vial and Cruzat siphoned cash to buy up manufacturers—then leveraged these assets with loans from foreign investors panting to get their piece of the state giveaways.

The banks' reserves filled with hollow securities from affiliated enterprises.

Pinochet let the good times roll for the speculators. He was persuaded that governments should not hinder the "logic" of the market. By 1982, the Chilean pyramid finance game was up. The Vial and Cruzat groups defaulted. Industry shut down, private pensions were worthless, the currency swooned. Riots and strikes by a population too hungry and desperate to fear bullets forced Pinochet to reverse course. He booted his beloved Chicago experimentalists.

Reluctantly, the general restored the minimum wage and unions' collective bargaining rights. Pinochet, who had previously decimated government ranks, authorized a program to create 500,000 jobs. The equivalent in the United States would be the government's putting another 20 million people on the payroll. In other words, Chile was pulled from depression by dull old Keynesian remedies—all Franklin Roosevelt, zero Ronald Reagan. The junta even instituted what remains today as South America's only law restricting the flow of foreign capital.

New Deal tactics rescued Chile from the Panic of 1983, but the nation's long-term recovery and growth since then is the result of—*cover the children's ears*—a large dose of socialism. To save the nation's pension system, Pinochet nationalized banks and industry on a scale unimagined by the socialist Allende. The general expropriated at will, offering little or no compensation.

While most of these businesses were eventually reprivatized, the state retained ownership of one industry: copper.

University of Montana metals expert Dr. Janet Finn notes, "It's absurd to describe a nation as a miracle of free enterprise when the engine of the economy remains in government hands." (And not just any government hands. A Pinochet law, still in force, gives the military 10 percent of state copper revenues.) Copper has provided 30 to 70 percent of the nation's export earnings. This is the hard currency that has built today's Chile, the proceeds from the mines seized from Anaconda and Kennecott in 1973—Allende's posthumous gift to his nation.

Agribusiness is the second locomotive of Chile's economic growth. This is a legacy of the Allende years as well. According to Professor Arturo Vasquez of Georgetown University, Allende's land reform, that is, the breakup of feudal estates (which Pinochet could not fully reverse), created a new class of productive tiller-owners, along with corporate and cooperative operators, who now bring in a stream of export earnings to rival copper. "In order to have an economic miracle," says Dr. Vasquez, "maybe you need a socialist government first to commit agrarian reform."

So there we have it. Keynes and Marx, not Milton Friedman, saved Chile.

Half a globe away, an alternative economic experiment was succeeding quietly and bloodlessly. The southern Indian state of Kerala is the laboratory for the humane development theories of Amartya Sen, winner of the 1998 Nobel Prize for economics. Committed to income redistribution and universal social services, Kerala built an economy on intensive public education. As the world's most literate state, it earns its hard currency from the export of technical assistance to Gulf nations. If you've heard little or nothing of Sen and Kerala, maybe it is because they pose an annoying challenge to the free market consensus.

In the year Sen won the prize, the international finance Gang of Four—the World Bank, the IMF, the Inter-American Development Bank and the International Bank for Settlements—offered a $41.5 billion line of credit to Brazil, which was then sinking in its debts. But before the agencies handed the drowning nation a life preserver, they demanded that Brazil commit to swallowing the economic medicine that nearly killed Chile. You know the list by now: fire-sale privatizations, flexible labor markets (that is, union demolition) and deficit reduction through savage cuts in government services and social security.

In São Paulo, the public is assured that these cruel measures will ultimately benefit the average Brazilian. What looks like financial colonialism is sold as the cure-all tested in Chile with miraculous results.

But that miracle was in fact a hoax, a fraud, a fairy tale in which no one lived happily ever after.

Madhouse

It's been twenty-five years since I sat with Milton Friedman and the Chicago Boys as they planned our new world. The Chicago Boys' grouping, officially called the "Latin American Finance Workshop," was directed by Professor Arnold Harberger; Friedman's was the "Money and Banking Workshop." I worked my way in with both of them—even then I was undercover, operating for the electrical and steelworkers' union leaders Frank Rosen and Eddie Sadlowski. Frank told me, "Keep your mouth shut, put away the childish Mao buttons, put on a suit and *find out what these guys are up to.*"

I wouldn't call Milton Friedman a midget, but what sticks in my mind is that his feet didn't touch the floor from the built-up chair in which he presided.

In those years, Rhodesia (now Zimbabwe) was a hot topic. The nation was controlled by whites, 5 percent of the population, who kept the 95 percent Black population in virtual slavery, without hope and certainly without the right to vote. Professor Friedman opined from his high chair, "Why are people attacking Rhodesia, the only democracy in Africa?" And I remember that, at the time, the professor was driven around in a black limousine by a Black chauffeur.

So, while the other students—the budding bankers and dictators-in-training—are drooling in admiration, I'm reporting back to the unions, "This Friedman is *one sick puppy.* And no one's going to buy this self-serving 'laissez faire' free market mumbo jumbo from some ultra-right wing-nut."

But now, two decades later, Bush and Clinton and Putin and Wolfensohn open their mouths and out comes Milton Friedman. And everywhere I turn, the guys running the show are wearing their Golden Straitjackets and grinning and groping and agreeing with each other. And all I can think of is something another professor of mine, Allen Ginsberg, once said: *The soul should not die ungodly in an armed madhouse.*

INSIDE CORPORATE AMERICA

When a poseur like former CBS news reporter Bernard Goldberg says the media is "biased," he means there are more journalists registered as Dems than Repugs. But that's meaningless. They may vote *D* or *R*, but their real affiliation is to Hezb'Shekel—the Party of Money. Over the last two decades, when it comes to covering corporate America, our press poodles have spent their working hours curled up at the feet of "entrepreneurs" like Jack Welch of GE and Ken Lay of Enron, panting and drooling and scribbling songs of puppy love to the miraculous work of the new breed of get-it-while-you-can CEO centi-millionaires. "Liberal bias," my ass, Mr. Goldberg. Just try taking on a corporate power, Bernard, and see how long you hold a network post.

Since the apotheosis of Ronald Reagan, the American media has fed us tales of the titanic struggles between these innovative, progressive corporate chiefs and their Enemy. And we all know the name of that Enemy: the bureaucrat, that paunchy apparatchik with the thick rule book, his fat bottom spreading behind the paper-choked desk, scheming up ways to pick the pockets of the productive class and get in the way of business doing business. Even government tells us: The enemy is government. Politicians, whether Democrat or Republican, compete to lash him at the whipping post. Our only chance of rescue is a cavalry of inventive creative private-sector samarai: Wackenhut Corporation, Monsanto, Enron, Reliant, Wal-Mart, Novartis—these are just a few of the knights errant of the New Order.

But as Butch said to Sundance, "Who *are* these guys?" In 1998, I was hired by the *Observer* of London to find out. I began an ongoing series of investigative and analytical reports titled "Inside Corporate America." My mission, banished from U.S. happy-talk business newsrooms, was to enter the bodies and souls of world-spanning corporations, many you've never heard of, who had taken extraordinary control of our health, our culture, our pocketbooks and our freedoms. *Who are these guys* who would govern us better than government?

I began with a corporate hero larger than life, even in death.

What Price a Store-gasm?

At Wal-Mart's 1992 general meeting, company founder Sam Walton asked his shareholders to stand and sing "God Bless America." The 15,000 Wal-Martians responded emotionally to Sam's call, even though Mr. Walton had been dead for two months.

Walton's request to the stockholder-cum-revival meeting in rural Arkansas—channeled through an executive, spotlit and on bended knee, speaking to the departed Deity of Retail—was not surprising. Wal-Mart is the most patriotic, flag-waving company in America.

Until you look under the flags. Stores are decked out like a war rally, with Stars and Stripes hung from the ceiling and cardboard eagles shrieking BUY AMERICA! But one independent group sampled 105,000 store items and found only 17 percent made-in-the-USA items. Many gewgaws on sales carts marked "Made in

America!" came from such red-white-and-blue locales as Honduras and Indonesia.

Wal-Mart's annual sales far exceed the GDP of the old Warsaw Pact. Where does all that stuff come from? Avid Wal-Mart shopper Wu Hongda can tell you.

"Harry" Wu is famous in the United States. Although he escaped China after nineteen years in a prison camp for "counterrevolutionary" views, Wu conned his way back into the prisons to document *laogai,* the misery of forced labor. In 1995, Wu was caught and rejailed, then released again after an international campaign.

Wu told me another part of the tale that no U.S. television station would report. Just before his last arrest, he set up a fake commercial front and sent a confederate to Guandong Province posing as a wholesale clothes buyer looking to contract with Shantou Garment Trading Company. The trading company uses factories in both Shantou town and within nearby Jia Yang prison. Shantou gave Wu's operatives "references" from another customer: Wal-Mart.

I asked Wal-Mart directly if they used incarcerated gangs in Guandong to stitch T-shirts, breaking U.S. law. The company responded, inscrutably, that its contracts prohibit slaves, prisoners or little children from making its products.

How does Wal-Mart know if company contractors with plants in China's gulag use captive labor? They can't know. Wu's associate was told Chinese authorities prohibit monitoring production inside the prison.

Of course, asking Wal-Mart if shirts are made by workers shackled or "free" is merely playing China's game. To the workers, whether inside or outside the barbed-wire enclosures, China is a prison economy. What wage can a worker expect when competing prison factories pay an effective wage of zero—and when the price for complaining about the system is made so starkly visible?

Wu, now back in the United States, continues to shop at Wal-Mart, just to check labels.

He has discovered bicycles, condoms and other necessities manufactured by the Chinese People's Liberation Army under the aptly named brand "New Order." Outside China, who makes the dirt-cheap clothes? The answer depends on how you define "children." When reporters confronted CEO David Glass with photos of fourteen-year-old children locked in his Bangladesh factories, he said, "Your definition of children may be different from mine." But those were the bad old days, back in 1992, before Wal-Mart published its Code of Conduct, which ended contractor abuses.

Or maybe not. According to the highly reliable National Labor Committee of New York, Wal-Mart contractor Beximco paid teenage seamstresses in Bangladesh eighteen cents an hour and their helpers fourteen cents an hour for an eighty-hour, seven-day week. That's half the legal minimum wage and way beyond the legal work week of sixty hours.

Wal-Mart told me this could not happen. But the company has a bad habit of trying to put one over on reporters. In 1994, former *Wall Street Journal* reporter Bob Ortega, author of the fearsome exposé *In Sam We Trust,* was taken on a dog and pony show of Wal-Mart's Guatemalan contract factories filled with smiling adult workers. But Ortega had arrived secretly two weeks earlier to speak with the child seamstresses hidden from the official tour. Later, human rights activists flew Guatemalan Wendy Diaz to the United States, where she testified about the sweatshop where, as a thirteen-year-old, she earned thirty cents an hour making Wal-Mart label clothes.

Regarding abuse of child workers, I tried but failed to reach Wal-Mart's former lawyer, Hillary Rodham. We now call her Senator Clinton, but Sam just called her "my little lady" when he appointed her to the Wal-Mart board of directors, a well-paid honor left off her official White House biography.

Despite the bothersome gripes of a few skinny kids from Guatemala, Wal-Mart maintains a folksy image based on Sam

Walton's aw-shucks six-pack Joe Bloke manner. Joyous clerks, say the company, chant pledges of customer service, which end with shouts of *"So help me Sam!"* The multibillionaire took time to go into his shops and warehouses, put on a name tag and chat with employees over doughnuts. An employee told me about these folksy chats. In 1982, well on his way to becoming America's richest man, Sam dropped by an Arkansas distribution center and told the loaders, as one regular guy to another, that if they voted to join a union in a forthcoming representation ballot, he would fire them all and shut down the entire center.

The words, corroborated by eight witnesses, may have been in violation of U.S. labor law, but they were darned effective. The workers voted down the union, keeping Sam's record perfect. Out of 2,450 stores in America today, exactly none is unionized.

Who needs a union anyway? Arkansas headquarters would not tell me the company's wage rate for clerks. So my paper arranged for volunteers to call Wal-Marts nationwide to apply for cashier jobs. In 1999, offers averaged a big $6.10 an hour, though in deference to an old American tradition, the corporation offered only $4.50 an hour near Indian reservations.

But these wages are before Wal-Mart deducts for health insurance "copayments." Because the deductions could wipe out their cash paychecks, most workers cannot accept this "benefit."

There is a pension plan and profit sharing. But Sam Walton didn't make his billions by sharing profits. Wal-Mart invented the disposable workforce. About a third of the workers are temporary and hours expand, shift, contract at whim.

The workforce turns over like the shoe inventory, so few ever collect full pensions or profit shares.

But Wal-Mart does provide free meals—sort of. Most workers' salaries are near or below the official U.S. poverty line, so those without second jobs qualify for government food stamps. With 1.3 million workers, Wal-Mart has the nation's largest payroll, if you call that pay. Taking over the care and feeding of the Wal-Martyred workforce is a huge government welfare program. It could have been worse, but the courts rejected Walton's plea for exemption from the U.S. minimum wage.

Wal-Mart does respond to workers who plead for an extra bowl of porridge.

When employee Kathleen Baker handed her store manager a petition from eighty workers hoping for a little raise, she told me, she was fired on the spot for *theft* of the use of the company typewriter to write up the petition. The charge ruined her ability to get another job.

In 1994, Linda Regalado was threatened with loss of her job if she continued to talk to fellow "associates" about their right to join a union. She persevered and Wal-Mart made good on its illegal threat. Shortly thereafter, her husband, Gilbert, working at the same store, was seriously injured and Wal-Mart refused to pay for surgery. The government sued the company, but the United Food and Commercial Workers, which backed Linda's cause, threw in the towel. The Commercial Workers' organizer told me that "the Fear Factor had become so widespread" that the union had no choice but to abandon all hope of signing up any Walton operation.

Down the road from my home, sixty miles from New York City, Wal-Mart has built a "Sam's Club." Upon entering for the first time, even my reason could not withstand the pressure of seventy thousand Standard Commercial Product Units, lit by the fluorescent sun, moaning *you want me, take me, have me*—fulfilling my nastiest human desire for Cheap and Plenty.

But my store-gasm has a cost. I step out of the Big Box and into the Pine Barrens, the last scrap of woodland left on Long Island's suburban moonscape, which Wal-Mart, despite a thousand urban alternatives, insisted on cutting up for its parking lots.

Thirty miles east in my small farming hamlet, one in four shop windows on Main Street says "For Rent." Maybe we'll end up like Hudson Falls, New York, once called "Hometown, USA." Planning expert James Howard Kunstler told me, "That town's main street is now a pitiful husk of disintegrating nineteenth-century buildings." After Sam Walton's Big Box landed outside the town, Hudson Falls was "sprawled into extinction."

No more cheap commercial thrills for me. I'm staying out of the Box, *so help me Sam*.

Gilded Cage: Wackenhut's Free Market in Human Misery

One of the hottest stock market plays of the 1990s was the investment in hotels without doorknobs: privately operated prisons. And the hottest of the hot was a Florida-based outfit, Wackenhut Corporation, which promised states it would warehouse our human refuse at bargain prices. In 1999, I thought it worth a closer look.

That year, New Mexico rancher Ralph Garcia, his business ruined by drought, sought to make ends meet by signing on as a guard at Wackenhut's prison at Santa Rosa, New Mexico, run under contract to the state. For $7.95 an hour, Garcia watched over medium-security inmates. Among the "medium security" prisoners were multiple murderers, members of a homicidal neo-Nazi cult and the Mexican Mafia gang. Although he had yet to complete his short training course, Garcia was left alone in a cell block with sixty unlocked prisoners. On August 31, 1999, they took the opportunity to run amok, stabbing an inmate, then Garcia, several times.

Why was Garcia left alone among the convicts? Let's begin with Wackenhut's cutrate Jails "R" Us method of keeping costs down. They routinely packed two prisoners into each cell. They posted just one guard to cover an entire "pod," or block of cells. This reverses the ratio in government prisons—two guards per block, one prisoner per cell. Of course, the state's own prisons are not as "efficient" (read "cheap") as the private firm's. But then, the state hadn't lost a guard in seventeen years—where Wackenhut hadn't yet operated seventeen months.

Sources told me that just two weeks prior to Garcia's stabbing, a senior employee warned corporate honchos that the one-guard system was a death-sentence lottery. The executive's response to the complaint? "We'd rather lose one officer than two."

How does Wackenhut get away with it? It can't hurt that it put Manny Aragon, the state legislature's Democratic leader, on its payroll as a lobbyist and used an Aragon company to supply concrete for the prison's construction.

"Isn't that illegal?" I asked state senator Cisco McSorley. The Democratic senator, a lawyer and vice chairman of the legislature's judiciary committee, said, "Of course it is," adding a verbal shrug, "Welcome to New Mexico."[1]

Wackenhut agreed to house, feed, guard and educate an inmate for $43 a day.

But it can't. Even a government as politically corroded as the Enchanted State's realized Wackenhut had taken them for a ride. New Mexico found it had to maintain a costly force of experienced cops at the ready to enter and lock prisons down every time Wackenhut's inexperienced "green boots" lost control. A riot in April 1999 required one hundred state police to smother two hundred prisoners with tear gas—and arrest one Wackenhut guard who turned violent. The putative savings of jail privatization went up in smoke, literally.

The state then threatened to bill Wackenhut for costs if the state had to save the company prison again. In market terms, that proved a deadly disincentive for the private company to seek help. On that fateful August 31, during a phone check to the prison, state police heard the sounds of the riot in the background. Wackenhut assured the state all was well. By the time the company sent

---

[1] Tell me about it, Senator. In 1985, I was hired by New Mexico's attorney general to look into a merger agreement between the state's electric and gas companies. As the daisy chain of self-dealing by corporate chiefs and politicos began to unravel, the AG's office gave me $5,000 to bury my files and leave the state. I did; it's the only time I've ever taken a dive to the mat on an investigation. There, I've confessed.

out the Mayday call two hours later, officer Garcia had bled to death.

Why so many deaths, so many riots at the Wackenhut prisons? The company spokesman told me, "New Mexico has a rough prison population." No kidding.

My team at the *Observer* obtained copies of internal corporate memos, heartbreaking under the circumstances, from line officers pleading for lifesaving equipment such as radios with panic buttons. They begged for more personnel. Their memos were written just weeks before Garcia's death.

Before the riots, politicians and inspectors had been paraded through what looked like a fully staffed prison. But the inspections were a con because, claim guards, they were ordered to pull sixteen- and twenty-hour shifts for the official displays.

One court official told me that Wackenhut filled the hiring gap, in some cases, with teenage guards, several too young to qualify for a driver's license. And because of lax background checks, some ex-cons got on the payroll.

A few kiddie guards and insecure newcomers made up for inexperience by getting macho with the prisoners, slamming them into walls. "Just sickening," a witness told me in confidence. Right after the prison opened, a pack of guards repeatedly kicked a shackled inmate in the head. You might conclude these guards needed closer supervision, but that they had. The deputy warden stood nearby, arms folded. One witness to a beating said the warden told the guards, "When you hit them, I want to hear a *thunk*." The company fired those guards and removed the warden—to another Wackenhut prison.

Conscientious guards were fed up. Four staged a protest in front of the prison, demanding radios—and union representation. Good luck. The AFL-CIO tagged Wackenhut one of the nation's top union-busting firms. The guards faced dismissal.

Senator McSorley soured on prison privatization. New Mexico, he says, has not yet measured the hole left in its treasury by the first few months of Wackenhut operations. After the riots, the company dumped 109 of their problem prisoners back on the government—which then spent millions to ship them to other states' penitentiaries.

Still, let's-get-tough pols praise Wackenhut's "hard time" philosophy: no electricity outlets for radios, tiny metal cells, lots of lockdown time (which saves on staffing). And, unlike government prisons, there's little or no schooling or job training, no library books, although the state *paid* Wackenhut for these rehab services.

The company boasted it could arrange for in-prison computer work, but the few prisoners working sewed jail uniforms for thirty cents an hour. Most are simply left to their metal cages. Brutality is cheap, humanity expensive—in the short run. The chief of the state prison guards' union warns Wackenhut's treating prisoners like dogs ensures they lash out like wolves.

Wackenhut Corporation does not want to be judged by their corrections affiliate only. Fair enough. Following the *Exxon Valdez* disaster in Alaska, an Exxon–British Petroleum joint venture wiretapped and bugged the home of a whistleblower working with the U.S. Congress. This black-bag job was contracted to, designed by, and carried out by a Wackenhut team.

Wackenhut did not have a very sunny summer in 1999. Texas terminated their contract to run a prison pending the expected criminal indictment of several staff members for sexually abusing inmates. The company was yanked from operating a prison in their home state of Florida. Mass escapes in June, July and August threatened Australian contracts. In New Mexico, Wackenhut's two prisons, which had barely been open a year, experienced numerous riots, nine stabbings and five murders, including Garcia at Santa Rosa. Wackenhut's share price plummeted.

But there was a ray of hope for the firm. At the end of Wackenhut's sunless summer, between the fourth and fifth murder in New Mexico, the office of Britain's Home Secretary announced he would award new contracts to the company. Wackenhut opened a new child prison in County Durham one month after Texas prosecutors charged executives and guards at Wackenhut's juvenile center with "offensive sexual contact. Deviant sexual intercourse and rape were rampant and where residents were physically injured, hospitalized with broken bones."

Based on its stellar performance in the United States, Wackenhut has become the leading operator of choice in the globalization of privatized punishment.

It wasn't a convict but an employee who told me, "My fifteen months in the prison were hell on earth. I'll never go back to Wackenhut." Those sentiments need not worry the company so long as they are not shared by governments mesmerized by the free market in human misery.[2]

How the Filth Trade Turned Green

British Petroleum has repainted all their U.S. gas stations green, and if that isn't enough to convince you that Big Oil is the environment's best friend, then just consider corporate USA's plans, endorsed by our biggest environmental groups, to bring market mechanisms to the rescue of Mother Earth.

It began in Tennessee. Up in them thar hills, they just *love* air pollution. Can't get enough of it. In fact, they'll spend hard cash for more of it.

In May 1992, the Tennessee Valley Authority paid a Wisconsin power company for the "right" to belch several tons of sulphur dioxide into the atmosphere, allowing the TVA to bust above-contamination limits set by law. Wisconsin cut its own polluting

---

[2]Following my initial report on Wackenhut, I was flooded with whistleblowers, insiders and professionals in the incarceration "industry" who piled papers on me, internal company and government documents from three continents, pleading that I keep their names concealed. To be honest, I hated it. I felt weighed down, responsible and guilty as hell because I couldn't report it. There was the story of Wackenhut's juvenile center in Louisiana, where guards beat a seventeen-year-old boy so severely that part of his intestines leaked into his colostomy bag. But that's not exactly attractive television. Editor after editor said, "No thanks."

to offset Tennessee's. This was the first-ever trade in emissions credits, an experiment in using market mechanisms to cut nation-wide pollution overall.

Why should you care if Billy Hill is paying good money to suck soot? Because trading rights to pollute, as first tried in Tennessee, was the cornerstone for implementing the Kyoto Protocol, the global warming treaty, which proposed rules for industrial production worldwide for the next three decades. The Kyoto Protocol aimed to slash emissions of "greenhouse gases" that would otherwise fry the planet, melt the polar caps and put Los Angeles under several feet of water. (It will also have negative effects.)

As you can imagine, industry's big lobbying guns beat the protocol senseless. Leading the charge against the treaty is Citizens for a Sound Economy, an ultra-right pressure group chaired by corporate super-lobbyist Boyden Gray.

Squaring off against CSE was the influential Environmental Defense Fund of Washington, DC. So committed were EDF's greens to the treaty that they set up a special affiliate to help implement the protocol's trading system. EDF's Environmental Resource Trust was first chaired by Boyden Gray.

Huh?

How did Gray, top gun of big industry's antitreaty forces, become chief of a respected environmental group? Did he have a deathbed conversion? No, Mr. Gray's in fine health, thank you. Someone far more cynical than me might suggest that Mr. Gray and his polluting clients, unable to halt the clean air treaty during the Clinton administration, perfected a new way to derail the environmental movement: If you can't beat 'em, buy 'em. By covering themselves in the sheep's clothing of a respected green organization, polluters can influence treaty talks to make darn certain they do not have to change their dirt-making ways.

That's where the Tennessee model comes in. By insinuating into the protocols a company's right to meet pollution targets by buying unused emissions allotments, U.S. industry can blow up the treaty from the inside. Fronting the filth-trading scheme is the

Environmental Defense Fund. The idea of contamination credits did not come from the greenies. It originated with the corporate lobby Business Roundtable. We know this because the Roundtable left a memo to that effect in a photocopy machine at a Kyoto follow-up meeting in Buenos Aires.

Other than the plain creepiness of selling rights to pollute, what is wrong with such trades if they painlessly cut emissions overall? Well, keep your eye on that "if." I haven't yet found a single trade that took an ounce of pollution out of the atmosphere. The free market fix for dirty air was rotten from the first deal. In the 1992 Wisconsin "sale" of pollution to Tennessee, the Wisconsin company's right to sell sulphur dioxide was based on their agreement not to build another power plant. But state authorities in Wisconsin would never have permitted building the new plant. Therefore, the seller's supposed reduction in pollution was a sham; however, the additional spume of poison from the Tennessee mountains is real and deadly.

Despite this sorry record, U.S. negotiators for the Bush administration continue to push emissions trading as a take-it-or-leave-it condition of America's participation in any new global warming treaty. Emissions trading, as a so-called market mechanism for saving the biosphere, is the pride and joy of the Third Way, the means by which both Republicans and Democrats hoped to replace those nasty old rule-by-command laws—"THOU SHALT NOT POLLUTE"—with efficient retail transactions, possibly at your local Toxins "R" Us. (America already has a "stock exchange" where 15 million tons of sulphur dioxide are traded each year.)

Under U.S. treaty proposals, any U.S. or European manufacturer who wants to crank up their earth-baking discharges will have to buy up rights from a green-minded company that has cut emissions. But where in the world will they find earth-friendly industries willing to sell their rights to pollute? You'll never guess: Russia.

In case you were on vacation when Russia became an eco-paradise, I'll fill you in. The Kyoto treaty's rights to pollute were allocated based on the level of air trash pumped out in 1990. Up to that year, remember, Russians were under Communist rule, forced to work in grimy, choking factories. Now they are free not to work at all. The post-Communist Russian industrial depression cut that nation's emissions by 30 percent. Thus, the bright side of starvation on the steppes: a bountiful supply of pollution "credits," enough to eliminate 90 percent of U.S. industries' assigned reduction in pollution.

Is anyone fooled? Did tree hugger Al Gore, vice president when the scheme was proposed, jump up and holler "Fraud!"? Not a chance. To corporate applause, the VP blessed the bogus trading in filth credits. Gore even used the pollution trading scam to enhance his green credentials by posing for photo ops surrounded by members of that most revered environmental organization, the Environmental Defense Fund.

It gets worse. The Clinton-Gore administration, before taking its final bow, announced a scheme to give "early credits" to U.S. companies that cut emissions before any treaty takes effect. So, for example, if a chemical company shuts a plant to bust its trade union, they get credits. A dozen top environmental groups are up in arms about this windfall for phantom reductions in pollution— but not EDF, which takes pride in crafting the proposal's details.

How did EDF come up with this bizarre idea? Apparently, under the tutelage of some of America's most notorious polluters, at least according to internal documents faxed to my newspaper from a source (whom, as you undoubtedly understand, I cannot name) inside the Environmental Resource Trust, the EDF unit chaired by Boyden Gray.

One memorandum, dated October 21, 1997, states: "At the present time, most of the major utilities have been regularly meeting with EDF staff to discuss this concept." Another memo indicates the group could cash in on the credits, opening the door to an environmental group profiting by selling rights to increase pollution. An EDF staffer admitted the plan was drafted with Southern Company and American Electric Power, notorious polluters, "looking over our shoulders."

Why do some enviros appear to act like Rent-a-Greens for the Boyden Grays and corporations they once blasted? It's not just the loot. Rather, genteel alliance with industry is the ticket that lets them hang out with Gore or Bush and the industry Big Boys in the deal-making loop. They believe that, from the inside, talking the "market" lingo, they can change policy. They certainly are allowed to *feel* important. Unfortunately, the collaborationists have confused proximity with influence.

The filth trade is the ugly stepchild of the new mania to replace regulation with schemes that pose as "market" solutions. We know the attractions of the filth trade to politicians of any party: It provides a pretense of action to the public while giving winking assurance to industry that the status quo is not disturbed. The sale of crud credits is chopping the legs off America's antipollution laws and it will be used to sabotage any new global warming treaty.

Marketing-not-governing gimmicks spread like Tenneessee kudzu. And it's not limited to the trade in pollution. Don't be surprised when General Pinochet claims to have purchased unused bone-cracking rights from Pol Pot.

The Non-Proliferation Trust Drops the Big One on Russia

If pollution speculators won't save the plant, how about this idea from corporate America: Why don't we send ten thousand tons of high-level uranium waste to Russia? You'd rather not? Not until you buy your lead suit?

Okay then, how about we send ten thousand tons of radioactive garbage to Russia *and* throw in $15 billion for Vladimir Putin. For the cash, President Putin must solemnly promise to store the bomb-making material safely and not let any of it slip into the hands of the Iranians or the IRA.

Just when I thought the Bush administration had adopted every crackbrained idea that could threaten Mother Earth, along comes another. This send-uranium-to-Russia scheme is the creation of something called the Non-Proliferation Trust (NPT Inc.), a Washington group that says it "grew out of extensive dialog with . . . the arms control community and the environmental community."

If by "arms control community" you were thinking of Greenpeace, you'd be a bit wide of the mark. The chairman of NPT Inc. is Admiral Daniel Murphy, once deputy director of the CIA and Bush Sr.'s chief of staff. The other seven listed board members and executives include former CIA chief William Webster, two nuclear industry executives, one former Nixon administration insider, the general who commanded the U.S. Marine Corps, and, indeed, one certified greenie tree hugger.

It may not be your typical save-the-world lineup, but their idea is worth a hearing. Russia has a huge hot pile of "fissile material"— bomb fixings and old nuclear plant rods—sitting in polluted Siberian towns whose very names, like Chelyabinsk-14, sound radioactive. NPT Inc.'s idea is that if we send them more radioactive garbage, plus cash, Russia will then have the means and obligation to store theirs, and ours, safely.

In July 2001 the scheme got a big boost when the Duma, under pressure from Putin, abolished the Russian law that barred the nation's importing most foreign nuclear waste.

NPT Inc.'s assemblage of ex-spooks and militarists (and their lone green compatriot) control the operation through three nonprofit trusts. But nonprofit does not mean that no one gains.

So after no small amount of digging and several pointed questions by my associate Oliver Shykles, this self-described charity admitted it will pay a British-American wheeler-dealer, Alex Copson, some unidentified percentage of the deal. NPT has been reluctant to give details of Copson's potential gain from the success of NPT, possibly because the polo and sports car aficionado with the posh accent lacks the diplomatic gloss appropriate to this sensitive enterprise. Copson once described the natives of the Marshall Islands as "fat, lazy fucks" when they nixed one of his nuke dump schemes.

Contractors will share a few billion from this scheme, including German power consortium Gesellschaft für Nuklear-Behälter mbH (GNB). By the way, Dr. Klaus Janberg of GNB is director of "not-for-profit" NPT International.

But the real winner, should NPT succeed, would be the long-dead nuclear industry, which George Bush hopes to bring back from the crypt. There is one huge obstacle to Bush's radioactive dream: disposing of the nuclear waste. If you think about it, the only indispensable appliance for a kitchen is a toilet (presumably in another room); so too, one cannot build a nuclear plant without planning for the end product.

At $15 billion, dumping in Russia is a bargain. Since Russia is already a nuclear toilet, who would notice a little more hot crud?

Russia's own environmentalists have noticed, but objections from their Ecological Union are smothered by the ringing endorsement of the nuclear issues chief of one of America's richest environmental groups, the Natural Resources Defense Council. NRDC's Dr. Thomas Cochran sits on NPT Inc.'s MinAtom Trust board of directors, painting the project with a heavy coat of green.

What on Mother Earth would drive the NRDC man to front for NPT?

Bernardo Issel, director of the Washington-based Non-Profit Accountability Project, sent me a copy of NPT Inc.'s draft "Long-term Fissile Materials Safeguards and Security Project." At page eighteen, one finds arrangements for the NRDC to administer a $200 million Russian "environmental reclamation fund," for which the green group will receive a fee of up to 10 percent of expenditures—a cool $20 million.

NRDC's Cochran insists his group would have never taken that role. An NPT spokesman says the clause has been removed from a new draft contract, though they have refused my request to see the document.

Is this another case of greens selling out for greenbacks? It's not that simple.

The NRDC's Dr. Cochran is as straight a shooter as you'll ever meet. The problem here is not payola, but philosophy. The NRDC represents the new wave of environmental organization enchanted with the use of market mechanisms. Like the Environmental Defense Fund with its goofy pollution-trading scheme, these groups are mesmerized by can-do entrepreneurs with access to huge mounds of capital and sold on the pleasant if naïve idea that the profit motive can be bent to the public good.

The NRDC and other pro-market environmentalists are always on the hunt for what their prophet, Amory Lovins, calls "win-win" cases—deals that aid the environment while making big bucks for the corporate players. To the horror of many consumer advocates, NRDC stood with business lobbyists to push both the trade in "pollution credits" and promote deregulation of electricity in California, though the group did a quick flip on deregulation when it flopped.

The NPT uranium scheme is the quintessential public-private partnership that business greens find irresistible. For Dr. Cochran, the uranium-dumping deal's attraction is NPT Inc.'s promise, which cannot be easily dismissed, to provide billions to clean up Russia's radioactive hellholes. And NPT also promises to toss in $250 million to a Russian orphans fund.

Environmental cleanup, nonproliferation and orphans. Why would Russia's green activists turn away from this obvious win-win? The answer, in a word, is "MinAtom." MinAtom, Russia's Ministry of Atomic Energy, is, of course, the agency that created the nuclear mess in the first place. Can MinAtom be trusted to safely handle both the nuclear fuel and faithfully use the several billion for environmental cleanup, not to mention the orphans?

As soon as I heard "MinAtom," I ran to my notes of my 2001 interview with Joseph Stiglitz, the former World Bank economist. The economist told me about an incident involving MinAtom that disturbs him to this day.

In July 1998, the Clinton administration privatized the United States Enrichment Corporation, USEC. According to Stiglitz, the privatized USEC proved inefficient at enriching uranium, but exceptionally efficient at enriching several Clinton associates. Hillary's sidekick Susan Thomases was a USEC lobbyist. The law firm that defended the president in one of Bill's bimbo lawsuits picked up $15 million for work leading up to USEC's flotation. A federal judge concluded, after reviewing documents USEC tried to conceal, that the privatization decision was influenced by "bias, self-interest and self-dealing."

To sell privatization, Clinton's buddies at USEC promised their corporation would buy up tons of Russia's old warhead uranium from MinAtom. As with NPT, the sales pitch went that by taking over government enrichment operations, private industry could reduce the amount of bomb ingredients in Russia's hands at no cost to the U.S. Treasury. Another public-private win-win.

But Stiglitz, ever the hard-nosed economist, could not fathom how this new profit-making corporation could pay the Russians an above-market price for their uranium.

The answer was, USEC couldn't. In 1996, when Stiglitz was Clinton's chief economic advisor, some honest soul dropped a damning document on Stiglitz's White House desk. It was a memo indicating that MinAtom had demanded USEC buy about double the amount of uranium originally expected. Rather than take the costly deliveries, USEC quietly arranged a payment to MinAtom of $50 million. Stiglitz called it "hush money." USEC says it was a legitimate prepayment for the hot stuff.

However one describes it, MinAtom was more than happy to play along, for a price.

Yet NPT Inc. tells us MinAtom and U.S. private enterprise can now form a trustworthy partnership to safeguard nuclear material for the next few thousand years. At first, this puzzled me: NPT Inc.'s board is led by the CIA and military men who pushed Star Wars, which they sold on the premise that Russia has probably let slip nuclear material to unnamed "rogue states."

But I think I've solved this puzzling conundrum. What we have here is the ultimate, and very green, recycling program: NPT ships America's uranium to the Russians . . . which then falls into the hands of a rogue state . . . which then returns it to the United States perched atop an intercontinental ballistic missile . . . which is shot down by the trillion-dollar Star Wars defense system. Win-win for everyone.

Neither Bodies to Kick nor Souls to Damn: Government versus the New Corporate Prometheus

Ronald Reagan warned us: Look out for the man from the government who says, "We're here to help." Here, for example, is the government's idea of help: *The federal government payroll includes 150 bureaucrats whose job is measuring the space between a mattress and the railings on a bunk bed.*

While the rest of America is busy making things people can use, these ruler-armed squadrons launch surprise raids on shopping malls and furniture stores hunting for the latest threat to society: the killer kiddy bed. If a railing is even a half inch off the specifications in their little rule books, the bed is put under arrest and removed. Altogether the bureaucrats have saved us from 513,000 criminal beds, costing manufacturers nearly $100 million. Never mind that the industry issued its own strict safety standards voluntarily without help from the little men with rulers. Maybe the way for the government to "help" is to get the hell out of the way.

That's Version A. Now try Version B:

One evening in May 1994, Sherrie Mayernik put her visiting young nephew, Nicholas, into the top cot of a brand-new bunk bed. Ten minutes later, hearing her own son's screams, she rushed to the children's room to see Nicholas hanging. When the boy struggled to free himself, the railing pushed his head into the mattress. The gap between rail and mattress, an inch more than allowed by regulation, permitted his body to slip through, but not his head. Nicholas suffocated, the fifty-fourth child to die trapped in bed rails before the government sweep.

So which version tickles your fancy? In the Version A world-view, the United States has become America the Panicked, where self-serving lawyers and journalists have created a lucrative industry of scaremongering, hunting down dangers rare or nonexistent. The result of all this misguided hysteria, say the Version A advocates—the Deregulators—is the mushrooming of giant bureaucracies whose sole effect is to hog-tie business with red tape and maddening, nitpicking regulations.

Deregulation promoters say America, which touts itself as the land of free-enterprise cowboys, John Wayne individualism and capitalism unfettered, has the most elaborate, pervasive, rule-spewing system of regulating private industry on the face of the earth. U.S. government agencies such as the Consumer Product Safety Commission—the bed police—have exploded to a scale unimagined in Europe.

For example, in 1999 the United Kingdom had 265 nuclear plant inspectors. The United States, with not many more operating plants than Britain, had 4,000.

America regulates industry like no other nation on Earth—and for good reason. America tried it the other way, hoping the marketplace would reward enlightened producers and drive out the rogues. Not a chance.

The Mayerniks' bed, which smothered their nephew, was manufactured by El Rancho Furniture of Lutts, Tennessee, long after the industry published its "voluntary standards" for bed designs.

How did America become international headquarters for corporate capitalism and, at the very same time, the society with the world's tightest constraints on private industry? It all goes back to the beginning of the nineteenth century, when Andrew Jackson ran for president on the platform of outlawing that dangerous new legal concoction called the "Corporations."

Jackson and his ally, Thomas Jefferson, feared this faceless, heartless creature made of stock certificates. Before the advent of the stockholder corporation, business owners had names and faces. They could be held personally accountable for their evils before courts or mobs or the Lord in His Heaven or at society dinners. But, ran Jackson's manifesto, "Corporations have neither bodies to kick nor souls to damn." President Jackson could not stop the corporate dreadnought. Instead, as historian Arthur Schlesinger put it, Jackson established government regulation as the means by which the democracy would impose a sense of morality upon these amoral entities.

The regulatory reform gang argues that in the twenty-first century we no longer need reams of rules and phalanx of agency inspectors. Enlightened corporations now understand the long-term advantage of protecting the public interest voluntarily. *Oh, please*. Catalina Furniture of California resisted the government order to recall five thousand of its bunk beds despite a report that, as happened to the Mayernicks' nephew, a three-year-old child was caught between mattress and rails on the thin beds. The company protested at the recall on the grounds that the first trapped child survived.

Recently, I was nauseated by a full-page ad run by Mobil Oil (now ExxonMobil) topped with the banner "Two of the Safest Ships Ever Built." It announced the launch of a new, double-hulled oil tanker which, trumpeted Mobil, would "have prevented most of history's collision caused oil spills."

Indeed, it would have. However, the ExxonMobil PR people, preening and prancing in their double-hulled self-congratulations, failed to mention that in the 1970s the oil giants successfully sued the government of Alaska, blocking a law requiring they use double-hull ships when moving oil out of the port of Valdez. As a direct consequence, the single-hulled *Exxon Valdez* destroyed twelve hundred miles of Alaska's coastline. ExxonMobil now sees the light—but only because, after the great spill and under public pressure, congress rammed the double-hull rule down Big Oil's corporate throats.

Today, the Jacksonian compact is under assault, and not just from the Republicans—we expect them to be craven toadies to business interests—but from that Democratic coulda-been Al Gore. As vice president he pushed a program called "Re-Inventing Government," which all but dynamited Jefferson's head off Mt. Rushmore.

Gore's "Re-Inventing Government" program repackaged in Democratic sheep's clothing all the hate-the-government blather that spewed from Republican hyenas like Newt Gingrich. Gore's cute anecdotes about red tape and goofy rules masked his treacherous proposals for industry to "peer review" any new government regulation. Peer review would *add* new levels of bureaucracy, procedural delay and red tape, but it would accomplish the goal of General Motors and Alliance USA, a business lobby that devised the plan for Gore, to choke off tougher safety and environmental rules.

I spoke with one of the little bureaucrats with a ruler, Consumer Product Safety Commission inspector Robin Ross. Measuring bed rails "is one of the things I like best" about the job, she says. It is a nice break from her main chore, taking evidence from families of children hung, sliced, drowned and burned.

Sometimes, when her day is done, "I just sit in my car and cry." I asked her about the best-selling book called *The Death of Common Sense: How Law Is Suffocating America*. The author, tobacco industry lawyer Philip K. Howard, Al Gore's deregulation guru, is especially fond of jokes about government agents "who even measure the number of inches surrounding a railing." Robin acknowledges the need for a second look at rule making, but she notes that it wasn't the law that suffocated Nicholas Mayernik.

"Two Symbols of American Capitalism": September 11, 2001

And while we're on the subject of little government payrollers sucking up our tax bucks and hog-tying American business, let me tell you about two of them: Greg O'Neill and Clinton Davis.

Before the World Trade Center hit the ground, professional U.S. television hairdo Tom Brokaw announced that the Twin Towers had been attacked because they are Symbols of American Capitalism. As we were watching humans jump to their deaths from burning windows, Tom had already appropriated them as martyrs to a rising stock market and the enterprising spirit of his advertisers.

He wasn't alone. Much of the pus-for-brains European Left agreed with him. In my own paper, the *Guardian*, one Rana Kabbani wrote with ill-disguised glee that this mass murder was aimed at "two symbols of American hegemony."

So let's talk about those two symbols of American capitalism, O'Neill and Davis. I recognize that Kabbani, the smarmy little terror tart, and Brokaw, big-business booster, were referring to the two towers of the Trade Center, but it wasn't an architectural artifact that was crushed lifeless.

Davis worked in the basement of the Trade Center; O'Neill on the fifty-second floor of the South Tower. (And until I started spending too much time in London, my office was on the fiftieth floor of the North Tower.)

Here's what O'Neill did in Suite 5200. As a lawyer, he represented local government. When O'Neill learned a power company had faked safety reports on a nuclear plant, he hit them with a civil racketeering suit and ultimately helped put the creeps out of the nuclear racket. That's right, O'Neill's job was to impede business. We're lucky he succeeded. Davis worked in the cops' division of the state's port authority.

In other words, those skyscrapers were filled with the bureaucrats that the Bushes love to hate. Well, Mr. Bush, while the bankers were running out of the building (I would have too!), the bureaucrats—government payrollers, firefighters and rescue workers-ran *in*.

If anything, the Trade Center was a symbol of American *socialism*. These towers were built by New York State in the 1970s. The towers' owner, the New York–New Jersey Port Authority, generates the revenue that keeps the city's infrastructure—subways, tunnels, bridges, and more—out of the hands of the ever-circling privatizers. Convincing capitalists that publicly owned operations are as good an investment bet as General Motors fell to government securities market-makers Cantor Fitzgerald (one hundredth floor, 658 workers, no known survivors).

Public ownership of the Trade Center is no anomaly. Capitalization of corporations owned by the U.S. federal government exceeds $2.85 *trillion*. Add to that state and local operations, like water systems, and the total invested in public enterprise eclipses the stock market, making the United States one of the most socialized nations left on this sad planet. If you're not American, you wouldn't know that. And if you are, you probably wouldn't know that either. There's a lot you probably don't know about America that would surprise you.

That terrible Tuesday evening, I had to call O'Neill's home. He answered the phone. "My God, you're safe!"

O'Neill replied, "Not really."

Davis was safe too, in the towers' basement. But he chose to go up into the building to rescue others. Today, Davis, the guy living high on our tax dollars, is listed as missing.

Heartbreaker: How the Maker of Viagra Saved My Romance with Attorneys

No, there aren't a million lawyers in America. Only 925,671. But that's not nearly enough, according to Elaine Levenson.

Levenson, a Cincinnati housewife, has been waiting for her heart to explode. In 1981, surgeons implanted a mechanical valve in her heart, the Bjork-Shiley, "the Rolls-Royce of valves," her doctor told her. What neither she nor her doctor knew was that several Bjork-Shiley valves had fractured during testing, years before her implant. The company that made the valve, a unit of the New York–based pharmaceutical giant Pfizer, never told the government.

At Pfizer's factory in the Caribbean, company inspectors found inferior equipment, which made poor welds. Rather than toss out bad valves, Pfizer management ordered the defects ground down, weakening the valves further but making them *look* smooth and perfect. Then Pfizer sold them worldwide.

When the valve's struts break and the heart contracts, it explodes. Two-thirds of the victims die, usually in minutes. In 1980, Dr. Viking Bjork, whose respected name helped sell the products, wrote to Pfizer demanding corrective action. He threatened to publish cases of valve strut failures.

A panicked Pfizer executive telexed, "ATTN PROF BJORK, WE WOULD PREFER THAT YOU DID NOT PUBLISH THE DATA RELATIVE TO STRUT FRACTURE." The company man gave this reason for holding off public exposure of the deadly valve failures: "WE EXPECT A FEW MORE." His expectations were realized. The count has reached eight hundred fractures, five hundred dead—so far.

Dr. Bjork called it murder, but kept his public silence.

Eight months after the "don't publish" letter, a valve was implanted in Mrs. Levenson.

In 1994, the U.S. Justice Department nabbed Pfizer. To avoid criminal charges, the company paid civil penalties—and about $200 million in restitution to victims. Without the damning evidence prized from Pfizer by a squadron of lawyers, the Justice Department would never have brought its case.

Pfizer moans that lawyers still hound the company with more demands. But that is partly because Pfizer recalled only the *unused* valves. The company refused to pay to replace valves of fearful recipients.

As we've all learned from watching episodes of *LA Law*, in America's courtrooms the rich get away with murder. Yet no matter the odds for the Average Joe, easy access to the courts is a right far more valuable than the quadrennial privilege of voting for the Philanderer-in-Chief. This wee bit of justice, when victim David can demand to face corporate Goliath, makes America feel like a democracy.

We can even vent our fury on the führer. Figure 5.1 is a letter from Hitler. He's agreeing to Volkswagen's request for more slave laborers from concentration camps. This evidence would never have come to light were it not for lawsuits filed by bloodsucking lawyer leeches, as the corporate lobby would like to characterize class-action plaintiffs' attorneys. In this case, the firm of Cohen, Milstein, Hausfeld & Toll, Washington, DC, outed this document in a suit on behalf of slave workers whose children died in deadly "nurseries" run by the automakers VW, Ford, Daimler and others. (If Hitler had been captured, he might have used the defense, "I was only taking orders . . . from Volkswagen.")

But the Nazi profiteers have their friends in the corporate lobby. Victims' rights are under attack. Waving the banner of "Tort Reform," corporate America has funded an ad campaign portraying entrepreneurs held hostage by frivolous lawsuits. But proposed remedies stink of special exemptions from justice. One would give Pfizer a free ride for its deadly heart-attack machines. A ban on all lawsuits against makers of parts for body implants, even those with deadly defects, was slipped into patients' rights legislation by the Republican Senate leader. The clause, killed by exposure, was lobbied by the Health Industries Manufacturers Association, which is supported by—you guessed it—Pfizer.

At their best, tort lawyers are cops who police civil crime. Just as a wave of burglaries leads to demand for more policemen, the massive increase in litigation has a single cause: a corporate civil crime wave.

Six years ago, after eighteen buildings blew up in Chicago and killed four people, I searched through the records of the local private gas company on behalf of survivors. What I found would make you sick. I saw engineers' reports, from years earlier, with maps marking where explosions would be likely to take place. The company, People's Gas, could have bought the coffins in advance.

Management had rejected costly repairs as "not in the strategic plan." It's not planned evil at work here, but the enormity of

Fig. 5.1. Hitler taking orders from Volkswagen.

corporate structures in which human consequences of financial acts are distant and unimaginable.

I admit, of the nearly one million lawyers in the United States, you could probably drown 90 percent and only their mothers would grieve. But as Mrs. Levenson told me, without her lawyer, who worked for a percentage of her settlement, Pfizer would not have paid her a dime of compensation.

The tort reformers' line is that fee-hungry lawyers are hawking bogus fears, poisoning Americans' faith in the basic decency of the business community, turning us into a nation of people who no longer trust each other. But whose fault is that? The lawyers? Elaine Levenson put her trust in Pfizer Pharmaceutical. Then they broke her heart.

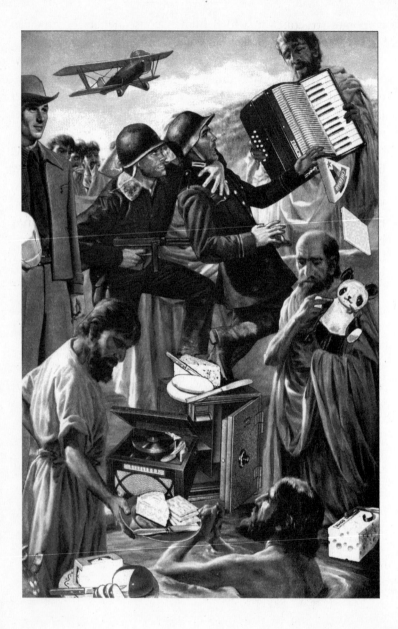

PAT ROBERTSON, GENERAL PINOCHET, PEPSI-COLA AND THE ANTI-CHRIST:
Special Investigative Reports

Papers fly out of filing cabinets and land on my desk. Voices whisper phone numbers of corporate, government and even church insiders. People talk and my tape recorder happens to be rolling. I guess I'm a lucky guy.

I've tried to carry over to journalism the techniques of in-depth investigation I used in gathering intelligence for government racketeering cases. While there's the cloak-and-dagger fun stuff (setting up false front organizations as I did for my newspaper in the Lobbygate sting), most of it involves hours, days and weeks lost in piles of technical and financial papers. Glamorous it ain't. It is expensive and time-consuming—not exactly attractive to editors for whom Quick and Cheap are matters of principle, both professional and personal. Bless those editors who've tolerated my deviant journalistic behavior.

Almost all the stuff in this book is "investigative"; that is, it's revealing information the subjects of the stories assumed and hoped had been well hidden.

These reports were a bit more difficult to tease out, especially when the subject of one, through divine communication, learned that I was a correspondent for a newspaper, the *Observer*, founded by an agent of Lucifer. But I knew that already.

Sympathy for the Banker: Anti-Christ Inc. and the Last Temptation of Pat Robertson

It's time someone told you the truth. There is an Invisible Cord easily traced from the European bankers who ordered the assassination of President Lincoln to German Illuminati and the "communist rabbi" who is the connecting link to Karl Marx, the Trilateral Commission, the House of Morgan and the British bankers who, in turn, funded the Soviet KGB. This is the "tightly knit cabal whose goal is nothing less than a new order for the human race under the domination of Lucifer."

You don't know about the Invisible Cord? Then you haven't read *New World Order* by the financier named chairman of the Bank of Scotland's American consumer bank holding company: Dr. Marion "Pat" Robertson.

In May 1999, the oldest financial enterprise in the English-speaking world, the Bank of Scotland, decided to launch into the cyber-future with the largest-ever telephone and Internet bank operation, to be based in the United States. Their choice of partner and chairman for the enterprise, U.S. televangelist "Reverend" Robertson, raised some eyebrows in Britain. But the United Kingdom's business elite could dismiss objections with a knowing condescension. To them, Robertson was just another Southern-fried Elmer Gantry bigot with a slick line of Lordy-Jesus hoodoo who could hypnotize a couple of million American goobers into turning over their bank accounts to the savvy Scots.

I had a different view of the Reverend Pat. For years, I'd kept tabs on the demi-billionaire media mogul who had chosen one president of the United States (named Bush) and would choose another (same name) . . . and who left a scent of sulphur on each of his little-known investments from China to the Congo. The Feds were already on his case, but I had a line to insiders in the born-again Christian community who, once high in Reverend Pat's billion-dollar religious-commercial-political empire, would never speak to officialdom. Their evidence suggests the Reverend broke a number of commandments handed down by the Highest Authority: the IRS.

Interestingly, the Scottish bank's official biography of Robertson failed to mention *New World Order*, the 1991 bestseller that a *Wall Street Journal* review uncharitably described as written by "a paranoid pinhead with a deep distrust of democracy." The bank left out much about this man of wealth and taste. For example, they failed to mention that Dr. Robertson is best known to Americans as the leader of the 1.2-million-strong ultra-right political front Christian Coalition. The Bank of Scotland says it is not concerned with Dr. Robertson's religious beliefs. Nor, apparently, is Dr. Robertson concerned with theirs. He has called Presbyterians, members of Scotland's established Church, "the spirit of the Anti-Christ."

What would entice the Bank of Scotland to join up with a figure described by one civil liberties organization as "the most dangerous man in America"? Someone more cynical than me might suspect that the Bank of Scotland covets Dr. Robertson's fiercely loyal following of 2 million conspiracy wonks and Charismatic Evangelicals. A former business partner of Robertson's explained the Reverend's hypnotic pull on their wallets: "These people believe he has a hotline to God. They will hand him their life savings." Robertson drew believers to his other commercial ventures: "People remortgaged their homes to invest in his businesses," the insider told me. If he did use his ministry to promote his business, this would cross several legal boundaries.

When we finally met, Dr. Robertson swore to me he would keep bank commerce, Christianity and the Coalition completely separate.

But a look into the Robertson empire, including interviews

with his former and current business associates, reveals a hidden history of mixing God, gain and Republican campaign. Not all has been well concealed. Tax and regulatory authorities have tangled for decades with his supposedly nonpartisan operations. But government gumshoes still missed some of the more interesting evidence of self-dealing, and worse.

The combination of Christianity and cash has made Dr. Robertson a man whose net worth is estimated at somewhere between $200 million and $1 billion. He himself would not confirm his wealth except to tell me that his share in the reported $50 million start-up investment in the bank deal is too small for him to have taken note of the sum.

Neil Volder, president of Robertson's financial business and future CEO of the bank venture, emphasizes Robertson's having selflessly donated to his church 65 to 75 percent of his salary as head of International Family Entertainment. I was surprised: That amounted to only a few hundred thousand dollars yearly, pocket change for a man of Dr. Robertson's means. There was also, says Volder, the $7 million he gave to "Operation Blessing" to help alleviate the woes of refugees fleeing genocide in Rwanda. Or did he? Robertson's press operation puts the sum at only $1.2 million—and even that amount could not be corroborated.

More interesting is how the Operation Blessing funds were used in Africa.

Through an emotional fundraising drive on his TV station, Robertson raised several million dollars for the tax-free charitable trust. Operation Blessing purchased planes to shuttle medical supplies in and out of the refugee camp in Goma, Congo (then Zaire). However, investigative reporter Bill Sizemore of the *Virginian-Pilot* discovered that, except for one medical flight, the planes were used to haul heavy equipment for something called the African Development Corporation, a diamond-mining operation distant from Goma. African Development is owned by Pat Robertson.

Did Robertson know about the diversion of the relief planes? According to the pilots' records, he himself flew on one plane ferrying equipment to his mines. One of Robertson's former business partners speaking on condition of anonymity told me that, although he often flew with Dr. Robertson in the minister's jet, he never saw Robertson crack open a Bible or seek private time for prayer. "He always had the *Wall Street Journal* open and *Investor's Daily*." But on the Congo flight, Robertson did pray. The pilot's diary notes, "Prayer for diamonds."

Volder told me that Robertson's diverting the planes for diamond mining was actually carrying out God's work. The planes, he asserts, proved unfit for hauling medicine, so Robertson salvaged them for the diamond hunt which, if successful, would have "freed the people of the Congo from lives of starvation and poverty." Nonetheless, the Virginia state attorney general opened an investigation of Operation Blessing.

Volder asserts that Robertson was "not trying to earn a profit, but to help people." As it turned out, he did neither. The diamond safari went bust, as did Robertson's ventures in vitamin sales and multilevel marketing. These disastrous investments added to his losses in oil refining, the money pit of the Founders Inn Hotel, his jet-leasing fiasco and one of England's classier ways of burning money, his buying into Laura Ashley Holdings (he was named a director). One cannot term a demi-billionaire a poor businessman but, excepting the media operations handed him by his nonprofit organization, Robertson the "entrepreneur" seems to have trouble keeping enterprises off the rocks. Outside the media, Robertson could not cite for me any commercial success.

Undeniably, Dr. Robertson is a master salesman. To this I can attest after joining the live audience in Virginia Beach for *700 Club*, his daily television broadcast. The day I arrived, he was selling miracles. Following a mildly bizarre "news" segment, Dr. Robertson shut his eyes and went into a deep trance. After praying for divine assistance for his visions, he announced, "There is somebody who has cancer of the intestines . . . God is healing you right now and you *will* live! . . . Somebody called Michael has a deep chest cough . . . God is *healing* you right *now*!"

It is not clear why the Lord needs the intervention of an expensive cable TV operation to communicate to Michael. But more intriguing theological issues are raised by the program hosts' linking miracles to donations made to Robertson's organization. In a taped segment, a woman's facial scars healed after her sister joined the 700 Club (for the required donation of $20 per month). "She didn't realize how close to her contribution a miracle would arrive." It ended, "Carol was so grateful God healed her sister, she increased her pledge from the 700 Club to the 1000 Club," which means kicking up her monthly payout to Pat to $84.

The miracles add up. In 1997, Christian Broadcast Network, Robertson's "ministry," took in $164 million in donations plus an additional $34 million in other income.

Earlier tidal waves of tax-deductible cash generated by this daily dose of holiness and hostility paid for the cable television network, which was sold in 1990 to Rupert Murdoch, along with the old sitcoms that filled the nonreligious broadcast hours, for $1.82 billion. Seven years prior to the sale of this media bonanza, the tax-exempt group "spun it off" to a for-profit corporation whose controlling interest was held by Dr. Robertson. Lucky Pat.

Robertson donated hundreds of millions of dollars from the Murdoch deal to both Christian Broadcast Network (CBN) and CBN (now Regent) University. That still left Robertson burdened with a heavy load of cash to carry through the eye of the needle.

Cosmetics for Christian Crusaders

In his younger days, Robertson gave up worldly wealth to work in the Black ghettos of New York. But, says former Coalition executive Judy Liebert, "Pat's changed." She noted that he gave up his ordination as a Baptist minister in 1988. (He is still incorrectly called "Reverend" by the media.) His change in 1988 was accelerated when, says his former TV cohost Danuta Soderman Pfeiffer, "he was ensnared by the idea that God called him to run for president of the United States."

The 1988 run for the Oval Office began with Robertson's announcing his endorsement by the Almighty. I asked Volder how Robertson could have lost the Republican primary if God was his campaign manager. But the Lord did not tell Robertson to *win*, He told Pat to *run*. And this "losing" race generated a mailing list of 3 million sullen Americans of the heartland whose rage was given voice by Robertson forming, out of defeat, the Christian Coalition. Volder offers that this may have been, in fact, the Lord's stratagem: to generate the fearsome lists. The Coalition lists, like the CBN lists, are worth their weight in gold. One doubts the Lord would permit the use of this list of Crusaders to line the Reverend's pockets. Indeed, Robertson swore to me they would not be used for the banking business. And whatever the Lord's intent, to dip into the Coalition lists uncompensated to promote the new bank would breach the law.

But abuse of these lists lies at the heart of charges by ex-partners. Two former top executives in the for-profit operations who have never previously spoken to media (or government) state that Robertson personally directed use of both the tax-exempt religious group's lists and the "educational" Christian Coalition lists to build what became Kalo-Vita, the Reverend's pyramid sales enterprise, which sold vitamins and other products.

Kalo-Vita collapsed in 1992 due to poor management amid lawsuits charging deception. A former officer of the company alleges some operations were funded, without compensation, including offices, phones and secretarial help, by the ministry, stretching laws both secular and ecclesiastical. When insiders questioned Robertson's using viewers' donations for a personal enterprise, Robertson produced minutes of board meetings that characterized the Kalo-Vita start-up capital obtained from CBN as "loans." According to insiders not all board members were made aware of these meetings until months after they were supposedly held. Could Dr. Pat have manufactured records of nonexistent meetings? His spokesman responds that they are unfamiliar with the facts of the allegation.

The executives were also alarmed about Dr. Robertson's preparing to use the twenty-thousand-strong and growing Kalo-Vita sales force as "an organizational structure to back his political agenda"—and partisan ambitions. U.S. federal investigators never got wind of this alleged maneuver. (U.S. law bars corporations from giving direct aid to political candidates.)

"Why Not Just Blow My Brains Out?"–The Missing Bush Papers

Besides the Kalo-Vita lists, there is evidence Robertson used Christian Coalition mailing lists to help political candidates, especially one named Bush. A September 15, 1992, memo from the Coalition's then-president, Ralph Reed, to the coordinator of President George Bush Sr.'s reelection campaign says Robertson "is prepared to assist . . . [by] the distribution of 40 million voter guides. . . . This is a virtually unprecedented level of cooperation and assistance . . . from Christian leaders." Unprecedented and *illegal*, said the Federal Elections Commission, which sued the Christian Coalition, technically a tax-exempt educational corporation, for channeling campaign support worth tens of millions of dollars to Republican candidates. The action was extraordinary because it was brought by unanimous vote of the bipartisan commission, which cited, among other things, the Coalition's favoring Colonel Ollie North with copies of its lists for North's failed run for the U.S. Senate.

Records subpoenaed from the Christian Coalition contain a set of questions and answers concocted by the Coalition and the Republican Party for a staged 1992 "interview" with Bush broadcast on the *700 Club*. This caught my eye: first, because it appears to constitute a prohibited campaign commercial, and second, because Robertson months earlier claimed Bush was "unwittingly carrying out the mission of Lucifer." With Bush running behind Bill Clinton, Robertson must have decided to stick with the devil he knew.

But the government will never see the most incriminating documents. Judy Liebert, formerly chief financial officer for the Christian Coalition, told me she was present when Coalition president Reed personally destroyed documents subpoenaed by the government. Also, when Liebert learned that the Coalition had printed Republican campaign literature (illegal if true), she discovered that the evidence, contained in the hard drive of her computer, had been removed. Indeed, the entire hard drive had been mysteriously pulled from her machine—but not before she had made copies of the files.

When Liebert complained to Robertson about financial shenanigans at the Coalition, "Pat told me I was 'unsophisticated.' Well, that is a strange thing for a Christian person to say to me." The Christian Coalition CFO told me that Ralph Reed, a big Republican operative even today, "would go through [the subpoenaed documents] and throw everything on the floor—I mean just pitch it—just take it and throw it on the floor." As Arthur Andersen executives can now attest, that's called Obstruction of Justice. When challenged on the legality (and Christianity) of such actions, Reed reportedly said, "Why don't you just take a gun and blow my brains out."

The Coalition has attacked Liebert as a disgruntled ex-employee whom they fired. She responded that she was sacked only after she went to government authorities—and after she refused an $80,000 severance fee that would have required her to remain silent about the Coalition and Robertson. The Feds, notes the Coalition, have never acted on Liebert's charge of evidence tampering.

Little of this information has been reported in the press. Why? The three-hour dog and pony show I was put through at the CBN-Robertson financial headquarters in Virginia Beach culminated in an hour-long diatribe by CEO Volder about how Robertson was certain to sue any paper that did not provide what he called a "balanced" view. He boasted that by threatening use of Britain's draconian libel laws and Robertson's bottomless financial treasure chest, one of his lawyers "virtually wrote" a laudatory profile of Robertson in a U.K. newspaper. As in the days when the Inquisition required recalcitrants to view instruments of torture, I was made to understand in detail the devastation that would befall me if my paper did not report what was "expected" of me.

This was said, like all the Robertson team's damning anthems, in a sweet, soft Virginia accent.

Would Dr. Robertson use his ministry's following to promote the Bank of Scotland operation (a legal no-no)? Despite Robertson's protests to the contrary, his banking chief Volder laid out a plan to reach the faithful, including appearances of bank members on the *700 Club*, mailings to lists coincident with their own, and "infomercials" just after the religious broadcasts. This is just the type of mixing that has so upset the election commission and the Internal Revenue Service, which in 1998 retroactively stripped Christian Broadcasting of its tax-exempt status for 1986 and 1987.

What My Cigarette Lighter Overheard

It was most difficult to convince the Reverend's protectors to let me speak directly to "the Doctor" (as they call him) at his compound in Virginia, and once there, to get my wire through the metal detector. ("Officer, could you please hold my cigarette lighter?")

I met the Doctor in his dressing room following his televised verbal intercourse with God. Robertson, though three hours under the spotlight, didn't break a sweat. He peeled off his makeup while we talked international finance.

Here was no hayseed huckster, but a worldly man of wealth and taste.

And, despite grimacing and grunts from Volder, Dr. Robertson told me he could imagine tying his Chinese Internet firm ("The Yahoo of China," he calls it) into the banking operation. Picking up Volder's body shakes, Dr. Robertson added, "Though I'm not supposed to talk about Internet banking." And he wasn't supposed to mention China. His fellow evangelists are none too happy about his palling around with Zhu Rongji, the communist dictator who gleefully jails Christian ministers. Volder defends Dr. Robertson's friendship with Zhu (and associations with deceased Congo strongman Mobutu) on the grounds that "Pat would meet with the Devil if that is the only way to help suffering people." The fact that the political connections assisted in obtaining diamond (Congo) and Internet concessions (China) is secondary.

The enterprising minister planned to launch his bank through his accustomed routes: phone and mail solicitations. But had he hit the Net, with or without the Chinese, this bank deal would have made Pat Robertson the biggest financial spider on the World Wide Web. Yet, his choosing the Bank of Scotland as his partner is surprising because, in *New World Order*, he singled out one institution in particular as the apotheosis of Satan's plan for world domination: the Bank of Scotland.

In the fevered coils of *NWO*, Robertson explains that Scotsman William Paterson first proposed the creation of the satanic "central banks"—specifically the Bank of England and Bank of Scotland—who were manipulated by the Rothschilds to finance diamond mines in Africa which, in turn, funded the satanic secret English Round Table directed by Lord Milner, editor of the London *Observer* (Ah-*ha*!) a century ago. Furthermore, the Scottish banker's charter became the pattern for the U.S. Federal Reserve Board, a diabolic agency created and nurtured by the U.S. Senate Finance Committee, whose chairman was the evil Money Trust's dependable friend, Senator A. Willis Robertson—Pat Robertson's father.

That's right. Pat is the scion of the New World Order, who gave up its boundless privileges to denounce it.

Or did he?

I had done some research on the Anti-Christ. How would we recognize him? How would the Great Deceiver win over God-fearing Christians? What name would he use? As I drove away from the chapel-TV studio-university-ministry-banking complex,

I realized I'd forgotten to ask a key question: Why does the ex-
Reverend go by the name Pat—not his Christian name, Marion?
It struck me that "Pat Robertson" is an obvious anagram for the
Devil's agent, Paterson of the Scottish bank. My silly thoughts
piled higher, fueled by staying up all night to finish *New World
Order.* Suddenly, like Robertson, I too had a vision of an Invisible
Cord that went from Lucifer to Illuminati to Scottish bankers to
African diamonds to the Senate Finance Committee to commu-
nist dictators to the World Wide Web. . . . Ridiculous, I know, but
strangely, though I thought I'd turned off the radio, it continued
to play that damned Rolling Stones song . . .

> *Pleased to meet you!*
> *Hope you've guessed my name . . .*

The Almighty Moves Mysteriously, and Swiftly

Within a week of the *Observer* completing our series of exposés,
Robertson abandoned the "dark land" of Scotland, and his big
banking dream went poof! Robertson fled Darkest Scotland. He
even resigned from the board of Laura Ashley, the U.K. fashion
house.

But our exposing of evidence that Robertson had used the
"educational" foundation mailing lists of the Christian Coalition
not only for political purposes (as the U.S. government charged)
but to promote the failed Kalo-Vita cosmetics pyramid marketing
operation opened up whole new possibilities of investigation into
whether the pastor sheered his flock. Add to that the allegations
that Reed destroyed subpoenaed documents. Public interest
lawyers with People for the American Way announced they would
take our discoveries to the U.S. Federal Elections Commission and
the Internal Revenue Service.

More questions arose. I discovered the Bank of Scotland had
appointed Robertson chairman of the bank venture. How odd.
Usually such things are announced with fanfare. It seems the Feds

have lots of problems granting bank charters to persons under investigation for misuse of assets. The Bank of Scotland made the "Reverend" chairman of the *holding* company; his name could not be found listed as a member of the board of the subsidiary that applied for the banking charter. Was the venture group trying to hide Robertson's role from the banking regulator through this odd corporate structure? That would not be cricket—nor would its revelation help their cause.

But Robertson is one swift character and quickly came up with a plan for his financial and legal salvation. It centered on the weird fact that the Christian Coalition's tax-exempt status had been in limbo for an unprecedented ten years. Apparently, no U.S. government had the guts or cold evidence to take it away—nor could authorities in good conscience grant it. After the *Observer* stories ran, Robertson simply withdrew the application for tax-exempt status, costing him virtually nothing in cash but thereby pulling the plug on all the investigations of the use or misuse of the Coalition's assets.

And within days, on June 10, 1999, Robertson announced the shutdown of the Christian Coalition. The *New York Times*, National Public Radio and *60 Minutes*, the infotainment flagship of the CBS network, all gleefully announced that Robertson and his Coalition were *finis*, his political machine sunk. This was a sure signal that Robertson would rise again, and stronger. The wily shape-shifter closed the Christian Coalition (a Virginia organization) only to establish "Christian Coalition of America" (from a Texas base).

Within a year of his demise as announced by the media establishment, which will forever underestimate Robertson's strategic brilliance, the Doctor was again positioned as America's kingmaker. His old family chum, George H. W. Bush, would need his help again. The Bush-Robertsons go way back. Pat's dad, Senator Willis Robertson, saw himself as a kind of mentor to Senator Prescott Bush, father of President Bush the First. In the 1960s, Senator P. Bush, a wealthy banker, sat on the Senate committee that oversaw banking regulations, chaired by Robertson. This time, it was Prescott's grandson, Dubya Bush, who was in hot water. In January 2000, Senator John McCain beat the Dim Son in the New Hampshire Republican presidential primary. McCain was being hailed as a real American hero, calling for an end to the corporate "soft" money that fueled the Bush campaigns. McCain looked unstoppable in the race for the Republican nomination . . . until the Virginia and South Carolina primaries.

This was Christian Coalition turf. Advertisements secretly paid for by Bush's buddies smeared McCain; but the final blow was a whisper campaign among the Believers that tagged McCain, a red-white-and-blue war veteran, as Satan's stand-in. McCain lost those primaries, and that's how Dr. Pat chose our president (with a little help from his friends in Florida).

The Cola-Nut Coup: Pinochet, Nixon and Pepsi

"It is the firm and continuing policy that Allende be overthrown by a coup . . . please review all your present and possibly new activities to include propaganda, black operations, surfacing of intelligence or disinformation, personal contacts, or anything else your imagination can conjure. . . .
—"EYES ONLY" "RESTRICTED HANDLING"
"SECRET" message from CIA headquarters to U.S.
station chief in Santiago, October 16, 1970

"SUB-MACHINE GUNS AND AMMO BEING SENT BY REGULAR COURIER LEAVING WASHINGTON 0700 HOURS 19 OCTOBER DUE ARRIVE SANTIAGO. . . .
—Message from CIA, October 18, 1970

You would be wrong to assume this plan for mayhem (figure 6.1) had anything to do with a cold war between the Free World

RUESNA-2FF 9

RESTRICTED HANDLING

CLASSIFIED MESSAGE

Copy ____ of ____

S-E-C-R-E-T

ORIG
UNIT
EXT
DATE 18 October 1970

(CLASSIFICATION)   (DATE AND TIME FILED)

MILITARY

S-E-C-R-E-T
431   18 23   11z Oct 70 CITE HEADQUARTERS - 856

TO IMMEDIATE SANTIAGO (EYES ONLY

REF: SANTIAGO 562

SUB-MACHINE GUNS AND AMMO BEING SENT BY REGULAR
COURIER LEAVING WASHINGTON 0700 HOURS 19 OCTOBER DUE ARRIVE
SANTIAGO LATE EVENING 20 OCTOBER OR EARLY MORNING 21 OCTOBER.
PREFERRED USE REGULAR COURIER TO AVOID BRINGING UNDUE
ATTENTION TO OP.

END OF MESSAGE

DECLASSIFIED - E.O. 12953 Sec 3.4
EXEMPTIONS EXEMPTED
E.O. 12356, Sec. 1.3 (a) (4)

MR 89-38 #11 CIA ltr 1/29/94

By M34 NARA, Date 3/16/95

COORDINATING OFFICERS

C/WHD
RELEASING OFFICER

AUTHENTICATING OFFICER

THIS FORM FOR USE BY AUTHORIZED RESTRICTED HANDLING MESSAGE USERS ONLY!

3205

Fig. 6.1. In the fall of 1970, the CIA planned to prevent Salvador Allende from taking office as president of Chile, by assassination, if necessary. This CIA cable was obtained by the National Security Archive.

and Communism. Much more was at stake: Pepsi-Cola's market share and other matters closer to the heart of corporate America.

In over six hours of an intense, tape-recorded debriefing, the U.S. ambassador to Chile at the time of the attempted coup d'état, Edward Malcolm Korry, interpreted these and other chilling CIA, State Department and White House top secret cables for me. Korry literally filled in the gaps, describing cables still classified and providing information censored by black lines in the documents made available to the National Security Archive. Korry laid out this hidden history of CIA-corporate complicity in mayhem— but he didn't mean to. In fact, when I went public with this info, he screamed bloody murder, not about Pinochet, but about me. He complained to my editor at the *Observer* he'd been had, bamboozled, set up, conned into talking. The old ambassador is a fervent anticommunist who thought most highly of the "Chicago Boys," the University of Chicago economic free market shock troops that pillaged and impoverished Chile (my view) or saved the South American country (his view). He had been under the impression that I was one of the "Boys," a student of Milton Friedman and crew, and so the curmudgeon—whose hatred of, and threats against, journalists are notorious—let down his guard. I had not lied to him, I really *had* been one part of the closed little Chicago Boys study group. Just because he convinced himself that I was a fellow free market fruitcake . . . well, there's nothing I could do about that.

It was 1998 when we spoke, the month Chile's former dictator Augusto Pinochet, on one of his many shopping trips to London, was arrested for murder and held for extradition to Spain to face charges of killing Spanish citizens during his regime's slaughtering spree. I thought I might track down some of Pinochet's alleged accomplices. This led to that embarrassing historical factotum, Henry Kissinger—no surprise there—and behind him the real Mr. Bigs of the operation: ITT Corporation, Anaconda Copper, Citibank and Pepsi-Cola.

Korry, an ambassador who served Presidents Kennedy, Johnson and Nixon, gives a picture of U.S. companies, from cola to copper, using the CIA as a kind of international collection agency and investment security force. Indeed, the October 1970 plot against Chile's president-elect Salvador Allende, using CIA "sub-machine guns and ammo," was the direct result of a plea for action one month earlier by Donald M. Kendall, chairman of the board of PepsiCo, in two phone calls to Pepsi's former lawyer, President Richard Nixon.

Kendall arranged for the owner of the company's Chilean bottling operation to meet National Security Adviser Henry Kissinger on September 15. Some hours later, Nixon called in his CIA chief, Richard Helms, and according to Helms's handwritten notes, ordered the CIA to prevent Allende's inauguration.

But this is only half the picture, according to Korry. He revealed that the U.S. conspiracy to block Allende's election did not begin with Nixon, but originated—and read no further if you cherish the myth of Camelot—with John Kennedy.

In 1963, Allende was heading toward victory in Chile's presidential election.

Kennedy decided his own political creation, Eduardo Frei, could win the election by buying it. Our president left it to his brother, Bobby Kennedy, to put the plan into motion.

The Kennedys cajoled U.S. multinationals to pour $2 billion into Chile—a nation of only 8 million people. This was not benign investment, but what Korry calls "a mutually corrupting" web of business deals, many questionable, for which the U.S. government would arrange guarantees and insurance. In return, the American-based firms kicked back millions of dollars toward Frei's election. This foreign cash paid for well over half of Frei's successful campaign.

By the end of this process, Americans had gobbled up more than 85 percent of Chile's hard-currency-earning industries. The U.S. government, on the hook as guarantor of these investments, committed extraordinary monetary, intelligence and political resources for their protection. Several business-friendly U.S. government fronts and operatives were sent into Chile—including the

APL-CIO's American Institute for Free Labor Development, infamous for sabotaging militant trade unions.

Then, in 1970, U.S. investments both financial and political faced unexpected jeopardy. A split between Chile's center and right-wing political parties permitted a Communist-Socialist-Radical alliance, led by Salvador Allende, to win a plurality of the presidential vote.

That October, Korry, a hardened anticommunist, hatched an admittedly off-the-wall scheme to block Allende's inauguration and return Frei to power. To promote his own bloodless intrigues, the ambassador says he "back-channeled" a message to Washington warning against military actions that might lead to "another Bay of Pigs" fiasco. Korry retains a copy of this still-classified cable.

But Korry's prescient message only angered Kissinger, who had already authorized the Pepsi-instigated coup, scheduled for the following week.

Kissinger ordered Korry to fly in secret to Washington that weekend for a dressing-down. Korry arrived at the White House after his eleven-thousand-mile flight, still clueless about the CIA plan. Strolling the White House corridor with Henry Kissinger, Korry told Kissinger that "only a madman" would plot with Chile's ultra-right generals. As if on cue, Kissinger opened the door to the Oval Office to introduce Nixon.

Nixon once described Korry, his ambassador, as "soft in the head," yet appeared to agree with Korry's conclusion that, tactically, a coup could not succeed. A last-minute cable to the CIA in Santiago to delay action was too late: The conspirators kidnapped and killed Chile's pro-democracy armed forces chief, Rene Schneider. The Chilean public did not know of Nixon's CIA having armed the general's killers. Nevertheless, public revulsion at this crime assured Allende's confirmation as president by the Chilean Congress.

Even if Nixon's sense of realpolitik disposed him to a modus vivendi with Allende (Korry's alternative if his Frei gambit failed), Nixon faced intense pressure from his political donors in the business community who had panicked over Allende's plans to nationalize their operations.

In particular, the president was aware that the owner of Chile's phone company, ITT Corporation, was channeling funds—illegally—into Republican Party coffers. Nixon was in no position to ignore ITT's wants—and ITT wanted blood. An ITT board member, John McCone, pledged Kissinger $1 million in support of CIA action to prevent Allende from taking office. McCone was the perfect messenger: He had served as director of the CIA under Kennedy and Johnson.

Separately, Anaconda Copper and other multinationals, under the aegis of David Rockefeller's Business Group for Latin America, offered $500,000 to buy influence with Chilean congressmen to reject confirmation of Allende's electoral victory. But Ambassador Korry wouldn't play. While he knew nothing of the ITT demands on the CIA, he got wind of, and vetoed, the cash for payoffs from the Anaconda gang.

Over several days of phone interviews from his home in Charlotte, North Carolina, Korry revealed, among other things, that he even turned in to Chilean authorities an army major who planned to assassinate Allende—unaware of the officer's connection to the CIA's plotters.

Once Allende took office, Korry sought accommodation with the new government, conceding that expropriations of the telephone and copper concessions (actually begun under the U.S.-installed Frei regime) were necessary to disentangle Chile from seven decades of "incestuous and corrupting" dependency. U.S. corporations didn't see it that way. While pretending to bargain in good faith with Allende on the buyout of their businesses, they pushed the White House to impose a clandestine embargo of Chile's economy.

But in case all schemes failed, ITT—charges Korry—paid $500,000 to someone their intercepted cables called "the Fat Man." Korry identified the Fat Man as Jacobo Schaulsohn, Allende's supposed ally on the compensation committee.

It was not money well spent. In 1971, when Allende learned of the corporate machinations against his government, he refused compensation for expropriated property. It was this—Allende's failure to pay ITT, not his allegiance to the hammer and sickle—that sealed his fate.

In October 1971, the State Department pulled Korry out of Santiago. But he had one remaining chore regarding Chile. On his return to the United States, Korry advised the government's Overseas Private Investment Corporation to deny Anaconda Copper and ITT compensation for their properties seized by Allende.

Korry argued that, like someone who burns down their own home, ITT could not claim against insurance for an expropriation the company itself provoked by violating Chilean law. Confidentially, he recommended that the U.S. attorney general bring criminal charges against ITT's top brass, including, implicitly, the company's buccaneer CEO, Harold Geneen, for falsifying the insurance claims and lying to Congress.

Given powerful evidence against the companies, OPIC at first refused them compensation—and the Justice Department indicted two mid-level ITT operatives for perjury. But ultimately, the companies received their money and the executives went free on the not-unreasonable defense that they were working with the full knowledge and cooperation of the CIA—and higher.

As to Ambassador Korry, I look on him as heroic—despite his attacking me for reporting his words, and his holding political views that give me the shivers. He hated the Allende government, but would not countenance bribery or bloodshed, not even for Pepsi. And I thank the old diplomat for breaking, at the age of seventy-seven, his promise to the Kissinger–corporate complex to keep their secrets, a vow I found in a September 1970 declassified cable to the U.S. secretary of state, in which the ambassador quotes Jean Genet: "Even if my hands were full of truths, I wouldn't open it for others."

And the Ignoble Prize in Chemistry . . .
Goes to Monsanto!

Thirty-seven percent of Americans over the age of fifteen find sexual intercourse painful, difficult to perform or just plain don't feel like doing it. Who says so? Doctors Edward Laumann and Raymond Rosen, that's who. And because they said it in *JAMA*, the prestigious *Journal of the American Medical Association*, the story had enough white-lab-coat credibility to pop up in every U.S. newspaper suffering from Monica Lewinsky withdrawal pains.

Oh, did I forget to mention that the study's authors previously worked for Pfizer, maker of Viagra? *JAMA* forgot to mention it as well.

Maybe you don't care whether Americans are hot or not. But contamination by cash affects research on other organs as well. Calcium channel–blocking drugs reduce the risk of heart disease. But they may have an unfortunate side effect: They could give you a heart attack. But don't worry, an avalanche of learned articles in medical journals vouch for the drugs' safety and efficacy.

Now worry: According to an investigation by the *New England Journal of Medicine*, 100 percent of the scientists supporting the drugs received financial benefits from pharmaceutical companies, 96 percent from the manufacturers of these channel blockers. Only two out of seventy articles disclosed drug company ties to authors' bank accounts.

Surreptitiously putting a hunk of the scientific community on its payroll can help a manufacturer win government approval for human and animal drugs. But when suborning conflicts of interest fails to do the trick, one U.S. manufacturer, Monsanto Company, turns to more proactive means of influencing regulators.

In May 1999 a cache of documents fell out of a low-flying airplane and onto my desk at the *Observer*. However they ended up in my possession, they certainly came by an interesting route: from the files of WTO food safety regulators, where they had been filched by U.S. functionaries, and passed under the table to Monsanto. This was fresh evidence of a dangerous new epidemic: the infection of science by corporate cash.

The pile included copies of letters, memoranda and meeting notes indicating that Monsanto obtained crucial restricted documents from a key international regulatory committee investigating the company's controversial bovine growth hormone, called BST, as in BEAST. A shot of BST boosts a cow's milk output.

But European and American experts say BST has such yummy side effects as increasing the amount of pus in milk, promoting infection in cow udders and potentially increasing the risk of breast and prostate cancer in humans who drink BST-laced milk.

According to a November 1997 internal Canadian health ministry memo that came my way, Monsanto got its hands on advance copies of three volumes of position papers intended for review in closed meetings of the UN World Health Organization's Joint Experts Committee on Food Additives. This is one valuable set of documents. The European Community's ban on the genetically altered hormone was set to expire in 1999, and the Experts Committee advised the international commission that would be voting on whether to add Monsanto BST to something called the Codex Alimentarius—the international list of approved food additives. Codex listing would make it difficult for nations to block imports of BST-boosted foods.

Monsanto's cache included confidential submissions by the EC's directors general for food and agriculture as well as analysis by British pharmacologist John Verrall.

I spoke with Verrall just after he learned his commentary was passed to Monsanto. Verrall was stunned not just by selective release of reports he believed confidential—participants sign nondisclosure statements about the proceedings—but by the source of the leak. The memo identifies Monsanto's conduit from the UN experts' committee as Dr. Nick Weber of the U.S. Food and Drug Administration (FDA). Dr. Weber, it turns out, works at the FDA under the supervision of Margaret Miller. Dr. Miller, before joining government, headed a Monsanto laboratory studying and promoting BST.

After scouring the purloined committee documents, Monsanto faxed a warning to company allies in government that one participant on the Experts Committee, Dr. Michael Hansen, "is not completely on board." Indeed he was not. Hansen was furious. A BST expert with the Consumers' Policy Institute of Washington, Hansen interprets the memos to mean that some U.S. and Canadian authorities, supposedly acting as objective, unaffiliated scientists, were in fact working in cahoots with Monsanto as advocates for the producer.

Other memos discuss plans by U.S. and Canadian officials sympathetic to Monsanto, to "share their communication strategy" with industry. The plan was to lobby members of the Experts Committee. Monsanto would secretly provide help in preparing a response to critics of BST ahead of the vote of the experts panel scheduled for February 1998. Whether the scheme using inside information affected the outcome, we don't know. We do know Monsanto won that vote.

Because proceedings were confidential, we cannot know how a majority overcame objections of known dissenters. But we can presume Monsanto was not harmed by the late addition of BST defender Dr. Len Ritter to the deliberations. Ritter was the "Manchurian candidate" of Big Pharma on the committee. An intra-office memo obtained from Canada's Bureau of Veterinary Drugs states that Ritter's name was subtly suggested to the bureau's director in an August 1997 phone call from Dr. David Kowalczyk, Monsanto's regulatory affairs honcho.

Of course, there is not much value to Monsanto in obtaining government approvals to sell BST-laden milk if no one will buy the stuff. Luckily for Monsanto, the U.S. FDA not only refuses to require labeling hormone-laced products, but in 1994 published a rule that effectively barred dairies from printing "BST-free" on milk products. This strange milk carton exception to America's Bill of Rights was signed by Michael Taylor, deputy to the FDA commissioner. Prior to joining the U.S. agency, Taylor practiced law with the firm of King & Spalding, where he represented Monsanto. Taylor, no longer in government, did not return our calls to his office at his current employer—Monsanto Washington.

Monsanto does not just *place* friends in government, it likes to *make* friends.

Canadian Health Ministry researcher Dr. Margaret Haydon told me Monsanto offered her bureau $1 million in a 1994 meeting in return for their authorizing the sale of BST. Monsanto counters the funds were proffered solely to support the cash-strapped agency's research. When asked if he considered the Monsanto offer "a bribe," Haydon's supervisor replied, "Certainly!" though he said he laughed off the proposal.

No one's laughing now. Haydon and five other government scientists filed an extraordinary plea with Canada's industrial tribunal seeking protection for their jobs and careers. They feared retaliation for ripping the cover off long-hidden, highly damaging facts about BST. America's rush to approve the hormone in 1993 rested on a study published in the journal *Science* by FDA researchers, which concluded there were no "significant changes" in BST-fed rats. The rats tell a different tale. Their autopsies revealed thyroid cysts, prostate problems and signs of BST invading their blood. The Monsanto-sponsored U.S. researchers failed to publish these facts and the FDA sealed the complete study, saying its public release would "irreparably harm" Monsanto. Indeed it would.

The Canadian scientists, finally winning access to the full study, blew the whistle on the rat cover-up. The facts became public via their labor board action, a decade after the original, misleading report. By then BST had received U.S. FDA approval as safe.

I regret singling out Monsanto if only because I'm left with so little room to honor other corporate nominees for the Ignoble Prize in Chemistry. BST expert John Verrall, a member of the U.K. Food Ethics Council, says the Monsanto episode only illustrates a trend in which "Multinational corporations have let morals slide down the scale of priorities." He concludes—in what must be a sly reference to everyone's favorite White House intern—"The white coat of science has been stained."

A Well-Designed Disaster: The Untold Story of the *Exxon Valdez*

On March 24, 1989, the *Exxon Valdez* broke open and covered twelve hundred miles of Alaska's shoreline with oily sludge.

The official story remains "Drunken Skipper Hits Reef." Don't believe it.

In fact, when the ship hit, Captain Joe Hazelwood was nowhere near the wheel, but belowdecks, sleeping off his bender. The man left at the helm, the third mate, would never have hit Bligh Reef had he simply looked at his Raycas radar. But he could not, because the radar *was not turned on*. The complex Raycas system costs a lot to operate, so frugal Exxon management left it broken and useless for the entire year before the grounding.

The land Exxon smeared and destroyed belongs to the Chugach natives of the Prince William Sound. Within days of the spill, the Chugach tribal corporation asked me and my partner Lenora Stewart to investigate allegations of fraud by Exxon and the little-known "Alyeska" consortium. In three years' digging, we followed a twenty-year train of doctored safety records, illicit deals between oil company chiefs, and programmatic harassment of witnesses. And we documented the oil majors' brilliant success in that old American sport, cheating the natives. Our summary of evidence ran to four volumes. Virtually none of it was reported: The media had turned off its radar. Here's a bit of the story you've never been told:

- We discovered an internal memo describing a closed, top-level meeting of oil company executives in Arizona held just ten months before the spill. It was a meeting of the "Alyeska Owners Committee," the six-company combine that owns the Alaska pipeline and most of the state's oil. In that meeting, say the notes, the chief of their Valdez operations, Theo Polasek, warned executives that containing an oil spill "at the mid-point of Prince William Sound not possible with present equipment"—exactly where the *Exxon Valdez* grounded. Polasek needed millions of dollars for spill-containment equipment. The law required it, the companies promised it to regulators, then at the meeting, the proposed spending was voted down. The oil company combine had a cheaper plan to contain any spill—don't bother. According to an internal memorandum, they'd just drop some dispersants and walk away. That's exactly what happened. "At the owners committee meeting in Phoenix, it was decided that Alyeska would provide immediate response to oil spills in Valdez Arm and Valdez Narrows only"—not the Prince William Sound.

• Smaller spills before the Exxon disaster would have alerted government watchdogs that the port's oil-spill-containment system was not up to scratch. But the oil group's lab technician, Erlene Blake, told us that management routinely ordered her to change test results to eliminate "oil-in-water" readings. The procedure was simple, says Blake. She was told to dump out oily water and refill test tubes from a bucket of cleansed sea water, which they called "the Miracle Barrel."

• A confidential letter dated April 1984, fully four years before the big spill, written by Captain James Woodle, then the oil group's Valdez Port commander, warns management that "Due to a reduction in manning, age of equipment, limited training and lack of personnel, serious doubt exists that [we] would be able to contain and clean up effectively a medium or large size oil spill." Woodle told us there was a spill at Valdez *before* the *Exxon Valdez* collision, though not nearly as large. When he prepared to report it to the government, his supervisor forced him to take back the notice, with the Orwellian command, "You made a mistake. This was not an oil spill."

Slimey Limeys

The canard of the alcoholic captain has provided effective camouflage for a party with arguably more culpability than Exxon: British Petroleum, the company that in 2001 painted itself green (literally: all its gas stations and propaganda pamphlets now sport a seasick green hue). Alaska's oil is BP oil. The company owns and controls a near majority (46 percent) of the Alaska pipeline system. Exxon (now ExxonMobil) is a junior partner, and four other oil companies are just along for the ride. Captain Woodle, Technician Blake, Vice President Polasek, all worked for BP's Alyeska.

Quite naturally, British Petroleum has never rushed to have its name associated with Alyeska's recklessness. But BP's London headquarters, I discovered, knew of the alleged falsification of reports to the U.S. government *nine* years before the spill. In September 1984, independent oil shipper Charles Hamel of Washington, DC, shaken by evidence he received from Alyeska employees, told me he took the first available Concorde, at his own expense, to warn BP executives in London about scandalous goings-on in Valdez. Furthermore, Captain Woodle swears he personally delivered his list of missing equipment and "phantom" personnel directly into the hands of BP's Alaska chief, George Nelson.

BP has never been eager for Woodle's letter, Hamel's London trip and many other warnings of the deteriorating containment system to see the light of day. When Alyeska got wind of Woodle's complaints, they responded by showing Woodle a file of his marital infidelities (all bogus), then offered him payouts on condition that he leave the state within days, promising never to return.

As to Hamel, the oil shipping broker, BP in London thanked him. Then a secret campaign was launched to hound him out of the industry. A CIA expert was hired who wiretapped Hamel's phone lines. They smuggled microphones into his home, intercepted his mail and tried to entrap him with young women. The industrial espionage assault was personally ordered and controlled by BP executive James Hermiller, president of Alyeska. On this caper, they were caught. A U.S. federal judge told Alyeska this conduct was "reminiscent of Nazi Germany."

Cheaper Than Manhattan

BP's inglorious role in the Alaskan oil game began in 1969 when the oil group bought the most valuable real estate in all Alaska, the Valdez oil terminal land, from the Chugach natives. BP and the Alyeska group paid the natives *one dollar.*

Arthur Goldberg, once a U.S. Supreme Court justice, tried to help the natives on their land claim. But the natives' own lawyer, the state's most powerful legislator, advised them against pressing for payment. Later, that lawyer became Alyeska's lawyer.

The Alaskan natives, the last Americans who lived off what they hunted and caught, did extract written promises from the oil consortium to keep the Prince William Sound safe from oil spills. These wilderness seal hunters and fishermen knew the arctic sea. Eyak Chief-for-Life Agnes Nichols, Tatitlek native leader George Gordaoff and Chenega fisherman Paul Kompkoff demanded that tankers carry state-of-the-art radar and that emergency vessels escort the tankers. The oil companies reluctantly agreed to put all this in their government-approved 1973 Oil Spill Response Plan.

When it comes to oil spills, the name of the game is "containment" because, radar or not, some tanker somewhere is going to hit the rocks. Stopping an oil spill catastrophe is a no-brainer. Tanker radar aside, if a ship does smack a reef, all that's needed is to surround the ship with a big rubber curtain ("boom") and suck up the corralled oil. In signed letters to the state government and Coast Guard, BP, ExxonMobil and partners promised that no oil would move unless the equipment was set on the tanker route and the oil-sucker ship ("containment barge") was close by, in the water and ready to go.

The oil majors fulfilled their promise the cheapest way: They lied. When the *Exxon Valdez* struck Bligh Reef, the spill equipment, which could have prevented the catastrophe, wasn't there—see the Arizona meeting notes above. The promised escort ships were not assigned to ride with the tankers until *after* the spill. And the night the *Exxon Valdez* grounded, the emergency spill-response barge was sitting in a dry dock in Valdez locked in ice.

When the pipeline opened in 1974, the law required Alyeska to maintain round-the-clock oil-spill-response teams. As part of the come-on to get hold of the Chugach's Valdez property, Alyeska hired the natives for this emergency work. The natives practiced leaping out of helicopters into icy water, learning to surround leaking boats with rubber barriers. But the natives soon found they were assigned to cover up spills, not clean them up. Their foreman, David Decker, told me he was expected to report one oil spill as two gallons when two thousand gallons had spilled.

Alyeska kept the natives at the terminal for two years—long enough to help Alyeska break the strike of the dock workers' union—then quietly sacked the entire team. To deflect inquisitive inspectors looking for the spill-response workers, Alyeska created sham emergency teams, listing names of oil terminal employees who had not the foggiest idea how to use spill equipment, which, in any event, was missing, broken or existed only on paper. When the *Exxon Valdez* grounded, there was no native spill crew, only chaos.

The Fable of the Drunken Skipper has served the oil industry well. It transforms the most destructive oil spill in history into a tale of human frailty, a terrible, but onetime, accident. But broken radar, missing equipment, phantom spill personnel, faked tests— all of it to cut costs and lift bottom lines—made the spill disaster not an accident but an inevitability.

I went back to the Sound just before the tenth anniversary of the spill. On Chenega, they were preparing to spend another summer scrubbing rocks. A decade after the spill, in one season, they pulled twenty tons of sludge off their beaches. At Nanwalek village ten years on, the state again declared the clams inedible, poisoned by "persistent hydrocarbons." Salmon still carry abscesses and tumors, the herring never returned and the sea lion rookery at Montague Island remains silent and empty.

But despite what my eyes see, I must have it wrong, because right here in an Exxon brochure it says, "The water is clean and plant, animal and sea life are healthy and abundant."

Go to the Sound today, on Chugach land, kick over a rock and you'll get a whiff of an Exxon gas station.

Everyone's heard of the big jury verdict against Exxon: a $5 billion award. What you haven't heard is that ExxonMobil hasn't paid a dime of it. It's been a decade since the trial. BP painted itself green and ExxonMobil decided to paint the White House with green: It's the number-two lifetime donor to George W. Bush's career (after Enron), with a little splashed the Democrats' way. The oil industry's legal stalls, the "tort reform" campaigns and the generous investment in our democratic process has produced a Supreme Court and appeals panels that look more like luncheon clubs of corporate consiglieri than panels of defenders of justice. In November 2001, following directives of the Supremes, the Ninth Circuit Court of Appeals overturned the jury verdict on grounds the punishment was too dear and severe for poor little ExxonMobil.

The BP-led Alyeska consortium was able to settle all claims for 2 percent of the acknowledged damage, roughly a $50 million payout, fully covered by an insurance fund.

And the natives? While waiting for Exxon to make good on promises of compensation, Chief Agnes and Paul Kompkoff have passed away. As to my four-volume summary of evidence of frauds committed against the natives: In 1991, when herring failed to appear and fishing in the Sound collapsed, the tribal corporation went bankrupt and my files became, effectively, useless.

Coda: Nanwalek Rocks[1]

At the far side of Alaska's Kenai Fjord glacier, a heavily armed and musically original rock-and-roll band held lockdown control of the politics and treasury of Nanwalek, a Chugach native village.

According to not-so-old legend, rock came to the remote enclave at the bottom of Prince William Sound in the 1950s when Chief Vincent Kvasnikoff found an electric guitar washed up on the beach. By the next morning, he had mastered the instrument sufficiently to perform passable covers of Elvis tunes. Of all the lies the natives told me since I began work there in 1989, this one, from the chief himself, seemed the most benign.

When I first went to work there in 1989, I sat with the chief in his kitchen, across from an elaborate Orthodox altar. Russian icons were spread the length of the wall. It was a golden day, late summer at the end of the salmon run, but the chief's eighteen-year-old nephew hung out in the bungalow watching a repeating loop of Fred Astaire movies on the satellite TV.

Fishing was just excellent, the chief assured me. He'd taken twelve seals that year. I didn't challenge the old man, legless in his

---

[1]This diary of life in the native villages of the Prince William Sound was nearly censored out of *Index on Censorship*. The magazine had hired a guest editor for the "Tribes" issue, an amateur anthropologist. He'd been to the same group of Alaskan villages where I worked. The natives performed their special ceremony for him. Among themselves they call it "Putting on the feathers," in which they provide those quaint and expected lines that so please the earnest white men with 16mm Airflex cameras and digital tape recorders. The great white anthropologist wrote down "healing poems" about "our friend the bear." I imagined him with helmet and pukka shorts preserving in his leather notebook the words of the ancient, wizened Injuns. Stanley Livingstone meets Pocahontas.

It was my terrible, self-inflicted misfortune to spoil this delicate idyll of the Noble Savage by my reporting that Alaskan natives are, in fact, very much like us, if not more so.

wheelchair. Everyone knew he'd lost his boat when the bank re-possessed his commercial fishing license.

The village once had eight commercial boats, now it had three. Besides, all the seal had been poisoned eight years earlier, in 1989, by Exxon's oil.

It took an entire month for the oil slick from the *Exxon Valdez* to reach Nanwalek. Despite the known, unrelenting advance of the oil sheet, Exxon had not provided even simple rubber barriers to protect the inlets to the five lakes that spawned the salmon and fed the razor clams, sea lions, bidarki snails, seals and people of the isolated village on the ice. But when the oil did arrive, followed by television crews, Exxon put virtually the entire populace of 270 on its payroll.

"The place went wild," Lisa Moonan told me. "They gave us rags and buckets, $16-something an hour to wipe off rocks, to baby-sit our own children." In this roadless village that had sur-vived with little cash or store-bought food, the chief's sister told me, "They flew in frozen pizza, satellite dishes. Guys who were on sobriety started drinking all night, beating up their wives. I mean, all that money. Man, people just went berserk."

With the catch dead, the banks took the few boats they had, and Chief Vincent's sister, Sally Kvasnikoff Ash, watched the vil-lage slide into an alcohol- and drug-soaked lethargy. Sally said, "I felt like my skin was peeling off." Nanwalek's natives call them-selves Sugestoon, Real People. "After the oil I thought, this is it. We're over. Sugestoon, we're gone unless something happens."

Sally made something happen. In August 1995, the village women swept the all-male tribal council from office in an electoral coup plotted partly in the native tongue, which the men had for-gotten. Sally, who's Sugestoon name Aqniaqnaq means "First Sis-ter," would have become chief if Vincent, she says, hadn't stolen two votes. The rockers, Chief Vincent's sons, were out—so was booze (banned), fast food and the band's party nights in accor-dance with the new women's council cultural revolutionary diktats. The women returned native language to the school and replaced at least some of Kvasnikoff's all-night jam sessions, which had a tendency to end in drunken brawls, with performances of the traditional Seal and Killer Whale dances (figure 6.2).

They put the village on a health-food regimen. "We're fat," says First Sister, who blames the store-bought diet which, since the spill, must be flown in twice weekly from city supermarkets. To show they meant business on the alcohol ban, the women arrested and jailed Sally's disabled Uncle Mack for bringing a six-pack of beer into the village on his return from the hospital.

On Good Friday 1964, the snow-peaked mountains of Montague Island rose twenty-six feet in the air, then dropped back twelve feet, sending a tidal wave through the Prince William Sound. At the village of Chenega, Chugach seal hunter Nikolas Kompkoff ran his four daughters out of their stilt house, already twisted to sticks by the earthquake, and raced up an ice-covered slope. Just before the wall of water overcame them, he grabbed the two girls closest, one child under each arm, ran ahead, then watched his other two daughters wash out into the Sound.

Chenega disappeared. Not one of their homes, not even the sturdier church, remained. A third of the natives drowned. Survivors waited for two days until a postal pilot remembered the remote village.

Over the following twenty years, Chenegans scattered across the Sound, some to temporary huts in other Chugach villages, others to city life in Anchorage. But every Holy Week, these families sailed to the old village, laid crosses on the decaying debris, and Kompkoff would announce another plan to rebuild. Over the years, as the prospect of a New Chenega receded into improbability, Nikolas became, in turn, an Orthodox priest, a notorious alcoholic and failed suicide. He survived a self-inflicted gunshot to the head; however, he was defrocked for the attempt.

In 1982, Nikolas convinced his nephew, Larry Evanoff, to spend his life savings building a boat that could traverse the Sound.

Evanoff has four long scars across his torso. These wounds from

Fig. 6.2. Nanwalek, Alaska. Oil from the *Exxon Valdez* destroyed the fish and wildlife on which these Chugach native Alaskans survived. Here, Lisa Moonan, one of the leaders of the women's revolt, performs the Seal Dance. (© James Macalpine)

Vietnam helped him get a government job as an air traffic controller in Anchorage, but he was fired when his union went on strike. Larry had lost both his parents in the earthquake and tidal wave.

Larry's boat was not finished until the subarctic winter had set in. Nevertheless, he sailed to remote Evans Island with his wife and two children, aged nine and fourteen. They built a cabin and, for two years, without phone or shortwave radio, one hundred miles from any road, lived off nearby seal, bear and salmon while they cleared the land for New Chenega. Over the next seven years, twenty-six of Chenega's refugee families joined the Evanoffs, built their own homes and, with scrap wood from an abandoned herring saltery, built a tiny church with a blue roof for Nikolas, whom they still called "Father."

On March 24, 1989, the village commemorated the twenty-fifth anniversary of the tidal wave. That night, the *Exxon Valdez* oil tanker ran aground and killed the fish, smothered the clam beds and poisoned all the seal on which Chenegans subsisted.

In mid-century, the average life expectancy for Chugach natives was thirty-eight years. They had next to nothing by way of cash and the state moved to take even that away. In the 1970s, new "limited entry" laws barred natives from selling the catch from their traditional fishing grounds unless they purchased permits few could afford. The natives did have tenuous ownership of wilderness, villages and campsites. In 1969, America's largest oil deposit was discovered on Alaska's north slope. The Chugach campsite on Valdez Harbor happened to be the only place on the entire Alaska coast that could geologically support an oil tanker terminal. Their strip of land grew in value to tens or even hundreds of millions of dollars. In June of that year, Chief Vincent's father, Sarjius, representing Nanwalek, and Father Nikolas, representing the nonexistent Chenega, agreed to sell Valdez to British Petroleum and Humble Oil (later called Exxon)—for the aforementioned one dollar.

The one-dollar sale was engineered by the Chugach's attorney, Clifford Groh. Before he moved on to his next gig as an oil company lawyer, Groh transformed the Chugach utterly and forever. No longer would Chugach be a tribe; Groh *incorporated* them.

The tribe became Chugach Corporation. The villages became Chenega Corporation and English Bay (Nanwalek) Corporation. The chiefs' powers were taken over by corporate presidents and CEOs, tribal councils by boards of directors. The Sound's natives, once tribe members, became shareholders—at least for a few years until the stock was sold, bequeathed, dispersed. Today, only eleven of Chenega's sixty-nine shareholders live on the island. Most residents are tenants of a corporation whose last annual meeting was held in Seattle, two thousand miles from the island.

I first met the president of Chenega Corporation, Charles "Chuck" Totemoff, soon after the spill when he missed our meeting to negotiate with Exxon. I found the twenty-something wandering the village's dirt pathway in soiled jeans, stoned and hungover, avoiding the corporate "office," an old cabin near the fishing dock.

Years later, I met up with Chuck at Chenega Corporation's glass-and-steel office tower in downtown Anchorage. The stern, long-sober and determined executive sat behind a mahogany desk and unused laptop computer. Instead of photos of the village, a huge map of Chenega's property covered the wall, color-coded for timber logging, real estate subdivision and resort development.

He had penned a multimillion-dollar terminal services agreement with the Exxon-BP pipeline consortium. For Chenega Island, a forty-six-room hotel was in the works.

In 1997, I returned to Chenega. It was the worst possible day for a visit. Larry was out on "pad patrol," leading a native crew cleaning up tons of toxic crude oil still oozing out of Sleepy Bay eight years after the *Exxon Valdez* grounding. They'd already lost a day of work that week for Frankie Gursky's funeral, an eighteen-year-old who had shot himself after a drink-fueled fight with his grandmother.

Larry and his team continued to scour the oil off the beach, his family's old fishing ground, but it wasn't theirs anymore. The day before, the corporation had sold it, along with 90 percent of Chenega's lands, to an Exxon-BP trust for $23 million.

"Corporation can't sell it," Larry said, when I told him about the check transfer. "People really can't own land." He rammed a hydraulic injector under the beach shingle and pumped in biological dispersants. "The land was always here. We're just passing through. We make use of it, then we just pass it on." Nanwalek also sold. Chief Vincent's son, leader of the Nonwalek Village rock band and director of the corporate board, arranged to sell 50 percent of the village land to an Exxon trust.

I was in corporate president Totemoff's office the day Exxon wired in the $23 million. When Totemoff moved out of the village, he announced, "I hope I never have to see this place again." Now he doesn't have to. I asked Chuck if, like some city-dwelling natives, he had his relatives ship him traditional foods. "Seal meat?" He grinned. "Ever smell that shit? Give me a Big Mac any time."

Tony Blair and the Sale of Britain

On the first Wednesday of July 1998, on the floor of the House of Commons, Britain's prime minister rose to defend himself. According to the news reports, for the first time since his election the year before, Tony Blair's hands were shaking. The PM denounced the American reporter whose exposé of wholesale corruption in his cabinet "had not one shred of evidence." Meanwhile, Blair's press spokesman, a former pornographer named Alastair Campbell, grabbed every newsman he could find in the hallway to whisper that they should not trust a "man in a hat," while Peter Mandelson, known as Prince of Darkness, and the power behind the power of the prime minister, hissed a warning about "the man with an agenda."

Unfortunately, I didn't get to enjoy any of this. I could hardly keep my eyes open, half passed out after seventy sleepless hours in my "safe house" in Crouch End, a working-class neighborhood in London. I had moved in with sympathetic friends in the middle of the night because of a crank bomb scare at my hotel and to avoid camera crews.

But that's not why I didn't get any sleep. My paper, the *Observer*, had run a front-page story with detailed evidence that cronies of the prime minister, including his princeling and other cabinet members, had bartered policies for payola, cash for access. Our *Observer* team described lobbyists' special, secret access to ministers operating a flea market for favors out of 10 Downing Street.

Not a shred of evidence? My paper announced on page one that I had *tape recordings* of lobbyists explaining exactly how and when and to whom they made the fixes—for American power companies and banks, for friends of Clinton, friends of Bush, friends of Blair, for Australian-American media tycoon Rupert Murdoch, and others.

Until our story hit the headlines, Blair was seen as Britain's incorruptible new leader. He claimed to have put an end to "Tory sleaze," the cash payoffs to Margaret Thatcher's ministers that had tainted the conservative government. Prime Minister Blair's New Labour Party avoided the cash-in-envelope lobbyists. But like his good friend Bill Clinton, Blair hoped to turn his once-progressive party into the party of business. In particular, he had an almost fetishistic desire for the affection of U.S. corporations, the entrepreneurial stallions that would pull Olde England out if its tradition-shackled ways. What my *Observer* team had uncovered was a daisy chain of favors and inside access to confidential information in return for political support from these corporations (and a bit of cash for New Labour cronies). The prime minister's reputation as Mr. Good Government was on the line.

Blair's attack masters and the radio and TV stations demanded that I *play the tapes*. The tapes are phony, they said. They don't exist. Palast's a liar. And now the business editor of the *Observer*, the brilliant journalistic fanatic Ben Laurance, was shouting (much to the consternation of my friends, who were trying to block him at the door to my Crouch End hideaway) that I had to get out of bed, get to the BBC studios and confront—with tape—the number-one New Labour fixer, Derek Draper, on another live *Newsnight* broadcast.

But the truth was, I didn't have the tape.

The day before, I called my wife, who was back home in the States with our one-year-old twins, and told her to overnight to me the tape marked "Draper." It was right in the middle of my desk. Linda said, "I don't see any tape. There's no tape here." The next day was when the *Mirror* turned over its front page to a close-up of my leering face under the headline, "THE LIAR." (figure 6.3)

The story that became known as "Lobbygate" began innocently enough. Antony Barnett, Britain's best investigate journalist, got a tip that lobbying firms close to Blair's New Labour Party government were getting their hands on inside information to pass on to their clients. Along with editor Will Hutton, Antony had just asked if I would write for the *Observer*. He thought I might give a couple of these guys a call, maybe hinting to our targets that I needed a little influence.

At first, I said no. My idea had been to bring to journalism the full arsenal of weapons used in my official racketeering probes. No more quick and cheap. What I had in mind would take time and it would cost thousands of pounds.

To do this right, we needed a front, for which I enlisted a top U.S. business executive, Mark Swedlund, formerly with Booz Allen Hamilton, who mixes street smarts with boardroom savvy. We added a former Morgan Stanley executive (no name, sorry) and gave ourselves impressive legitimacy by tying up with one of America's white-shoe law firms well known to Her Majesty (no names, sorry again).

If Blair's cabinet was selling, it was corporate America buying. This would give me the chance to get myself inside the corporate influence machinery and see how the deals came down—something no American editor would dare do.

The most difficult fake-out was to re-create me. All these lobbyists knew me; it was their job to know. They knew I contributed to the *Guardian*, but more importantly, they knew that before the election I'd been one of Blair's much-displayed American policy advisers. I was in with Blair's trade and industry and energy ministers,

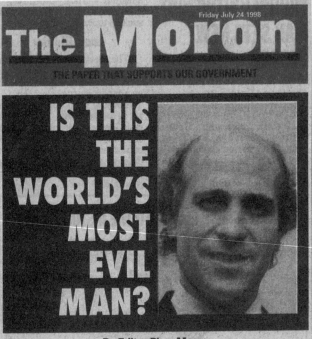

The Moron

Friday July 24 1998

THE PAPER THAT SUPPORTS OUR GOVERNMENT

IS THIS THE WORLD'S MOST EVIL MAN?

By Editor Piers Moron

THIS IS Greg Palast, better known to his friends (if he had any) as Lying Bastard!

He is the man who sought to bring down the greatest prime minister who has ever lived, i.e. Tony Blair.

It was his lies, spread all over down-market tabloids like the Observer, which tried to link Tony Blair with a bunch of seedy Soho bigmouths who call themselves lobbyists.

We have only one message for Greg (a convicted serial killer in his home state of New Dworkin, according to reports we've just made up):

Go back home to your own sleazy country, where the electric chair is waiting for you!

Hasn't Tony got enough on his plate trying to make this country the greatest in the world, without scumbags like you coming over there and making up a pack of lies?

If we want lies about prime minister, we'll make them up ourselves, thank you very much!

Leave the journalism to us, Greg.

Or should that be 'Dreg'?

Fig. 6.3. The magazine *Private Eye* thought the *Mirror*'s "LIAR" headline had not gone far enough.

described as "that influential American" by a big-shot British industrialist. It was bullshit, but now it would be useful bullshit.

I couldn't wear a false mustache and voice-coder—so I changed from Greg Palast, policy weanie and reporter, to Greg Palast, scuzz-ball, sleaze-o "consultant" on the take . . . *just like them*. I didn't get my beachfront estate and stable of ponies, I told them, by writing good government advice for the *Guardian*. I had a damn successful consulting firm that made *deals*.

At no time did we offer money in return for influence or access or favors (though they would be offered to us). I was looking for something else: what these lobbyists had already done for *others*. My line: "The Texans I'm working with don't want a lot of boasting horseshit, *these boys need hard, no-nonsense evidence of exactly what you've done, for whom. Names, dates, deeds, and solid proof, if you want our business*."

And they delivered . . . right to my fake office in New York and our "business suite" at the Tower of London Hotel. The spigot of evidence first opened on June 8, 1998.

A Fax for Enron

That morning, I found a surprise in my fax machine: a copy of the United Kingdom's Trade and Industry Select Parliamentary Committee Report on Energy Policy. What made it surprising was that the report had not yet been released to the public.

Attached to the fax was a short handwritten note to me from Karl Milner, a lobbyist with GJW Government Relations. During the 1997 general election that brought Tony Blair to power, Milner handled internal communications for Gordon Brown, now Chancellor of the Exchequer, the second most powerful man in government after Blair himself. Milner wrote, "Thought you may be interested." I was.

I called Milner. Maybe he had not filched the documents from the government but rather had committed the lesser offense of lifting a prerelease copy from a journalist. Milner assured me otherwise. His special access to policy papers for his clients was standard operating procedure. "We have many friends in government. They like to run things past us some days in advance, to get our view, to let them know if they have anything to be worried about, maybe suggest some changes." His operation represented U.S. power companies, like Pacificorp of Oregon, which had bought out almost the entire British electricity industry. The document, the inside info, would be especially helpful for the client he was pitching for, Enron of Houston, Texas. What a coincidence: Those were *my* Texans too. I was lying, but mentioning Enron was like saying "Abracadabra." Doors of the influential opened wide.

"I'm Very Excited"

June 11: Chancellor of the Exchequer Brown announced new government spending caps. I was trying to end my third phone call with Derek Draper, top lobbyist with GPC Market Access. Draper had been chief aide to the Dark Prince, "Minister-without-Portfolio" Mandelson. "I'm *very excited*," said Draper. "Very excited."

What had so excited Mr. Draper?

"Gordon Brown put the cap on total spending at 2.75 percent, not 2.5 percent, like everyone expected! And we said so! We said so last week!" This one-quarter percentage point difference may seem minuscule, but in the hands of securities traders and arbitrageurs, advance word could be parlayed into quite a windfall. Indeed, the week earlier, Draper had given the correct number to his client Salomon Brothers, the U.S. investment banking giant. I complimented Draper on his firm's extraordinary forecasting work. He responded, "No, I'm afraid it's inside information." In a voice crackling with schoolboy glee, Draper added, "If they [Salomon] acted on it, they'd have made a fortune!"

Indeed they would have. And under U.S. law, they would have risked jail time.

The *Observer* never asked any lobbyist to produce confidential government documents or information. We did not have to. Milner, Draper and others provided the evidence unrequested, meant to convince us they could deliver the goods from Tony Blair's government.

From our first New York–London call, Draper gossiped, gushed and ultimately could not resist revealing his special access to the treasury and 10 Downing Street, Britain's White House.

If we retained his firm, what could he deliver for our money? Could he secure a seat on one of the government's task forces? Done! "We just got the chief executive of British Gas on the government's Welfare to Work Task Force." Draper emphasized that winning this coveted spot at the elbow of the chancellor was an enormous achievement for a company once known in Labour circles as "the Fat Cats headed by Cedric the Pig" (an unkind reference to former British Gas chairman Cedric Brown).

What if my clients had reputations far less savory than BG? Not a problem.

In fact, Draper was about to sign up such a "challenging" client, U.S. lottery operator GTech Corp, a company whose lucrative links to Bush allies in Texas I was also investigating. GTech was in hot water. A jury had found GTech's CEO guilty of attempting to bribe British tycoon Richard Branson, hoping to buy him out of the competition to run Britain's lottery. While running for office, Blair had committed to oust these Ugly Americans from the consortium that had exclusive rights to operate the national lottery. Draper described his scheme-in-progress to waltz GTech around the official watchdogs and lure Blair's ministers into a sticky web of agreements with his new client.

"The government needed someone to sell tickets for this ridiculous Millennium Dome thing that my old boss is building. But GTech is offering to do that via the national lottery-selling equipment. Now it doesn't take a lot to work out that if the government thinks that GTech can sell government tickets for the Dome then it's got to be a legitimate firm to sell tickets for the lottery. See what I mean? Our forte, like, is to be *imaginative*." His "old boss" was the Dark Prince, Minister Peter Mandelson.[2] To call Draper and "Mandy" close would be a grievous understatement. Mandy had dedicated his book, *The Blair Revolution*, to the young man. In a profile in *Business on Sunday* Draper said his friendships with top officeholders were a "hindrance" to his lobbying business because his former workmates are "all so concerned to be ethical." Nevertheless, Draper assured me that, if we needed to change a law to our liking, "I can have tea with Geoffrey Robinson! I can get in to Ed Balls!" When Draper spoke of reaching Blair cabinet heavyweights Paymaster General Robinson and Balls, the chancellor's chief adviser, you could hear the exclamation points in his voice. He added, "Once someone pays us."

The Politics of Emptiness

While fielding calls and faxes from Draper and Milner, we reached Lawson Lucas Mendelsohn, a firm less than one year old yet already the hottest lobby group in town, collecting £2 million ($3 million) in billings in one year. LLM lists twenty powerful clients, including the RSPCA and Rupert Murdoch's News International, owner of America's Fox TV network. LLM, named for its three founders, is the definition of "inside."

Neal Lawson advised Tony Blair on campaign strategy, Ben Lucas conducted Blair's political briefings and Jon Mendelsohn handled the future prime minister's contacts with business.

But LLM is no influence-for-hire operation that can be purchased by anyone with a checkbook. To obtain their much-sought services, LLM clients are asked to review and embrace an eleven-page introductory statement of principles and methods, a some-

---

[2] The "Dome thing" was a tent set up in Greenwich to celebrate the big New Year. The tent, long ago taken down, cost the equivalent of one billion U.S. dollars. Blair had put Mandy in charge of finding the loot, which he took from taxpayers and from corporate "donors."

what chilling mix of Dick Morris and Nietzsche. A chart on page three or their booklet displays two columns labeled in bold face, "The Passing World" and "The Emerging World." To the Passing World belong "ideology," "conviction" and "politicians who lead." These will be replaced in the Emerging World by "pragmatism," "consumption" and "politicians who listen."

The sales brochure-cum-manifesto announces that the political terms Right and Left are now "obsolete." LLM promises to guide clients to understand "not only new Labour but more importantly the new world."

Partner Ben Lucas knows what government will do because "we know how they think." But what may seem like telepathic prognosticating comes down to harvesting insider leaks. Lucas knew, for example, that on June 11 Chancellor Gordon Brown would announce the creation of a new housing inspectorate. "The reason I knew that in advance is that I was speaking to people who were writing the chancellor's speech." He delivered the information to an LLM client and advised them on ways to capitalize on the early warning.

Also, like his competitor Draper, Lucas had several days' notice of details in the chancellor's public spending announcement. Lucas offered up other examples of "intelligence which in market terms would be worth a lot of money."

The inside track on decisions is one thing, influencing the outcome is another. Influence requires access. What could we obtain for our monthly retainer? LLM's Lawson trumped GPC's tea with Geoffrey Robinson by offering, if needed, to "reach *anyone*. We can go to [Chancellor] Gordon Brown if we have to." His partner Lucas commented, "We use relationships in a subtle way."

And how were these relationships subtly used? On behalf of Tesco, a supermarket chain, LLM were about to derail the chancellor's plan for a tax on parking lots. LLM was holding secret negotiations that very week with Policy Unit advisers to Blair, the ones who told Deputy Prime Minister John Prescott, nominally in charge of the issue, when to jump and how high. The tax, pushed by environmentalists to discourage excessive auto use, would have cost the supermarket giant more than £20 million ($30 million) annually.[3]

When I complimented Lawson for avoiding less reputable clients such as GTech, the U.S. lottery company, he countered that he had in fact lobbied for the bribery-tainted outfit. LLM used the Blair cabinet's trust in LLM to "assure the government how [GTech] will behave."

Lawson and Lucas were quick to point out that lobbying is not all about calls to the Treasury. Sometimes LLM recommends the indirect route, "placing things with columnists we know the chancellor reads." They called this "creating an environment." In addition, in deliberate imitation of U.S. lobbyists' methods, LLM operates a captive think tank, Nexus, to give their views (or their clients' views) the imprimatur of academic legitimacy. Sometimes they make use of the lefty-sounding Socialist Environmental Research Foundation, which, Lucas assured me, is a purchased front for retailers.

Lawson explained how LLM plays on what they call "politics without leadership." In a milieu in which a lack of conviction is deemed an asset, with no fixed star of principles by which to steer, policy is susceptible to the last pitch heard over cocktails. "The Labour government is always of two minds, it operates in a kind of schizophrenia. On big issues especially, they don't know what they are thinking. Blair himself doesn't always know what he is thinking."

It would be a mistake to view this politics of emptiness—in which ideals and beliefs are suspect—as a British invention, unique to Blair's "New" Labour Party. Blair and his buddy Clinton call this "the Third Way." The leaders of the world's "liberal" and "socialist" parties—Blair, Cardoso of Brazil, Frei of Chile—are all

---

[3]You have to admire these guys; they simply have no shame. Exposure was embarrassing for the flea market in favors, but not an impediment. Three weeks after we revealed in the *Observer* LLM's secret deal to get Tesco's supermarkets out of the parking lot tax, Blair's boys snuck the exemption into a white paper on transportation, even using the wording drafted by the lobbyists.

products of the factory that manufactured Bill Clinton, all bionic election machines who, in Mendelsohn's words, are "not ideologically constrained." LLM's manifesto dismisses "leaders who lead" as antique creatures of the Passing World. Today, markets lead. Industry CEOs lead. In the Emerging World, prime ministers and presidents merely "listen." Without the restraints of conviction, they are free to respond to the requests of the powerful while shifting their media images as the polling gurus dictate.

Lunch at Number 10

Draper was now aware that he had competitors for our business, and he determined to display his prowess at opening the doors to power. "I took the chief executive of the House Builders' Federation in to see Geoff Norris [a top Blair policy adviser] the other day, and that meeting *took place in the Downing Street dining room!* It's not difficult for me to take people into these people."

Sensing I was not impressed with merely breaking bread with ministers, he offered a story certain to leave an impression. Draper's client PowerGen PLC had long hungered to buy a regional electricity company, a deal even the probusiness Tories had killed off. And behind Britain's PowerGen was the secret Mr. Big: Reliant, the power giants out of Houston, which wanted to merge (that is, take over) the whole new super-utility. The British cabinet minister who would make the decisions, Margaret Beckett, head of the Department of Trade and Industry, was dead against the PowerGen proposals to create a super-monopoly in energy—especially one that would be owned by Texans. She'd publicly blasted new U.S. takeovers of U.K. electricity companies. Under the law, Beckett had final say; not even the prime minister could intervene.

The PowerGen-Reliant scheme seemed lost. Now Draper told me he'd steered the chairman of PowerGen, Ed Wallis, around Beckett and brought him directly into the treasury for a confidential meeting with Geoffrey Robinson, a top adviser to Chancellor Brown. The PowerGen merger deals are now locked, he told me.

Government rejection "will not happen again." Had Draper pulled off an extraordinary fix or was this merely hard-sell horsefeathers?

I told Draper my own clients, representing U.S. oil shippers and power plant builders, would need exemptions from environmental rules, in effect, a license to pollute England. Draper enthusiastically invited us over.

Two weeks later, in London, pouring sherry cocktails at my Tower of London Hotel suite—this front operation cost the *Observer* a pretty penny—I asked one of Draper's competitors, Rory Chisholm, if he could match Derek's setting up the meeting between PowerGen and Geoff Robinson to talk mergers. "Now hold on there!" Chisholm, a director of GJW and a lobbyist of the old school, put down his drink. "That's getting a bit *illegal*. It's a *judicial process. It's like approaching a judge.*" But Chisholm's partner Milner, who learned about lobbying U.S.-style while working for Hillary Clinton, was ready to match Draper's offers.

There Are Seventeen People That Count

Monday, June 23. Swedlund and I, fresh off the plane with fake business cards and references from big-name confederates, went to London's very soul, the Sanctuary building at Westminster Abbey. Within this historic courtyard at Number 7, GPC Access's Derek Draper guides us through the peculiarities of British democracy.

"There are seventeen people who count," Draper tells us. "And to say I am intimate with every one of them is *the understatement of the century.*" This intimacy is based on a web of favors of which the lobbyist keeps a careful mental inventory. At Chancellor Brown's confidential request, he put out a supposedly independent newsletter praising Blair's keeping the minimum wage low. Press control was especially valuable. In the *Sunday Telegraph*, Draper authored a two-thousand-word profile of Ed Balls, a Brown aide. He'd given Balls editorial control and the *Telegraph* was none the wiser.

As to Jonathan Powell, the prime minister's chief of staff, gatekeeper at Number 10, the corporate lobbyist "got him the job." My "business partner," Mark Swedlund, interrogated Draper. We Americans have come for access, not lessons in Labour rhetoric. We needed proof of Draper's insider bona fides.

Draper rose to the challenge, literally. He stood up from his chair, removed a phone pager from his belt and, holding it above his forehead, read off one phone message after another, nearly two dozen, from the powerful and near-to-power. "Ed Miliband—call me, Dave Miliband—please call, Andrew Hackett . . . that's [deputy prime minister] Prescott's office." The recitation continued. There were several messages from Liz Lloyd of the Downing Street Policy Unit, Balls from the Treasury and others, each pleading for a moment of the lobbyist's time for tea, advice or requests unknown.

The lobbyist was in a cheery mood. His walking the CEO of the Builders' Federation into Downing Street the week before was already paying dividends.

Blair's adviser Geoff Norris agreed to resurrect the Builders' plans to dig up several greenbelt areas for houses. "Just a bloody bunch of mud tracts at the edge of town," as Draper described the lands at issue, despite the claims of local councils.

Such favors must be returned. "Tony needed ten environmental gimmicks" for a news release to support the government's green image. Draper rapidly provided a list, "electric cars, silly things like that." Draper rolled his eyes. "They loved it."

Message to Murdoch

Our next stop, Soho. There, in the trendy loft offices of LLM lobbyists Ben Lucas and Jon Mendelsohn, we endured a mind-numbing two-hour lecture on the Third Way, "analytically driven evidence-based decision making," a solid wall of New Labour–speak (figure 6.4).

But what at first seemed like an aimless think tank seminar had purpose.

Lucas and Mendelsohn's point was to introduce us to a world in which, as their manifesto told us, message matters more than

"US Businessman" - You have a philosophy, you have
tremendous resumes and you know bios, but a little
bit about how you've been able to operate or what
you've been able to accomplish would be real
helpful.

Lucas - It's ... there are some examples which we
can give you, some of which are still quite
sensitive because the government is still
relatively new. There's a lot which is still as it
were, in negotiation. An example of this is, to
pick an example, the biggest food retailer in
Britain is called Tesco, they're a client of ours.
They have a concern about the government
potentially introducing a tax on all car parking
spaces in supermarkets in Britain which would cost
them about 20-30 million pounds. We've been
developing a strategy for them to head the
government off basically and push them in a
different direction in the plans which they're
about to announce next month and to get them to
effectively do a deal whereby   to
community transport   his
company is seen   g to
pay this tax and
represented in th
announced in July
KPMG a major acco
problem that they
the big six accoun
inadvertently iden
particularly anti-I
organised some tax
Labour government w
taxation. So six mor
Gordon Brown who was
press conference spe
black mark had been p
on to work for them a
refashioned the whole
to government and as a
that the morning of th
since the election his   ted us and said
that he would like to   special meeting with

Fig. 6.4. From the transcript of the June 11 call between a "US Businessman" (myself) and Ben Lucas, lobbyist. Photo: On June 23, 1998,
"Businessman" sets off to meet with Lucas. (Photo: Mark Swedlund)

content. For their fee of £5,000 to £20,000 per month, these two Professor Higginses would instruct us in the political grammar of the Emerging World of Tony Blair.

Our cover story was that we needed LLM's help in defeating environmental restrictions. Mendelsohn advised we must recast our plan for new power stations, noisy and polluting, into something that sounded earth-friendly. "Tony is very anxious to be seen as green. Everything has to be couched in environmental language—even if it's slightly Orwellian."

But LLM demands more of their clients than adopting new PR gloss. LLM clients are expected to "reshape their core corporate culture," to get in sync with New Labour's vision, as their client Tesco's Supermarkets had done to defeat the parking lot tax. Part of Tesco's cultural reshaping involved dropping £11 million ($16 million) into Mandelson's Millennium Dome project.

Once we have changed our culture, we asked, exactly how does LLM help us get a law changed? Lucas said, "This government likes to do deals."

He gave an example. Labour's antimonopoly competition bill threatened LLM client Rupert Murdoch. Murdoch, the American media baron, owns, in addition to Fox TV, Chinese satellite stations and those British tabloids that have the naughty "Page Six girls" with their boobies hanging out. In Britain that made him a power to be feared. But he had a little legal problem. Antitrust authorities were looking into Murdoch businesses' alleged predatory pricing practices. LLM carried the word from Downing Street to Murdoch's News International that, if their tabloids toned down criticism of the new antitrust legislation, the law's final language would reflect the government's appreciation.

On the other hand, harsh coverage in Murdoch's papers could provoke problems for the media group in Parliament's union-recognition debates. Kindly reporting would produce a kindly union bill (that is, one that would kill off unions) as well. The message to muzzle journalists was not, said Lucas, "an easy one in their culture." However, the outcome pleased all parties.

Unlike his wheeler-dealer partners, Jon Mendelsohn, aloof and intellectual, does not have an obvious ounce of fixer in him. Rather, he is their Big Idea man with a deep understanding of the modern politicians' obsession with corporate and media contacts. "[Tony Blair's] super-majority in Parliament means the only countervailing force is media and the business community. So when the economy turns soft, as it naturally must, we will make certain they stay with us. If we have business and media, the people will come along."

Lucas reviewed their awesome fee schedule, and we were on our way.

Rush hour in Soho. We walked down the street to the Groucho Club, where we would be guests of an operative with yet another lobby shop. He'd got word that these Americans were looking for political help. Over a bottle of overpriced claret, we listened to one more young Blairite make his pitch for our business.

We then detailed what his competitors had on offer: Milner's purloined reports for Enron, Draper's backroom deals for Reliant of Texas, LLM's insider information from the exchequer.

I waited for him to top their accomplishments. He put both hands over his eyes. "It's appalling," he said. "It's *disturbing*." If that's what we wanted, he'd have none of our business.[4]

Mr. Liddle's Offer

The next evening, GPC held its annual bash at the Banqueting Room in Whitehall Palace. Under vaulted ceilings inset with nine canvases by Rubens, GPC's two hundred guests washed down thin canapés with a never-ending supply of champagne (Lambray Brut) poured by discreet waiters. Lords, MPs and Downing Street powers by the dozen mixed with the nation's business elite. It was Derek Draper's phone pager come to life.

At the center of this swirl, Draper held court. Yet, he graciously

---

[4] I'm withholding the firm's name—exposing a lobbyist's rectitude could cost them business.

took the time to offer us free samples of his connections, introducing us to several government luminaries who could be useful to our projects, including more than half the prime minister's policy unit. From the member of Parliament who chaired the Select Committee on Trade and Industry we endured an earnest discourse on the development of Parliament's energy review (and we confirmed how lobbyist Milner of GJW received advance information of his committee's report for Enron, where this investigation began).

My confederate Swedlund asked Draper to point us to someone who could vouch for his influence with government. He reached out, seeming to pull at random the nearest figure from the crowd. He grabbed a short, balding man with sweat beaded on his forehead. Derek told the official we were potential GPC clients, then walked off.

Roger Liddle is one of the more important men in government, in charge of European affairs for the prime minister's Public Policy Unit, with an office near Blair's in 10 Downing Street. We talked about our power generators for our Texans—polluting and noisy and squandering resources, if we were honest about it. We needed the rules changed, and we asked Liddle if Draper was as influential as he claimed. Liddle leaned forward. "There is a Circle." Liddle was now whispering. "There is a Circle and Derek is part of the Circle. And anyone who says he isn't is an Enemy." He reassured us that, "Derek knows all the *right* people."

Could Draper introduce us to key policy makers? In response, Liddle handed us a card with his Downing Street and home phone numbers, and made this extraordinary offer: "Whenever you are ready, just tell me *what* you want, *who* you want to meet and Derek and I will make the call for you."

Derek and I. It was a strange locution. Swedlund remarked that Liddle sounded "more like a member of Derek's outfit than a member of the government." It was not until the next day we learned that Swedlund was not far off. Liddle had, until the general election, been managing director of Draper's firm.

Officially, he'd placed his 25 percent ownership interest in

GPC Access into a blind trust when he took the post at Downing Street. Any new business Liddle cooked up for Draper would go right into the minister's "blind" piggy bank.

Jail

The next morning I received a call from the persistent lobbyist from the Groucho Club. He still refused to match his competitors' offers. "If Draper and Lawson delivered half of what they promise *they'd be in jail!* Half of Downing Street would be in jail!"

Phone Call from Tony

"What I really am," said Draper the next day, "is a commentator-fixer. Your Mayor Daley has nothing on me." We were sitting in the exclusive Reform Club on Pall Mall, the kind of swanky, overwrought confection that could only be built by the overlords of an old empire. Draper sipped his trademark champagne and sank into a red leather armchair under a tall painting of an aristocrat from another century.

He tossed a copy of *Progress* magazine on the antique table. "I own it," he said of the Blairite journal, "one hundred percent of it, all the shares." The funds to launch the magazine came from a "Labour billionaire," a financial arrangement accomplished by "a single phone call from Tony." He meant the prime minister. In the lobbyists' world, there are no last names.[5]

Draper had just filed his weekly column published in the *Express* newspaper. His writings are edited in an unusual manner. "I

---

[5] The billionaire with the secret cash for the prime minister's use, my co-investigator Barnett discovered, was Lord Sainsbury. M'Lord owns the patent on a key element in creating genetically modified Frankenstein foods. Blair rewarded him by putting the lord in charge of "science" issues, including control over policy on selling the genetically manipulated products. See "And the Ignoble Prize in Chemistry Goes to . . . Monsanto!".

don't write that column without vetting it with [Minister] Peter [Mandelson]. They say, Oh [Chancellor] Gordon [Brown] will be mad at Derek, but he won't because his press secretary has vetted it."

It was June 25. For Draper, it was a day of miracles he had prophesied. Only two hours earlier, the government released its energy review. The coal industry would be saved if PowerGen agreed to sell a few generating plants. Simultaneously, newspapers reported PowerGen would buy Midlands Electricity for £2 billion, if the government approved. The suspicious alignment of the two announcements forced Trade Minister Beckett to deny categorically that a secret deal had been struck. "There has been no wink or nod to anyone about anything." But then, how would she know? The PowerGen meeting at the Treasury was a quiet affair, no record of it was kept and, as an LLM lobbyist assured me, Beckett is "out of the loop."

Draper should have been pleased with his success. But his mood was philosophical.

"I don't want to be a consultant," he said. "I just want to stuff my bank account at £250 an hour."

Beer at Crouch End

From the Reform Club, Swedlund and I took a cab for a get-together with Will Baker, another lobbyist of sorts. We joined up with Baker at a friend's flat in Crouch End. Baker works as an advocate for a large nonprofit organization based in Liverpool. The group was pleading with Blair to eliminate electricity and gas heating disconnections, and this puts them squarely up against Draper's and Milner's key clients, the American-owned utility companies. The antipoverty group lacks the £8,000 a month to hire an LLM or other professional consultants, so Baker and his colleagues must themselves act as lobbyists on behalf of their low-income constituents.

Over Budweisers at the kitchen table, Baker said his group failed to get a meeting with a single key minister during the government's energy review, not even contact with junior civil servants. "We can't get in the door. They tell us to submit our comments in writing. We are just totally excluded." He could not imagine getting an invitation to sit on a task force.

Ultimately, the government, despite campaign promises, chose to continue the system permitting private electricity, gas and water companies to disconnect poor customers behind in their bills—a big victory for Draper's and GJW's clients over Baker's group of clerics and poor people. Special access is not a victimless crime.

The Curtain Comes Down

It's hard not to like Draper, Milner and Lawson. They each have that Bart Simpson charm: mischievous, a bit immature, yet endearing. And they exude New Labour's *enthusiasm* for the New Britain. Do any of these young men harbor misgivings about renting out their contacts? They see no reason for apology. It's their world, after all. They are convinced that they crafted New Labour and now, through GPC, GJW and LLM, they are merely charging admission to enter the show they produced.

But even the best players of the game fear for its future. Derek Draper, in an unusually reflective moment, said he had worried thoughts about the inside access to government that goes under the rubric "public-private partnership."

Draper said, "I think there will be a scandal here eventually. The curtain is going to come down. I'm sure it will happen." Then he returned to discussion of fees and lunch.

And Inside the Newsroom...

Just before the story hit the streets, the *Observer* contacted Roger Liddle for his side of the story.

Liddle was the squat little man who offered to get "what you want and who you want to meet" at Downing Street. This was no small fish in the net. Liddle and Peter Mandelson had coauthored the book *The Blair Revolution*. The three of them were the key architects of that revolution-in-reverse, the program to seize the Labour Party, yank it to the right, and rename it "New" Labour. That was step one; step two was The Project—to merge New Labour with the Liberal Democrats, Liddle's political bailiwick. Big business would provide the gilded glue, shepherded by the lobbying firm set up by Liddle and Draper, GPC.

Blair moved Liddle right into 10 Downing Street, and made him the real power on European affairs. Liddle's equity in Draper's lobby shop went into a "blind trust." Liddle's wife was a dear friend of the wife of my editor, Will Hutton. When Liddle heard the story was about to break, he called Hutton at home, knowing full well that Will was about to turn Liddle's career into garbage with a pen stroke. Liddle begged. He claimed he was drunk, and when he's drunk he's a fool, everyone knows that, and he shot his mouth off, didn't mean it, didn't know what he was saying.

Hutton told me this on Sunday morning over croissants at a little bistro in the tony Belsize Park section of London. "Lobbygate" was on the streets, but we talked mostly, as we prefer, about industrial regulation and the political economy of Brazil. He was off that afternoon to São Paolo to meet President Cardoso—reluctantly, because of our influence-peddling story. I said, "Go. Brazil's the future, Britain's history." In Hutton's view, Liddle was pathetic and sincerely remorseful. So Will gave him the benefit of the doubt and did not call for Liddle's resignation in our paper's editorial. And besides, Liddle told him, he couldn't gain from swinging business to Draper: The blind trust had sold off his interest in Draper's lobby firm.

Hutton's as smart, maybe smarter, than his formidable reputation as Britain's leading intellect. So I paused to let him work it out himself. *Liddle knew his interest had been sold?* "So, Will, the blind trust ain't so blind." Hutton, a big man, laughed so hard he almost knocked over the metal table. He'd been had. Liddle was a weasel and a liar. But not a very good one.

In the newsroom the next day, I met the deputy editor. With Hutton away, the wan young corporation man now in charge preferred to meet surrounded by a guard of lawyers and marketing people. By Monday afternoon, the full force of the New Labour government and their running dogs at the other papers were tearing our journalistic flesh. And the deputy wanted to throw them something to chew on. Preferably me.

In the meantime, he'd *hand over our tapes* to the government. I said, "Well, that's nuts, that's just straight fucking insane nuts." But he'd made an Executive Decision. "So give us the tapes."

I explained about my wife. Didn't have 'em. He looked ready to die on the spot. He figured he would lose his job. (He did.)

In the meantime, he had another brainwave: He'd *tell* Alastair Campbell, Blair's press python, which accusations we had on tape, and which were "merely" backed up by witnesses and contemporaneous notes. How brilliant.

I opined: "The sleazy little shit-holes will talk away with excuses anything we have on tape then flat-out deny anything from notes, say we made it up." But there was no stopping him from stepping on his own dick.

At 4 A.M. London time, I reached Hutton in Rio. "There's a Concorde leaving São Paolo tomorrow. For Christ's sake, Will, *get on it.*"

Too late. The *Observer* showed our cards to Campbell, and immediately the government's guardians talked away what we had on tape, flat-out denied what we had from notes and witnesses, even though Swedlund—he was with me at the meetings with Draper and in the hugger-mugger with Liddle—gave us a sworn affidavit under penalty of perjury.

Liddle was no longer the pathetic drunk contrite over his corrupt offer. At first, he announced he couldn't remember meeting me, certainly couldn't remember what was said. Once he knew we had "only" a sworn affidavit of a witness, he grew bolder, and in his third version, he suddenly remembered it all clearly. And what he remembered was that I was a liar; I'd fabricated his words.

Then the next morning, a hand-scrawled note came through the *Observer*'s fax machine, no signature. "I've got your tape. What's it worth to you?" Linda thought she was quite droll.

Lobbyist Ben Lucas, smugly assured that I had no tape, flatly denied to BBC *Newsnight*'s cameras that he had detailed to me passing on advance information from the treasury to his client, the Government Association. Meirion Jones, one very smart producer at the program, let Lucas swallow that grenade—then played on air my tape of him saying the words he denied.

Then it was Draper's turn to step on a land mine. Assuming I had no tape of our chats, Draper denied the words I attributed to him, but that day, Linda relayed the tape via phone, and anyone could hear Draper's incriminating statements about Downing Street cronies on the *Guardian*'s Web site. Draper lost his job, but got a payout that will keep him in Lambray Brut for another decade. For two weeks, every paper in Britain ran nothing but Lobbygate stories on their front pages.

In that first week, while I was The Liar and Blair's hands were shaking, I was sure I'd nailed Liddle. The mendacious little scamp was drunk, was he? Didn't remember me, did he? Never offered to bring me into Downing Street, give me his private numbers? In fact, the next day after his offer, and sober as a deacon, *Liddle called me from 10 Downing Street* to set up a time to get together, to seal the deal. He denied it, and that stunned me. Now I had him! All I had to do was go over the Downing Street phone records and point to my mobile phone number . . . when I discovered that, in Great Britain, telephone records of a public servant from a public phone were "private," or confidential or some kind of state secret. I was screwed. Liddle walked away smelling like a rose; and Blair rewarded him with the highest increase in salary awarded anyone in government.

$ C H A P T E R   7 $

SMALL TOWNS, SMALL MINDS

My Mother Was a Hypnotist for McDonald's

I live one hundred miles outside of NYC, in the sticks. When McDonald's announced it was moving into Southold, NY, my little town in the woods, I had personal reasons, deep in my family history, for wanting to keep them out—My mother was a hypnotist for McDonald's. Really.

In 1970, one of the corporation's biggest franchisees, moving millions of burgers in Hollywood, California, feared for their crew leaders. Working fifteen-hour shifts scattered over nights and days for $3 an hour, some of these so-called managers took on that look of insomniac spookiness that could end with one of them "going postal," the colloquialism that describes what happens when the California penchant for self-expression meets the American fascination with automatic weapons. That wouldn't do. So my mother taught them self-hypnosis. "Twenty minute's trance is worth four hours' sleep!" Maybe that's why I don't eat clown meat anymore. I can't stand to look at those grinning, unblinking faces asking, "Do you want fries with that?"

To my friends in Paris and London, the opening of each new McDonald's under the Eiffel Tower or Big Ben heralds the horrid Bozo-headed déclassé Americanization of Europe. But to me, McDonald's represents something far more sinister: the frightening Americanization of America.

To understand what I mean, let's begin with this: The United States is *ugly*. A conspiracy of travel writers have sold the image of America the Beautiful: Georgia O'Keeffe sunsets over New Mexico's plateau, the wide-open vistas of the Grand Canyon. But to get there, you must drive through a numbing repetitive vortex of sprawled Pizza Huts, Wal-Marts, Kmarts, the Gap, Jiffy Lubes, Kentucky Fried Chickens, Starbucks and McDonald's up to and leaning over the Canyon wall.

From New Orleans jambalaya, to Harlem ham hocks, to New England crab boil, whatever is unique to an American region or town has been hunted down and herded into a few tourist preserves. The oppressive ubiquity of contrived American monoculture has ingested and eliminated any threat of character. The words of McDonald's late CEO Ray Kroc, *"We cannot trust some people who are nonconformists,"* have become our national anthem. Almost. One hundred miles dead east of New York City, a hamlet of farmers called Southold held out. Southold was the last place in New York State where you could look from a rolling road across an open cornfield uninterrupted by Golden Arches. The town board refused McDonald's request to build as "just not part of our rural character." A group of visiting English land-use experts had planted in our village the un-American idea of "stewardship" trumping property rights. In Britain, these battles are common stuff—in 1999, forty mums and kids in the Shakespearean hamlet of Shaftesbury marched against conversion of the local Hungry Horse pub into an Avaricious Clown—but in the USA in 1990, TINY TOWN RESISTS! was national news. The rebellion lasted six years. Then McDonald's huffed and puffed and threatened lawsuits, and Southold—my town—bowed down.

Today, Southold schools bus students to "instructional" outings at McDonald's.

The story of Mom and McDonald's is my contribution to the Great Bubble debate. A whole gaggle of Chicken Littles in the financial press have been cackling about the Bubble, the insupportable speculative rise in share prices that had to burst and spew out financial fire, brimstone and bankruptcies.

Yes, we've seen dot-coms vanish like backseat vows of eternal love. But stay calm. The sky is not, I repeat *not*, falling. The Bubble Theorem is the creation of good-hearted souls of the Left made ill by the orgy of monstrous increases in wealth for a few and begging bowls for the many. The world's three hundred richest people are worth more than the world's poorest three billion. The stock market could not rise indefinitely on the promises of dot-coms that sell nothing yet lay claim to a large share of the planet's wealth. From wise economists to complete cranks like Robert Schiller we heard sermons about the coming "Day of Reckoning." Yet the 2001–2002 "collapse" of the stock market barely dimpled the overall rise in equity values seen over the decade.

The belief that a Price Must Be Paid is religion, not economics—Calvinism dressed up in Marxist clothing. What the Bubble-heads fail to accept is that the class war, as Messrs. Bush and Clinton have told us, is indeed over—but not because we have reached a happy social entente. Let's face it, the working class has been defeated soundly, convincingly, absolutely.

Dr. Edward Wolff, director of the Income Studies Project at the Jerome Levy Institute, New York, tells me that between 1983 and 1997, 85.5 percent of the vaunted increase in America's wealth was captured by the richest 1 percent. In that time, overall U.S. income rocketed—of which 80 percent of America's families received *zero* percent. The market's up, but *who* is the market? According to Wolff, the Gilded One Percent own $2.9 trillion of the nation's stocks and bonds out of a total $3.5 trillion.

Not coincidentally, the rise in the riches of the rich matches quite well with the wealth *lost* by production workers through the shrinking of their share of the production pie. U.S. workers are producing more per hour (up 17 percent since 1983) while keeping less of it (real wages are down 3.1 percent). So there you have it: The market did not rise on a bubble of fictions but on the rock-hard foundation of the spoils of the class war.

What's going on here? Let's start with computers. Forget Robert Reich's sweet notion that computers can make work more meaningful and worthwhile. The purpose of every industrial revolution, from the steam-powered loom to the assembly line, is to make craft and skills obsolete, and thereby make people interchangeable and cheap. And now, computerization is speeding the industrialization of service work.

That brings us back to "Mickey D's." While Ray Kroc gets all the kudos for building the company, it was the genius of the brothers McDonald, Richard and Maurice, in 1948, to divide the production of restaurant food into discrete, skill-less tasks. McDonald's ruthlessly and methodically applied to the corner greasy spoon, the workingman's café, the techniques of Taylorism, the time-and-motion paradigm that rules factory assembly lines. No more cooks. Any clown can make a hamburger for McDonald's. Their machines are designed so that unskilled employees hired off the street can reach full speed within minutes. Politicians mesmerized by the modern are selling us on the wonders of the Knowledge Economy. Oh, yeah. At McD's, you can spend all day punching machine-portioned glops of ketchup onto burger buns.

In one of the *Observer*'s undercover investigations, I learned that McDonald's retained the notorious union-busting law firm Jackson Lewis of New York to take their search-and-destroy operations against union organizers to Europe. But why should McDonald's bother? Fast food operators report employee turnover averaging 300 percent per year—and, despite what the industry says, *they love it*. Workers out the door in four months don't demand pensions, promotions, training or unions. In 1996, a British civil court found McDonald's systematically exploited young workers, but that is a temporary situation. It won't be long before the majority of workers of *all* ages in every land will need no more experience than any seventeen-year-old slacker—and will be paid like one.

The real story of the "Bubble" is this: The stock market went up because the human market went down. Here in the twenty-first century, Blake's Dark Satanic Mills have been replaced by Bright Demonic Happy Meals as the factory for deconstructing work into a cheap commodity. It is estimated that one in eight American adults has worked at a McDonald's. This acts as a kind of moral instruction for the working class, as jail time does for ghetto residents. It is one reason behind America's low unemployment rate. As my old professor Milton Friedman taught me, unemployment falls when workers give up hope of higher pay.

How fitting that the Corcord Green of globalization, the 1999 Battle of Seattle, began when crazies threw a garbage can through the window of a McDonald's. The question is: Will it break the trance?

Things Like That Don't Happen Here

A couple of autumns back, one of my neighbors, Kenneth Payne, fortified by the courage available at one of our local bars, loaded his shotgun, walked across the road to the trailer home of his best buddy, Curtis Cook, and emptied both barrels into Cook's stomach. While his friend bled to death, Kenneth sat down on his porch and telephoned a local family to say, "No one's going to bother your little girl anymore." Kenneth claimed Curtis had earlier in the evening confessed to molesting the neighbor's eight-year-old child.

The next day, our town's burghers ran out to tell curious metropolitan reporters, "Things like that don't happen here." Really? None of my neighbors mentioned the story of our school principal's daughter, who hid her pregnancy from her parents then drowned her child right after its birth. I thought it worth reporting, so I did, in the London *Observer* and the *New York Times*.

"Here," by the way, is an archipelago of farm fields and hamlets of antique clapboard houses called the North Fork. While few

Americans have heard of it, it is quite well known in Britain as Peconic, the congenial, rural town lionized on BBC radio's "Letter from America," broadcast by Alistair Cooke, one of our few unarmed residents. Like Alistair, I've made shameless use of the cartoon imagery of this convenient exemplar of unspoiled, small-town America. I just told you about our town's heroic struggle to block McDonald's from opening a restaurant, a threat to our quaint rural character. The way I wrote it, we were gloriously defeated by the corporation's McLawyers, who bullied us into bending our preservation laws. I left out of the story of the part about our defense being sabotaged from within by that fifth column of small businessmen found in every American town—the local real estate agents, shopkeepers and farmers hoping to turn a quick buck on their properties once the planning rules are breached and broken.

I've written scores of bad-tempered columns about the brutish ways of America's biggest businesses. That viewpoint is admittedly a bit unbalanced. To be fair, we must recognize that for sheer narrow-minded, corrosive greed nothing can beat the grasping, whining, *small* businessmen. And within that avaricious little pack, none is so poisonously self-centered and incorrigible as the small-town businessman of rural America.

During the presidential debates, Al Gore opened the bidding to win this pampered demographic by promising to slash inheritance taxes, "to save our family farms and businesses." Until President Bush took office, if you inherited a farm or business worth up to $2.6 million you paid no tax at all. But that's just not enough for what the fawning candidates call "local entrepreneurs."

Gore promised to raise the exemption to $4 million—only to be trumped by George W. Bush, who promised to wipe away inheritance taxes altogether (one of the few promises he kept).

This group of small businessmen and farmers, so deserving of protection of their tax-free millions, is the same that defeated Bill and Hillary Clinton's 1993 proposal to require all businesses to provide bare-bones health insurance for their employees, an expenditure of only thirty-five cents per hour. Fortune 500 corporations expressed few qualms about the mandatory insurance plan, as most big firms already provide some health care coverage for their workforce. It was the swarm of Lilliputian entrepreneurs—those friendly local Fat Fritters franchisees, Gas'N'Chew owners and Mom's Hammer Drop Hardware Store operators, joined under the aegis of their National Federation of Independent Businesses— who blocked the Clintons' modest attempt to end medical care apartheid in America.

You name it—maternity leave, minimum wage, even health and safety inspections and rules barring racism in hiring—any meager proposal to protect the lives and families of working people, and the NFIB's small businesses legions have their swords out to kill it.

But we must never say so. Al Gore can shoot at big tobacco and big oil, Bush can vilify teachers and union workers, but any politician who breathes a word against rural businesses, farmers or the NFIB's Scrooge battalions ends up as electoral roadkill.

Ten years ago, our town convinced a charitable foundation with more money than wisdom to pay for experts from Britain to tell us how to preserve our area's rural character. We held meetings, referenda, elections. It was that active small-town American democracy that makes foreign writers like Tocqueville gaga with admiration. At the end, the town voted overwhelmingly to adopt what became known as the "U.K. Stewardship Plan" to protect our green fields and prevent ugly urban sprawl.

Come by my town today and count the pustules of strip malls and fluorescent signs directing you to *Bagels Hot! Cars Like New— No Down Payment! Dog Burger!* where cornfields once grew. Sensible British designs and a preservation-minded electorate could not overcome the me-first obstructionism of a hard core of small businessmen and farmers lusting to sell off their land to McDonald's, Wal-Mart and housing speculators.

In October, folks from the metropolis crowd our roads to buy Halloween pumpkins and gawk at farmers in overalls. In glossy magazine supplements, the North Fork is portrayed as a Norman Rockwell painting come to life, with Lake Woebegone characters and barbershop quartets. But look closely at the canvas and you'll get your first clue that something may be wrong: *Our fire trucks are very clean*. They stay clean because our firemen rarely put out fires. Yet the volunteer fire departments are quite busy. Rather than douse burning houses, firemen are more likely to be called out to stop Jimmy from beating in his wife's head again; to yank Fred from his wreck after a three-day bender, or, on occasion, to dissuade another grinning citizen from hanging himself from the porch awning. You will not read this in the tourist guidebooks.

A couple years ago, one of the firemen ran for town council. At a civic meeting, he won big applause for the usual speech about "preserving our unique way of life." Then he added, "And I think it's time we addressed another matter publicly. I intend to make domestic abuse a key issue in this campaign." The audience went dead, cold silent. Live here long enough and you discover that, at the heart of small-town life, there is a special form of communal cowardice. The enforced silence, this small-town *omerta,* is called "being neighborly."

I don't equate rural shotgun murders or child molesting to the small-town businessman's penchant for despoiling the rural landscape. But they are covered over by that same cowering silence. No politician, local or national, has the guts to break through the mythology, the legend of the struggling local businessman who cares and sacrifices for his community. This folkloric invention approaches saintliness when the discussion turns to rural, small-town America with its treacly images of barbershop quartets, Farmer Brown on his tractor and the Main Street parade after the strawberry harvest.

What makes this myth of happy small-town America off-limits to challenge is that it provides pleasant code words for the ugliest corner of the American psyche. When politicians talk about "small-town American values," "family values" and the "hardworking small businessman" everyone knows the color of that town, that family and that businessman—white. Pleasantville, USA, is implicitly placed against the urban jungle populated at the bottom by dark-skinned muggers and pregnant teenagers on the dole, and at the top by Jewish financiers of Hollywood pornography. It would dangerously undermine this politically useful imagery if the public were reminded that small towns like mine are filled with pale-faced citizens despairing and dangerous as any in the inner cities.

Nor could the NFIB win those special exemptions from taxes and planning regulations for small businesses and farms if they were seen not as struggling defenders of local communities, but as dollar-crazed and duplicitous operators who wouldn't care if McDonald's put a drive-through in the Lincoln Memorial.

Every landscape we build, wrote psychologist Norman O. Brown, is our re-creation of the interior of our mothers' bodies. What does it say about Americans when we look out over a natural vista and we are seized with psychic anguish if we cannot locate a throbbing neon sign flashing PIZZA HOT!? In our little town, it was George, the owner of the local lumberyard, who proudly organized successful business opposition to the U.K. Stewardship Plan. With dollar signs in his eyes, he welcomed McDonald's and the boxy shopping mall that replaced several hundred acres of raspberry fields.

But small-town Georges forget that, when they break down government regulations, it is *big* business that gleefully rushes through the breach. Last time I saw him, George the lumberman was stunned by the announcement that Home Depot, the Wal-Mart of do-it-yourself stores, would replace a nearby cornfield. And that means George is out of business.

In a small-town, neighborly manner, I expressed my sympathy to George.

If I were a better person, I would have meant it.

When I published a version of these stories in the New York Times, *my village's Pennysaver printed an editorial, for the second time, suggesting that I pack up and get the hell out of town. I did.*

Insane About Asylum

Nevertheless, I surprised myself by wanting to write something nice about my town, after reading this report: Near midnight on May 12, 2000, twelve Mexicans crossed the Rio Grande on the first leg of their journey to Farmingville, New York, where my town's tradesmen pick up their laborers. Abandoned in the Arizona desert, the twelve died of dehydration.

So here's me, using one of the lowest tricks in journalism—back in London, asking a cab driver to give his salt-of-the-earth opinion on one of the great issues of the day. He couldn't wait.

"Well, it's like you're ashamed to be English today! You're not supposed to be English!"

He was talking about the hot, hot topic of "asylum seekers"—refugees from the Bosnian wars, the Afghanistan wars, and the nearly-as-brutal economic wars of the Darker Continents. I had good reason to ask the cabby. As an American, I could not get my head around this whole issue of "asylum seeking"—which had seized the political stage in Europe. In Britain, France, Germany and even liberal Holland, candidates of parties whether right or left seemed to be running for the post of Great White Hunter, stalking "bogus" asylum seekers among the herd of "legitimate" ones.

In America, we don't have asylum seekers; we have *immigrants*. Lots of them—29 million by the lowball official census, with 1.2 million more coming in each year. U.S. cities compete for prime-pick foreign workers as they would for a foreign auto plant.

America certainly has had anti-immigrant politicians. In the nineteenth century we had the appropriately named Know-Nothing Party, and, in 1992 the New-Nothing candidate Pat Buchanan. And then there was Mike Huffington. In 1988, Huffington's wife, Arianna, famously convinced her overly-rich husband to run for the U.S. Senate on a rabid anti-immigration platform. It was a perplexing campaign for California, where whites are the minority race and the only true nonimmigrants are, if you think about it, a handful of

Shoshone Indians. Mrs. Huffington herself delivered the most viru-
lent antiforeigner speeches . . . in her thick Greek accent.[1]

After his demolition at the polls, the demoralized Mr. Huffington announced he could remain neither a Republican nor a
heterosexual.

Huffington's defeat also allowed George W. Bush to convince
his party to adopt hug-an-immigrant slogans. Bush would hold
open the Golden Door for immigrants, but not out of a weepy
compassion for the "huddled masses yearning to breathe free." Immigration is simply good business.

In fact, it's the deal of the millennium, says Dr. Stephen
Moore of the Cato Institute, a think tank founded by big-name
Republicans. "It's a form of reverse foreign aid. We give less than
$20 billion in direct aid to Third World nations and we get back
$30 billion a year in capital assets." By "assets" he means workers
raised, fed, inoculated and educated by poorer countries, then
shipped at the beginning of their productive lives to the United
States. (The average age of immigrants is twenty-eight.)

The Cato Institute reckons that the United States "imports"
about $25 billion a year in human "goods." "It is the lubricant to
our capitalistic economy," said Moore (as I eschewed thoughts of
the film *Modern Times*, in which Charlie Chaplin gets squeezed
through giant gears), "giving U.S. companies a big edge over
European competitors."

American industry saves a bundle due to its access to an army
of low-skill, low-wage foreign workers who can be hired, then
dumped, in a snap. U.S. industry also siphons off other nations'
best and brightest, trained at poor nations' expense.

The habit of brain-napping other countries' high-skilled
workers, let me note, permits America's moneyed classes to shirk
the costly burden of educating America's own underclass. So far,
this system hums along smoothly: Bangalore-born programmers in

---

[1]The lovely Ms. Huffington says I have her all wrong. Noted.

Silicon Valley design numberless cash registers for fast-food restaurants so they can be operated by illiterate Texans.

To get a closer understanding of the Cato Institute studies, I talked with a piece of imported human capital. His name is Mino (I can't disclose his last name). Mino first tried to get into the United States from Guatemala eleven years ago.

He paid thousands of dollars to a *gusano* (a "worm") to sneak him across the border. The cash bought Mino a spot in a sealed truck with one hundred other men. Mino felt lucky: He didn't die. But he did spend three days in jail when *La Migra* (the U.S. Immigration and Naturalization Service) grabbed him. Back in Guatemala, Mino next bought a plane ticket to JFK Airport—and a false visa. This time, no problems. Within days, Mino had a job washing dishes in the local café in my town here on the North Fork of Long Island. I asked the chief planner for our region, Dr. Lee Koppelman, about the role of "illegal" workers like Mino in our local economy. Koppelman laughed: "There wouldn't *be* an economy without the illegals." He estimates there are more than 100,000 "undocumented" workers in our county alone. Nationwide, undocumented workers total between 7 million and 11 million.

Our local businesses, says Koppelman, "turn a blind eye" to the suspect status of the workers stooping in our strawberry fields and clearing our construction sites. One local farmer tells me he gets his field hands from El Salvador—though I know this guest worker program ended more than twenty years ago.

Our business community's "blindness" goes beyond ignoring someone's counterfeit "green card." The local shop paid Mino the legal minimum wage, but worked him twice the legal number of hours.

And that's another advantage to U.S.-style immigration. "The workforce is flexible," says the expert from Cato. "Flexible" means millions of workers too scared of *La Migra* to blow the whistle on illegal working hours, or to join unions or make a fuss when, at the end of the harvest season (or tourist season or production run) they are told to get lost.

By keeping the Golden Door only slightly ajar, with a third of all immigrants fearful of deportation, America's employers profit from something that works quite a bit like the old South African system of migrant workers. "Workers just materialize," says Koppelman, then are expected to vanish, leaving neither businesses nor communities with any responsibility for their survival or their families' when work ends.

So why do Europeans fear this gloriously profitable scheme of importing valuable worker-assets? The politicians' claim that immigrants drain government resources is a laugh. The U.S. Senate immigration subcommittee tells me the government turns a nice profit on immigration, efficiently collecting in taxes from migrants roughly double what they get back in services.

But what about my cabby's fear of losing his English identity? Face it, Shakespeare's dead. England's cultural exports are now limited to soccer hooligans, Princess Di knickknacks and Hugh Grant.

Today, European pols from Blair to Berlusconi are kowtowing to the hysteria of brown-shirted antiforeign electoral mobs. Yet, despite the Know-Nothingtons and hooded crossburners infecting the U.S. body politic, despite a system so bent it is profitable to leave Mexicans to die in the border deserts. America's core decency, and the engine of our success, is in this: the United States approves 2.5 million applications to stay a year; Britain lets in a paltry 129,000.

Now for the happy American ending. Today, Mino owns a landscaping business, drives a flashy pickup truck, plans to buy a home, get rid of his accent and finish a degree in accounting. No one here resents Mino's success. His story is every American's story. It's my story. Anna Palast stole across the border in 1920. Luckily, *La Migra* didn't catch her until a few days before her one hundredth birthday.

And that's what Pat Buchanan and the Aryans-*über-alles* crowd on both sides of the Atlantic don't understand. It's not where you come from that counts. It's where you're going.

KISSING THE WHIP:
Reflections of an American in Exile

Napoleon said that England is a nation of shopkeepers, but then, the Little Corporal never tried to purchase simple dietary staples (organic milk, Merit Ultra Lites) from a supermarket in Islington, London.

I queried the manager as to why they were out of stock again.

"It's Friday," was the answer, as if that were an unforeseen occurrence, like a rogue tidal wave engulfing Trafalgar Square and preventing deliveries. I began to explain that "Friday" is what accountants call a "recurring event" and HAVEN'T YOU BRITONS EVER HEARD OF COMPUTERS? YOU KNOW THOSE THINGS THAT LOOK LIKE TELEVISIONS WITH TYPEWRITERS ATTACHED?!?

By then, everyone was looking around at that despised figure, the Complaining American.

I like that. In 1999, I left America in disgust, then discovered, to my surprise, I was some kind of freaking patriot.

Daniel Ellsberg, the man who made the Pentagon Papers public, feels the same way. After Richard Nixon had him charged with treason, he was beaten nearly to death on the courthouse steps. "God Bless America," he told me. Ellsberg's not as crazy as he sounds. In Britain, he noted, and in any other nation except the USA, he would have been thrown in the slammer and never heard of again.

The United Kingdom has an Official Secrets Act, libel laws that effectively privatize censorship of journalism, privacy laws protecting politicians—as do all nations in some form or other, except America. You may be surprised to learn that the mother of our Democracy has no legal freedom of the press, no First Amendment—no Bill of Rights. (Maybe they can borrow ours—we're not using it. And we may have no Official Secrets Act—yet—but we are on the cutting edge of creating an unofficial *corporate* secrets act.)

And that's why I'm so ornery about fighting for the First Amendment—which our president and bobbing heads in Congress would snatch from us in the name of "security." Just try working in a nation without the right to a free press, and worse, without the will to fight for it. I have. An unholy number of British journalists seem to have fallen in love with their shackles.

Truth Buried Alive

Of the thousands of bless you and f— you messages that arrived at the *Guardian* papers after we broke the Florida vote swindle story in November 2000, none ruffled my editors' English reserve but one: a letter demanding we retract the article *or else*. It was from Carter-Ruck, a law firm with the reputation as the piranhas of England's libel bar, a favorite of foreign millionaires unhappy about their press. Their letter stated they represented Barrick Corporation—whom you'll remember from Chapter 2 as the Canadian-American gold-mining operation that employed George Bush Sr.

Barrick particularly did not like my mention of the stomach-churning evidence that Sutton Resources, a Barrick subsidiary, had buried alive as many as fifty gold miners in Tanzania in August 1996, prior to Barrick's purchase of Sutton in 1999.

What set their complaint apart from the scores of others we receive from corporations bitching and moaning about my exposés was Barrick's extraordinary demand. They did not want their denial printed (I'd done that), nor their evidence the story was wrong (I would do that too, if they would provide it). They demanded my paper apologize and pay a tiny fortune for simply *mentioning* the allegations first reported by Amnesty International. And even that would not be enough. Barrick also demanded we print a statement vowing that my paper had confirmed that *no one was killed* at the Tanzanian site. Now, I would have been more than happy to confirm that—if I had evidence to that effect. The evidence was, in so many words, "We are billionaires—and you aren't."

Lacking a First Amendment, Britain has become the libel-suit capital of the world. Stories accepted elsewhere draw steep judgments in London. The *Guardian* papers receive notice of legal action about three times a day—that's *one thousand libel notices a year*. This creates a whole encyclopedia of off-limits topics, including an admonition from our legal department not to disparage the marriage of Tom Cruise and Nicole Kidman—sent the day *after* they announced their divorce. No paper can afford to defend against all these actions. The *Guardian* papers operate on a small budget from a not-for-profit foundation. No doubt about it, Barrick could break us in defense costs alone.

In Canada, where libel laws are similar to Britain's, *Frank* magazine had picked up my story. *Frank* swiftly grabbed its ankles by running that incredible retraction—that no one had been "killed or injured" in the mine clearance. The editor apologized to me; they simply had no resources to fight billionaires. Who could blame them?

The first report of the alleged killings in Tanzania came from Amnesty International, whom I quoted. I called their headquarters in London. Courageously, Amnesty refused to help. The organization whose motto is "Silence is complicity" announced that, on advice of lawyers, they would be silent.

Barrick made good use of Amnesty's self-censorship. The company told the court—and the many news outlets around the world that were sniffing around the story—that Amnesty had conducted an investigation and had concluded that "no one was killed in the course of the peaceful removal of miners." If this were true, I would have retracted the story immediately. I'm not infallible, and nothing would have been more joyous than to find out those miners were still alive. But Barrick could not produce this Amnesty clearance—no such report could be located. Amnesty said Tanzania had barred them from investigating, so the killings remained neither confirmed nor denied—in short, they had never cleared Sutton Resources. But that was off the record. Publicly, the Nobel Prize–winning organization (despite several angry calls to them from Bianca Jagger) continued to hide under a desk, knees knocking.

One excellent reporter, chosen Britain's journalist of the year, told me to just sign whatever it took to get out of trouble. "That's just how it's done here." Floyd Abrams, who defends the *New York Times* in the United States and Europe, explained to my astonishment that truth alone is not a defense in English courts. Photos of dead bodies and body parts in Tanzania meant nothing in our case.

I'm not a Man for All Seasons. Honestly, I was ready to go along with some kind of bum-kissing apology to Barrick, only because at the time I was living on Red Bull, potassium powder and no sleep trying to get out the Florida vote theft story, and I sure as hell didn't need another distraction.

But I had a problem. Our paper had encouraged an internationally respected expert on human rights and the environment, Tanzanian lawyer Tundu Lissu, familiar with the allegations, to go to the mine. If Lissu said no one died, I'd sign off as Barrick requested. Instead, over several missions to his home country, he sent back more witness statements, photographs of a corpse allegedly of a man killed by police during the clearing of the site, a list of the dead—and a *videotape* of bones, and a worker going into one pit to retrieve bodies buried, he says on tape, by "the Canadians." (Barrick says the bodies were not from its subsidiary's mine site or, if from the site, the deaths were not a result of the clearance of the site.) In April 2001, when Barrick found out Lissu was asking questions inside the mine site, they sent him and his employer, the World Resources Institute of Washington, DC, a letter outlining a lawsuit if he repeated the allegations concerning the removal of miners.

Then it turned grim. The Tanzanian police, we learned, were hunting for Lissu. Lissu, while in the Tanzanian capital of Dar es Salaam, told officials that the allegations of deaths should be *investigated*. Hardly an inflammatory statement; but the Tanzanian government determined that was sufficient grounds to charge him with sedition.

That's when I lost all sense of reason. I hinted that if the *Guardian* fabricated a lie to save a few coins, I might take action against my own paper for defaming me as a journalist. I'd never do it; the threat was nuts (and not exactly a career maker), but I couldn't let Lissu go to jail by going along with an easy lie. The *Guardian*'s good moral sense slowed the rush to the usual cheap exit from a suit. However, the money clock on legal fees was ticking, making me the most expensive journalist at the *Guardian* papers.

Bad news. In July 2001, in the middle of trying to get out the word of the theft of the election in Florida, I was about to become the guinea pig, the test case, for an attempt by a multinational corporation to suppress free speech *in the USA* using British libel law. I have a U.S.-based Web site for Americans who can't otherwise read my columns or view my BBC television reports. The gold-mining company held my English newspapers liable for aggravated damages for my publishing the story *in the USA*. If I did not pull the Bush-Barrick story off my U.S. Web site, my paper would face a ruinously costly fight.[1]

Panicked, the *Guardian* legal department begged me to delete not just English versions of the story but also my Spanish translation, printed in Bolivia. *(Caramba!)*

The Goldfingers didn't stop there. Barrick's lawyers told our papers that I personally would be sued in the United Kingdom over Web publications of my story *in America*, because the Web could be *accessed* in Britain. The success of this legal strategy would effectively annul the U.S. Bill of Rights. Speak freely in the USA, but if your words are carried on a U.S. Web site, you may be sued in Britain. The Declaration of Independence would be null and void, at least for libel law. Suddenly, instead of the Internet becoming a means of spreading press freedom, the means to break through censorship, it would become the electronic highway for delivering repression.

And repression was winning. InterPress Services (IPS) of Washington, DC, sent a reporter to Tanzania with Lissu. They received a note from Barrick that said if the wire service ran a story that repeated the allegations, the company would sue. IPS did not run the story.

I was worried about Lissu. On July 19, 2001, a group of Tanzanian public interest lawyers wrote the nation's president asking for an investigation—instead, Lissu's law partner in Dar es Salaam was arrested. The police were hunting for Lissu. They broke into his home and office and turned them upside down looking for the names of Lissu's sources, his whereabouts and the evidence he gathered on the mine site clearance. This was more than a legal skirmish. Over the next months, demonstrations by victims' families were broken up by police thugs. A member of Parliament joining protesters was beaten and hospitalized. I had to raise cash quick to get Lissu out, and with him, his copies of police files with

---

[1] See Joe Conason's "Exporting Corporate Control: A gold company with ties to the Bush family tries to muzzle a muckraking journalist" on Salon.com, July 20, 2001.

more evidence of the killings. I called Maude Barlow, the "Ralph Nader of Canada," head of the Council of Canadians. Without hesitation, she teamed up with Friends of the Earth in Holland, raised funds and prepared a press conference—and in August tipped the story to the *Globe & Mail*, Canada's national paper.

The Toronto-based newspaper was excited: This was big news about one of the richest men about town, Barrick CEO Peter Munk—not to mention their former prime minister Brian Mulroney, George Bush, repression, greed and blood. The rule in the news biz is, *if it bleeds, it leads*. So they promised Maude a front-page splash if she'd hold off on her public statement.

The *Globe & Mail* quickly put Mark McKinnon, their best reporter, on the case. Just as quickly, they yanked him off it and told him to fly home from Africa. From page one to page nothing. Barlow was incensed at the decision of the editor. According to Barlow, the editor pleaded that it wasn't his call—the spike came from "the highest levels."

While the big shots at the *Globe & Mail* dove to the mat, spunky little *Frank* magazine effectively retracted its retraction. They'd seen a videotape with bodies—spirited out of the country by Lissu—and would not stand silent. Barrick insisted the bodies in the films were not from the mine clearance—but *Frank* wasn't buying.

Meanwhile, not waiting on that palsied institution, the so-called free press, to act, I issued an alert to human rights groups worldwide. The *Guardian*'s lawyers went ballistic: In the United Kingdom, one can't complain of being sued for libel, because under their law, a paper is guilty of defamation until it proves itself innocent. Therefore, publicly defending oneself "repeats" the libel and makes the paper and reporter subject to new damages and court sanctions. Kafka had nothing on the British court system.

The pressure was on. I'm pleased to say that my editor refused to sign the abject, lying retraction—just fifteen minutes before the court-imposed deadline. He told me these encouraging words: "We are now going to spend hundreds of thousands on some fucking meaningless point you are trying to make. I hope you are happy."

World Bankenstein Goes for the Gold

Then came a new twist. Gold mining in Africa is risky stuff. Who would fund such a venture? I learned that to develop the site, the World Bank granted Barrick the largest loan guarantee in its history. That created a wee problem for these financiers of the new global order: The World Bank's own code bars it from aiding a project where local residents have been forcibly evicted from the site. If the photos, films and witness statements were to be believed, the loan guarantee would have to be withdrawn, and the project conceivably collapse, leaving the World Bank holding the bag financially. The result? Another organization with reason to bury the truth.

I contacted the World Bank about the Tanzanian mine, and one of their functionaries told me, in a snooty Oxford accent, that Black Africans had illegally "swarmed" over the mine site. (Actually, they had permits affirmed by a court.) Even if so, what of the reports of killings? Oh, that was looked into; it would be in Barrick's report.

But it wasn't. Any party seeking a loan or loan guarantee from the World Bank must file a report on the "social impact" of a project. There was a World Bank report on the mine—five thick volumes written by a Barrick contractor. Lissu, safely out of Tanzania, went through the "social development" section, which was supposed to disclose all information about the clearance of the site. The alleged killings? Not a single direct mention. And what happened to the 400,000 people on and near the site in August 1996? Barrick's 1999 report said,

> "One day after the order was made by the Shinyanga Regional Commissioner, artisanal miners . . . left."

Just got up and left. No mention of bulldozers; of police firing guns; of contemporary news reports of a lopsided battle between police and miners. Maybe those witnesses and news reports, as

Barrick claims now, manufactured an elaborate pack of lies. In its official report, Barrick did not trouble the World Bank with the photos of corpses that needed explaining.

Half a Hooray

British papers have made their peace with the libel laws: Except in rare cases where the story has a big national impact, they are resigned to symbolic payments, convoluted half retractions. My born-in-the-USA stance for freedom of speech only appeared to them as alien, grandiose and recklessly unsophisticated. Their instinct was to throw me to the dogs. And while I pounded the table, I understood that a British nonprofit paper couldn't spend half a million pounds sterling defending a story about a Canadian company's actions in Tanzania, dead bodies or no.

The truth was about to get bulldozed. But in July 2001, Maude Barlow's council and human rights groups worldwide bombarded Barrick's Toronto headquarters with petitions demanding they stop trying to censor the story and permit a public inquiry into the alleged killings. Barrick started to give, getting nervous, suddenly offering my paper a (relatively) cheap way out.

Would the *Guardian* still have to confirm no killings took place? Under the horrific British system, a statement that no one died, read in open court, would have given this factoid the virtual force of law, barring any paper from reporting otherwise. To prevent this, Friends of the Earth, Corner House (an English human rights group) and Britain's National Union of Journalists took the extraordinary step of approaching the judge directly under a rarely used provision of the law allowing third parties to argue against a legal settlement of a lawsuit in a manner that could harm the public interest. They presented the judge with the statements of Tanzanian witnesses and an explanation of the controversy surrounding the alleged killings, with pleas to keep the matter open for investigation.

To our astonishment, the judge adopted the activists' position, requiring Barrick to accept that the agreement with the *Guardian* could not be construed as a finding that no one died in the mines— the matter remained open for investigation. So that's how it ended: an apology and cash settlement from my paper[2] and Barrick frustrated, unable to extract a statement that no one died at the mine. Hooray.

Well, half a hooray. I faced personal ruin. The threat of a lawsuit against a reporter after settling with a paper was not cricket, even by English legal traditions. Barrick told my paper's attorneys the company would still sue me—depending on my behavior. So I immediately went on radio in Toronto, where Barrick is headquartered, to talk about their Tanzanian mine, and censorship—then flew to Vancouver to repeat the point on Canadian soil.

Ribbons Cut at the Golden Graveyard

On July 18, 2001, Barrick officially opened the mine, with George W. Bush's ambassador to Tanzania at the ceremony—as well as Andrew Young, former U.S. ambassador to the United Nations. Barrick had done the wise thing: With their subsidiary accused of killing Black people, they appointed Young to the advisory board position previously held by Bush. Here he joined fellow Atlanta Power broker Vernon Jordan, Bill and Hillary's African-American courtier and a member of Barrick's advisory board since its inception.

In March 2002, Dutch and Canadian human rights investigators were turned back from the mining towns by armed militia acting on government orders. Nevertheless, they filmed witness statements—for which they were expelled from the country.

---

[2] My paper apologized for any pains caused to Barrick and its CEO for misreadings of my article. For example, Barrick claimed my exposé could be read to assert that Bush pardoned Adnan Khashoggi's coconspirator in the Iran-Contra scandal as a favor to Peter Munk, that Bush personally ordered the grant of the gold mine in Nevada to Barrick or that the company made no substantial investment in the Nevada mine, or that Barrick owned the Tanzanian mine at the time of the alleged killings. Such readings of my words in the *Guardian* (or here) would be absurd, so I had no objection to my paper's prudent apology for such misreadings.

Barrick, once quite silent about the alleged deaths in Tanzania, was now on the defensive and loud in its responses. The company cited the Tanzanian police, concluding no one died. Of course, the police were themselves implicated in the killings. Barrick claimed the tapes were mistranslated, showed the bodies of ne'er-do-wells killed by local residents or victims of mine accidents distant in time or place from the clearances. That could be the case.

And the World Bank backed the company's view. In October 2002, the Bank issued a report in denying the need for full investigation. That is not surprising given the Bank's large investment in the mine as guarantor of the debt. What *was* unexpected was the vicious language used against Tundu Lissu and the human rights groups which had filed a formal demand with the Bank calling for an inquiry. The Bank attacked Lissu's human rights law firm, Amnesty International (which had recovered its voice), and others for "repeating an allegation which they know not to be true, especially of murder." At the core of the Bank's attack on the groups is their supposed failure to produce a list of the dead:

> The complaint alleges that 52 people were killed in the process of land clearance, trapped alive in their pits . . . as they plugged and filled mine shafts. This is allegation of pre-meditated murder. . . . The [Bank] asked for a list of the names of the 52 people who were killed. . . . Neither LEAT [Lissu's group] nor SSMC [other human groups] have been able to supply the list of names.

How odd. The list of alleged dead was, in fact, included in their complaint. I have the list; so does Barrick.

The Bank attacks the videotape as neither "new" (a Barrick line) nor substantiated, i.e., it could have come from other sites— though this would require evidence that the rescue worker on the tape was lying. And the Bank does assert that many Africans lie, and not just human rights lawyers. The Bank says that its investigation team talked to families who claimed to have lost people in

the mine, but dismisses these as mendacious because "their neighbors took pains to tell the [Bank] team that these relatives were
alive and well" and because in other cases, people who were alleged to have died were found to be alive by the Tanzanian press.

The Bank does not provide the names or the testimony of the
"neighbors" who challenge the claims of deaths. Stephen Kerr, reporting for Canadian Broadcasting and who followed the human
rights team in March, recorded statements from witnesses such as
William Musa. Musa says he stood in front of bulldozers, trying to
warn the drivers that people were in the mine, and he begged police to stop the mine plugging. Kerr reports that contemporaneous
documents and witnesses appear to support allegations of death—
but the killings were not deliberate. Miners, he found, bribed
guards to get back to the pits to obtain their gold and tools without realizing the bulldozers were rolling.

Most astonishing is that the World Bank gives support to the
charges of sedition against Lissu and the human rights lawyers by
stating, "it is the position of the CAO [the Bank's "Compliance
Advisor"] that those charges are not related to LEAT's position as
complainant before this office."

Despite their attack on human rights workers, I won't discount
all the Bank's claims. Still, I don't understand the Bank's goggle-
eyed rejection of independent investigation, a reasonable suggestion that would get me arrested if repeated in Dar es Salaam.

Former president George Bush Sr. (I should say, "Doctor" Bush
after his University of Toronto visit) left Barrick's payroll in 1999.
Let's not overstate Bush's role. What was Barrick to him, anyway?
A chat and chew, maybe a few rounds of golf with powerful
friends, a fistful of cash and stock, a billet-doux to a dictator, another forgotten honorary degree, and some gold diggers' loose
change dropped into the Republican campaign war chest maybe
without his notice. That's how gentlemen do these things.

Did the killings happen? Despite Barrick's bullying wage and
Tanzania's brutal attempt to silence protesters and halt investigations, we should not automatically assume their denials are false.

For example, Barrick has produced, alive, one of the dead men on Lissu's list. The issue here is the right to report evidence-backed allegations of political influence, murder and cover up.

In Washington, only one member of Congress raised questions about the foreign policy and human rights concerns brought on by our former president's work for the Canadian gold-mining company. In 2001, Congresswoman Cynthia McKinney chaired hearings taking testimony on Barrick's alleged role in stoking the civil war in the Congo. The evidence presented to McKinney and her committee is inconclusive, but certainly worth Congress' attention. Later, McKinney campaigned to protect Lissu's life. Then, in August 2002, the Democratic Party of Georgia used the full power of its political apparatus to defeat her in a primary election. The Democratic machine fought more aggressively than the party ever fought against George Bush and succeeded in removing her from office. The *New York Times* noted the Black congresswoman received no support from Atlanta's "prominent black figures."

And Lissu? There's no more work for him at the World Resources Institute. The Bush administration stripped the group of $1.3 million in funding after the group, says Lissu, refused officials' unsubtle requests to get out of mining issues. In April 2002, Lissu was officially charged with sedition. The Tanzanian government cites only his public call for investigation of the mine deaths. As I write this, Lissu's wife is about to give birth to twins—and he is packing to return to Tanzania. I've tried to talk him out of it. "If you go, they'll arrest you." "I know," he said, "but only if I'm lucky." We both know they might do much worse.

Kissing the Whip

On March 17, 1999, on an order from the London Metropolitan Police, my fellow reporter at the *Observer*, Martin Bright, our editors at the *Observer* and lawyers for the *Guardian* were called before a judge at the Old Bailey. On pain of imprisonment and unlimited fines, the British court ordered them to turn over all internal notes relating to stories about a former agent of MI5, the secret service that employs "James Bond." Bright and the editors, Roger Alton and Alan Rusbridger, refused.

One week later at a black-tie soirée at the Hilton Hotel, I found myself in a meandering, champagne-lubricated debate with a disturbingly articulate gent defending the government's right to censor and restrict news reports. My interlocutor (and my boss) was *Guardian* editor and *Observer* CEO Alan Rusbridger, the very man facing time in the Queen's dungeon for refusing the court order.

I was not surprised.

It is the subtle brilliance of British censorship and news suppression that its prime victims, the nation's editors and reporters, have developed a nodding acceptance of the principles justifying limits on their freedom, a curious custom of English journalists to kiss the whip that lashes them.

Rusbridger challenged me, "You wouldn't want a [news] photographer taking pictures of your family over your garden fence, would you?" Well, no. The death of Princess Diana—in the public's mind, a victim of invasive press hounds—has turned a concern for protecting privacy into a treacherous obsession. Privacy has become the first attractive step down that slippery slope to journalists' accepting state censorship.

Under this banner of respecting privacy, Prime Minister Tony Blair's government obtained a court order blocking publication of his children's nanny's diaries. The convenient tool of privacy also was the cloak to conceal public ministers' salaries. Even the records of a phone call from Downing Street in which a Blair adviser privately offered to sell me access to government office—that was private too.

The London news community's response to the writs against editor Rusbridger, reporter Bright and their papers was slow to form. In a land of cautious protest and measured defense, the *Observer* itself delayed for a week covering its own punishment, unsure whether readers found their paper's repression newsworthy.

Weeks passed. Finally, Stuart Weir, the first Briton since Tom Paine to understand the word "freedom," got up a petition signed by media notables. However, with their plea to the government to drop the prosecutions, the petitioners conceded, "We recognise the need to protect national security," a mannered diffidence to the state's ultimate authority over the printed word grating to my American ears. The journalists also demanded: "The Official Secrets Act should be reformed to allow a public interest defense." *Reformed?* The Official Secrets Act prohibits the publication of almost any document or fact that the government chooses to conceal, from crimes by MI6 to educational statistics. The polite protesters conceded the right of the Queen to arrest journalists. God forbid the pressmen should demand freedom of the press.

The *Guardian* had done nothing more than print a letter to the editor from former MI5 agent David Shayler. Shayler's a great guy, but more Maxwell Smart than James Bond. The *Observer's* crime was to note in print that a U.S. Internet site had posted information corroborating agent Shayler's accusations.

Apparently, Shayler had tipped the *Observer* to this public information. While any communication by an ex-agent violates the Official Secrets Act, the police did not need the reporter's letter files, as they claimed, as unique evidence of Shayler's alleged violation of the law—Shayler himself had sent the government copies of his messages to the paper.

Yet, the sheer foolishness of the government's demanding documents already in its possession is evidence of a more sinister aim. By showing it will punish minor infractions of its secrecy laws, government succeeds in freezing any journalist's attempt to dig out deeper and more dangerous truths concealed within secretive agencies. Worse, journalists, defending their minor infractions, trap themselves into justifying the greater censorship. "As a newspaper," wrote the *Observer*, "we have no difficulty with secrets or with the principle that secrecy, where necessary, should be protected by the law."

By acceding to limit itself to "legitimate" inquiries, to use the timid terminology of the journalists' petition, the papers open the door to state policing to root out the "illegitimate."

The United Kingdom remained one of the hemisphere's only nations without a written guarantee of free speech and press until October 1999. That month Article 10 of the European Convention on Human Rights became U.K. law. The convention allowed Britons, for the first time, "to receive and impart information and ideas without interference by public authority."

In the Crown versus the *Guardian* the court and government were quick to agree that the new human rights law applied to the current prosecution of reporter Bright and the newspapers.

This was not good news. Whereas the U.S. Constitution states "Congress shall not restrict the freedom of the press nor of speech"—no ifs, ands or buts—the European convention adds a nasty little codicil, "Part 2." In the March 17 hearing, the judge ruled that the right to "receive and impart information"—freedom of the press—was subject to Part 2's "restrictions and penalties in the interests of national security." How fitting that in the land of George Orwell, the law bars the government's controlling the press—unless the government decides to do so.

D-Notice Blues

On April 15, the censorship/self-censorship vaudeville opened a new act. That day, reporter Bright saw a copy of a four-year-old MI5 document detailing the security agency's bungled attempt to recruit a Libyan spy, a cock-up that appears to have led to the murder of a Libyan dissident living in London. The "TOP SECRET DELICATE SOURCE UK EYES" document can be read by anyone with a mouse and time on their hands at www.cryptome.org—see figure 8.1! *Observer* reporter Bright drafted a story (with Antony Barnett) about the information on the Web site.

Despite its open publication on the site, repeating this information invited criminal and civil penalties. (In fact, reading the Web site's content is a crime in the United Kingdom.) And if you think that's a joke, the prime minister's thought Gestapo arrested college student Julie-Ann Davies for reading letters from Agent Shayler published on his French Web site. To avoid another writ, the *Observer* contacted the Defence Advisory Committee, the "D-Notice" Committee, a kind of government confessional where journalists may whisper their unpublished thoughts and information and ask, in confidence, "If we publish, will we have sinned against the state?" The agency suggested that if our paper could prove our news report contained no new news—an interesting restriction for a newspaper—then prosecution might not follow.

Laudably, the paper went ahead with publication for its last edition, though it "voluntarily" left off the Web site's address (which I've included above). Reporter Bright finds the procedure deadly to the ethics of news coverage. "It's crazy, but the law says

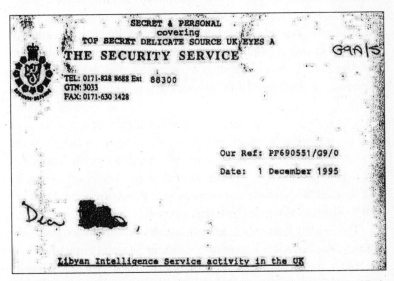

Fig. 8.1. An MI5 document regarding an attempt to recruit a Libyan spy, Khalifa Ahmad Bazelya, allowing him to stay in Britain. Reporter Martin Bright and the editors of the *Guardian* and *Observer* were hauled into court for mentioning the existence of the document, a violation of the Official Secrets Act, and refusing to turn over information on sources. By the way, the MI5 documents can be seen at www.cryptome.org.

we can't do what journalists should always do: Check with the sources, review the key documents. We have to break the law to break the news."

Self-Censorship Is in the Breeding

The D-Notice Committee, the reluctance to ban publication outright, and the seemingly sympathetic bargaining all serve to foster the habit of self-censorship.

Rarely does government have to brandish the implements of coercion because British news people are bred to a strong sense of the boundaries of public discourse. In this class-poisoned society, elite reporters and editors are lured by the thrill of joining the inner circle of cognoscenti with ministers and titled military intelligence men. The cost of admission is gentlemanly circumspection.

Britons, as they constantly remind me, are subjects—not citizens. British-born journalist Christopher Hitchens, scourge of authorities on two continents, stunned Americans by submitting to deposition by U.S. government prosecutors during the impeachment trial of President Bill Clinton. Clearly, habits of subjugation die hard.

The state extends its power to punish unruly reporters through libel laws, which, in effect, privatize enforcement of state censorship. I have yet to publish a single column in a British newspaper as written, uncarved by lawyers fearful of ruinous court action by well-funded litigious bullies running the gamut from McDonald's Corporation to the prime minister himself.

These libel laws, while crippling the work of investigative reporters (the *Guardian*'s computer won't accept any copy prior to a reporter's answering the machine's query, "LAWYERED?") hardly protect the public. England's tabloids like the *Daily Mirror* are notorious cesspools of character assassination, rumor and vicious fabrications.

When other arguments against unfettering the press fail, the ultimate defense by officials eager to censor and journalists ready to comply is that a government open to scrutiny is "not British." Certain freedoms offend what some Britons call their "culture," which, on examination, is nothing more than a debilitating combination of long-established habits of subjugation mixing too comfortably with the preferences of the powerful.

Hot Water and Hitchens

Talk about hot water, we'd done it now. I published the above story in *Index on Censorship* magazine, London. Frank Fisher, managing editor and the type of troublemaker journalism desperately needs, was left in charge of publication while his superiors were out of London. Frank slipped into the piece the actual Web site address where anyone can read MI5 and MI6 documents. In case readers missed the point, he illustrated the story with a secret service document marked confidential.

When the chief editors returned to find the thousands of copies already printed, they called a meeting. Should Frank be boiled in oil or merely turned over to the authorities with a note pinned on him, "Do as you will"? How can we preserve the computer disks, keep the magazine running, out of bankruptcy, when the Metropolitan Police come to take the computers as they had done to the student arrested earlier? How do I prevent seizure of my passport?

No matter the consequences, the issue would go out.

But we were not prepared for the stunning attack about to come by electronic post:

> Greg Palast's hastily-written article entitled, *Kissing the Whip* . . . What on earth is *Index* doing when it allows its space to be wasted, and its reputation for seriousness lowered, by ignorance and pettiness of this sort?

Christopher Hitchens, a British transplant in America, whose posh accent and carefully hedged nastiness made him New York's favorite cocktail party revolutionary, was in high dudgeon. The mild reproving mention of his collaboration with Republican politicians would not be countenanced.

> *Everything in this passage is either false or irrelevant. The House Judiciary Committee, which prepared the case against Clinton, is not an arm of the U.S. government. . . . I did not "submit" to any process, but freely agreed to a request for my testimony. . . . If Mr. Palast does not understand the impeachment provisions of the U.S. Constitution, he has no business patronising the hapless Brits for their lack of a Bill of Rights.*

Chastened by this dressing-down, I replied with humility:

Mr. Christopher Hitchens
Washington, DC

Dear Sir,

I write to you to offer a sincere apology for my words in print which appear to have deeply wounded your pride and your justly earned sense of your own worth. I did not mean to offend a person as important and accomplished as yourself in the arts of essay and condescension.

I often say that social critics such as ourselves, whose profession it is to censure others, should withstand with grace and humor that which we dish out so easily. But, given your stature and deserved celebrity, I agree we should make you an exception, and grant you an immunity from any and all criticism. For though your work seldom discomfits the powerful, it does flatter the Left at a time when we so need an appreciation of our prejudices.

I must admit that had I edited, as well as authored, the piece, I would not have concluded with any mention of your story . . . your antics in Washington were not as noteworthy in my estimation as you believe.

Forgive us, for we had other things on our mind as we approached publication. *Index* exposed the vicious system of British censorship—and came close to crossing the line of the Official Secrets Act as interpreted by MI5 and MI6. We ad long discussion about what to do in case *Index* were charged under the Act, our computers seized or the editors and I arrested. I admit, while focusing on the difficulties of facing down state repression, I did not give more careful attention to your personal feelings.

I am horrified that in what you rightly term my "ignorance and pettiness," I stated you "submitted" to a request to provide testimony in Kenneth Starr's prosecution of President Clinton. Had you done so, it would have been a violation of American journalistic ethics: reporters must never provide source information to aid a state prosecution. I now gladly correct the record. You did not "submit" to testify but, as you say, "freely agreed" to take part in Kenneth Starr's official witch-hunt.

Therefore, I would ask *Index* to run the following retraction:

Mr. Greg Palast wishes to apologize unreservedly to Mr. Christopher Hitchens whose actions are at all times honorable, commendable and always, without exception, beyond the criticism of so-called investigative reporters such as Mr. Palast. Mr. Palast is terribly ashamed.

Sincerely, . . .

In the end, Her Majesty's intelligence services and Christopher Hitchens backed off. An English court of appeals ruled that the new European human rights law trumped British official secrets hysteria in this silly matter of publishing information already public, though the pernicious Act remains to punish those who cross a line, drawn at a place unknown, in revealing official evils. So I decided to head back to the USA, where nothing can be censored—but where nothing printed is worth censoring.

Death Wish Under the Palm Trees

Very unlike the subjects of the monarchy we divorced, Americans bitch, moan, complain and *demand our rights*. Sometimes. When our TV infotainment hypnosis wears off, when "Have a nice day" is an insufficient answer to getting screwed by the powers that be, Americans can surprise themselves, rise up and say, No thanks, we won't eat shit.

You can read my chapters up to here and get darned depressed: The big boys, the bullies, the brutal always seem to win. When your daddy was a president and your brother, the governor of Florida, counts the ballots, you don't have to win an election to become president yourself. They don't call it the "privileged" class for nothing. Corporate cash beats democracy every time. So it seems.

But not always. It may appear like a battle of bears versus bunnies, but sometimes we little critters stand on our hind legs, fight it out and win. There's a long history in the United States of biting back, from Andrew Jackson's challenge to the creation of these creatures called "corporations" to the Populist Movement's demand for public utilities commissions to limit monopolists' price gouging. In the USA, trade unions may fall, but credit unions rise.

The point of this chapter is that America has something to offer the planet besides McBurgers, cruise missiles and Madonna: When we've had enough, we kick ass.

In Chapter 2 I told you how San Diego's 3 million residents had been involuntarily enrolled as laboratory rats in a scary economic experiment: ending regulation of electricity prices. The power companies promised the free market would cut prices "at least 20 percent." By 2000, the price for energy rose by 379 percent.

Then something extraordinary happened. Where the bilious tumble of freeways, McDonald's and Wal-Marts smash up against the Mexican border, laid-back Californians leapt off their surfboards and out of their hot tubs waving their middle finger in the air, chanting, "Boycott! Boycott!" San Diego Gas and Electric sent out their bloated bills, but in the summer of 2000 the tanned masses wouldn't pay. By the tens of thousands, customers simply continued to pay only the old, lower prices. Joining the boycott: the city's school system, the Council of Churches and even, without a hint of shame, the state senator who sponsored the original deregulation law.

In Bolivia, you'll remember, when British-American owners of Cochabamba's utility kicked up prices and customers boycotted bill payments, government confronted protesters with bullets and martial law. But in California, protesters were met by panicked, genuflecting politicians. The governor of California, Democrat Gray Davis, drafted an emergency law to knock back prices retroactively by 60 percent. The state's utility regulators effectively endorsed the revolt by barring San Diego Gas and Electric from cutting off service to customers who refused to pay.

The power pirates were stunned by the public revolt. After all, though San Diego prices skyrocketed to about fifteen cents per kilowatt hour, this is no more than U.S. power companies typically charge their customers in Europe—who endure the fleecing with a stoic shrug.

So what got the beach bunnies up in arms? America's little secret is that the New World Order of free markets and deregulation is for export only; the free-market snake oil is applied almost exclusively to obtaining foreign plunder. Americans have always expected that, within our borders, the public, through state power, should squeeze down the prices and profits of monopoly service companies.

The city of Los Angeles owns its own electricity and water system and virtually gives the stuff away. Good. We don't have to put up with World Bank dicta for privatization and "market pricing" designed for the schmucks on lesser continents.

Thick as we are, when Americans get kicked in the head like this, our eyes blink and our heads begin to think. Deep in our commercialized, Disneyfied heart, America still throbs with a certain democratic spirit. Not the spirit of Thomas Jefferson and the Bill of Rights, of toleration and of public discourse; I'm talking the spirit of Charles Bronson and *Death Wish*, the coiled snake on the Revolutionary Flag—*don't tread on me*. Since long before the deregulation price hikes, 46,000 San Diegans voluntarily paid $15 a year to belong to the Utility Consumers Action Network (UCAN), whose sole work is to harass, challenge, sue and otherwise drive electricity and phone companies up against the wall. UCAN sponsored the can't-pay-won't-pay radio adverts. An older group, The Utility Reform Network (TURN) has another 20,000 angry members. Toqueville called it the American "genius for association": what he meant was, the working stiffs' commitment to *getting even*.

Hence, the class-action suit, antitrust laws, public service commissions, the Consumer Product Safety Commission (thanks, Ralph), the Food and Drug Administration, the Occupational Safety and Health Administration, state universities, the Voting Rights Act (thanks, Martin) and . . . and, yes, I know, every one of these institutions gets infiltrated by corporate stooges, turns rotten, then toothless and so we have to rise up again. That's what makes America great, not innovations in the derivatives market.

After I relocated to Britain four years ago, I covered a story about an auto dealership price-fixing ring. Volvo, a division of Ford Motor, confessed that a bunch of their English dealers had conspired to jack up car prices by as much as $6,000 each. The British government was very proud of itself, nailing the bad guys. Of course, the government would not dream of requiring the crooked corporation to give back the money—nor would they name the dealership crooks (that was a "commercial secret"). And the ripped off consumer found it quite impolite to request refunds. As jackbooted imperialists, the English were damn good at kicking brown people around but at home, they are well trained to kiss the whips of their betters. Sue the bastards, you say? It's against the law to fix prices in Britain, but in the past one hundred years, the number of price-fixing victims who have won compensation is exactly zero.

The big names in British thinking postulate that America's tougher, citizen-friendly antitrust laws are rooted in the progressive theories of enlightened turn-of-the-century capitalists seeking to keep the marketplace free and fair. Washington antitrust lawyer Kenneth Adams has a closer view. "Americans have 200 million handguns. We've always had guns. If we didn't have a way for the average guy to get his money back, there'd be war."

No question, if Ford Motor confessed in the USA to taking down its buyers for six grand each, then refused to return the loot, there would be bullet holes in the salesrooms and blood on the bumpers. The 1890 Sherman Anti-Trust Act was the desperate defense of America's monied class against the Populist Movement, a million angry farmers on the verge of insurrection against the railroad barons.

Guns scare me; violence is a loser. In fact, it's the ingenious no-bullets reforms that give Americans a fighting chance against the wealthy few. American farmers did it one hundred years ago on the Great Plains; and here's an example of how the lowlifes in my old neighborhood, Manhattan's Lower East Side, are doing it.

Ni Tuya, Ni Mia, De Todos

New York, New York, it's a helluva town. Just fifteen years ago, you could walk down Third Street on the Lower East Side and count twenty-three boarded-up, abandoned buildings and only seven buildings inhabited. On the corner at Avenue B, the awnings of the local bank provided shelter for the open-air market where you could buy smack, crack, angel dust—you name it. In 1984, one of those dealers (no longer in the business) took over the bank and heralded a revolution in U.S. finance.

Mary Spink, out of prison for running a drugs network, heard news that the bank, a branch of Manufacturers Hanover Trust, was about to shut its doors and reopen in a tony Midtown location. "Manny Hanny" was the last bank on the "Loees-Side-a," if you don't count the loan sharks. Without a bank, the neighborhood would finally die. Spink teamed up with the parish priest and local housing activists (including a former Weather Underground wannabe terrorist) and picketed Manufacturers Hanover's Manhattan headquarters. They won a face-to-face meeting with the bank's executives hosted by the Federal Reserve Board.

In the Fed's elegantly appointed Wall Street conference room, the Lower East Side crew demanded that the $80 billion bank corporation hand over their branch building to the group to house a community credit union. They also demanded the bank kick in several hundred thousand dollars to get the credit union off the ground. The executives balked, but the Federal Reserve reminded them of the power of the Invisible Hand of the Marketplace (that is, the iron fist of Alan Greenspan) and the Community Reinvestment Act, CRA, a new law obliging banks to serve the credit needs of communities in their areas of operation. Manufacturers Hanover caved in. The launch of the Lower East Side Peoples Federal Credit Union, a novel use of the CRA, quietly marked an extraordinary shift in political power from boardrooms to the public. Their slogan: *Ni Tuya, Ni Mia, De Todos*—"Not Mine, Not Yours, But Ours."

Today's monster-sized mergers of financial behemoths, such as the Citicorp/Travelers Group combination, are akin to elephants mating. It is such a fascinating spectacle, we forget about the effect on the ants below, the poor and working-class customers for whom bank consolidation usually means bank abandonment.

But the ants are fighting back and their weapon of choice is the Community Reinvestment Act. Activists armed with CRA are holding mega-mergers hostage until banks cough up millions, and sometimes billions, of dollars for loan funds pledged to low-income borrowers. In March 1998, following the success on the Lower East Side, 130 angry citizens in Philadelphia testified at Federal Reserve Board hearings against the takeover of local

CoreStates by First Union Corporation. To avoid further challenge under the CRA, the banks settled with community groups by pledging to make $5 billion in low- and moderate-income loans over five years, a huge jump over current lending rates. Then Bank of America made the mother of all pledges, $350 billion over ten years, in return for the right to gobble up NationsBank. In all, merger-bound banks have signed 360 agreements to provide $1.04 *trillion* in targeted financing to underserved communities.

But Matthew Lee isn't satisfied. Lee, now head of New York's Community on the Move, rejected a plea by Citibank and Travelers to end his challenge to their merger in return for the new bank's establishing a $115 billion ten-year loan program for low-income customers and small businesses in poor neighborhoods.

An alumnus of the Lower East Side Peoples Credit Union, Lee is the Che Guevara of poor folks' banking rights. Like Che, he sports a beard. Unlike Che, he puts fear into the hearts of American capitalists. His only armament is convincing, detailed analysis of banks' lending patterns that expose the dark, racist side of "redlining," the practice of cutting off credit to deteriorating neighborhoods, thereby accelerating the deterioration. Lee wrested a commitment of $1 billion for loans to low-income customers from Charter Bank of Ohio after he exposed data showing the bank was three times as likely to reject loan applications from Blacks and Hispanics as from whites, despite little discernible difference in creditworthiness.

Lee, in rejecting the $115 billion offer from Citigroup, emphasized that CRA compliance is not a game of piling up gargantuan loan funds, but a matter of justice for the poor in the provision of credit. He cites a case of unscrupulous treatment of an African-American family, the Harrises, by Citigroup's Commercial Credit Unit. While homeowners in white neighborhoods receive mortgages at 7 percent interest, the Harrises paid 12 percent despite their solid credit rating. The Harrises had signed blank loan forms, counting on the integrity of the world's largest financial institution. That was a mistake, one that Lee himself did not make by signing off on the Citigroup merger deal. Lee insists that the Harrises' predicament is not isolated, that Citigroup operations systematically overcharge and underfund poor and minority communities.

It would be easy to list CRA's weaknesses; biased access to capital remains a fact of American life. Nevertheless, CRA has helped boost the total number of home mortgages for Black Americans by 72 percent in its first four years on the books. The Republicans' chief banking spokesman charges that the loan funds are simply extortion payments to activists. Yet he could not find a single banker to testify against CRA's continuation. No mystery there: Banks turn a profit on these mandatory low-income loans.

Back on the no-longer-mean streets of the Lower East Side, Mary Spink, dealer-turned-banker (today she's treasurer of the National Federation of Community Development Credit Unions) warns against the new "volunteerism." The credit union is not one of the Bushes' thousand pointless lights; it was not created by the charity from Big Brother Banks. Our president has pumped hot gas into the already bloated egos of America's CEOs, cooing to them that he knows they are good and honest and decent and will do the right thing without the government telling them they have to. The grinning public relations flacks tell us that corporate financial institutions will do the right thing, voluntarily putting money back into our inner cities instead of into international hedge funds. The free markets elixir salesmen say we can win over the hearts and minds of the banking community with sweet talk of profits from lending to the working poor. But Spink suggests that the Community Reinvestment Act succeeds because it obeys the dictum of General Westmoreland, "When you've got 'em by the balls, their hearts and minds will follow."

Victory in the Pacific

Sometimes, the protests that liberate us are quieter.

In 1995, in Chicago, veterans of Silver Post No. 282 celebrated the fiftieth anniversary of their victory over Japan, marching around a catering hall wearing their old service caps, pins, ribbons and medals. My father sat at his table, silent. He did not wear his medals.

He had given them to me thirty years earlier. I can figure it exactly: March 8, 1965. That day, like every other, we walked to the newsstand near the dime store to get the LA Times. He was a Times man. Never read the Examiner. He looked at the headline: U.S. Marines had landed on the beach at Danang, Vietnam.

As a kid, I was fascinated by my dad's medals. One, embossed with an eagle and soldiers under a palm tree, said "Asiatic Pacific Campaign." It had three bronze stars and an arrowhead.

My father always found flag-wavers a bit suspect. But he was a patriot, nurturing this deep and intelligent patriotism. To him, America stood for Franklin D. Roosevelt and the Four Freedoms. My father's army had liberated Hitler's concentration camps and later protected Martin Luther King's marchers on the road to Birmingham. His America put its strong arm around the world's shoulder as protector. On the back of the medal, it read "Freedom from Want and Fear."

His victory over Japan was a victory of principles over imperial power, of freedom over tyranny, of right over Japan's raw military might. A song he taught me from the early days of the war, when Japan had the guns and we had only ideals, went,

> We have no bombers to attack with . . .
> . . . but Eagles, American Eagles,
> fight for the rights we adore!

"That's it," he said that day in 1965, and folded the newspaper. The politicians had ordered his army, with its fierce postwar industrial killing machines, to set upon Asia's poor. Too well read in history and too experienced in battle, he knew what was coming. He could see right then what it would take other Americans ten years of that war in Vietnam to see: American bombers dropping napalm on straw huts, burning the same villages Hirohito's invaders had burned twenty years earlier.

Lyndon Johnson and the politicians had taken away his victory over Japan.

They stole his victory over tyranny. When we returned home, he dropped his medals into my twelve-year-old hands to play with and to lose among my toys.

A few years ago, my wife Linda and I went to Vietnam to help out rural credit unions lending a few dollars to farmers so they could buy pigs and chickens.

On March 8, 1995, while in Danang, I walked up a long stone stairway from the beach to a shrine where Vietnamese honor their parents and ancestors.

Halfway up, a man about my age had stopped to rest, exhausted from his difficult, hot climb on one leg and crutches. I sat next to him, but he turned his head away, ashamed of his ragged clothes, parts of an old, dirty uniform.

The two of us watched the fishermen at work on the boats below. I put one of my father's medals down next to him. I don't know what he thought I was doing. I don't know myself.

In '45, on the battleship *Missouri*, Douglas MacArthur accepted the surrender of Imperial Japan. I never thought much of General MacArthur, but he said something that stuck with me. "It is for us, both victors and vanquished, to rise to that higher dignity which alone benefits the sacred purposes we are about to serve." (figure 8.2)

"Your Book Is Depressing": A Conclusion

I've got a stack of letters that read, "Your book is depressing." True, but only if you put your hands in your pockets, look at your shoes and whistle. Here's your choices: You can shut the book and use the binding to scratch your nether parts or you can *do* something. Read, learn, join, holler, act. *Sue* something. The NAACP has:

Fig. 8.2. When war was heroic. Gil and Gladys Palast in 1943. Dad was in the 716th Tank Battalion in the Philippines. Mom was in the SPARS, the U.S. Coast Guard women's unit.

Katherine Harris for violating the civil rights of Floridians, Black and white, who were illegally denied the vote. Join them. If you live in downtown New York, yank your shriveled 401(k) from Citibank and join the Lower East Side Peoples Credit Union. If not, then don't come crying to me; I don't have time for the corporate abuse enablers. I told you about TURN, the organization that fights the electricity barons. If you're in California, send them a check for $25. Right *now*. Their address is at the back of this book, along with a sampler of other great American troublemakers who can inform you and get you in *motion*.

Even our president's caught the spirit, asking every American to volunteer and turn in the names of "suspicious" people requiring closer scrutiny. Okay: Let's all write in "Dick Cheney."

And whatever you do . . .

DON'T THROW AWAY THAT PAPER!

Do you have a document marked "confidential" your boss would rather the planet not see? Were you told to shred, deep six, eat, destroy or erase that report/file/e-mail/photo that would save a life if shown on TV?

Don't waste it, *paste it*! To:

Greg Palast at www.GregPalast.com

Hit the home page button that says "Tell me about it!"

Whistleblowers welcome. *Don't* break the law. (You can check the rules at my site.) And *don't* jeopardize your job. But, for the sake of this sorry planet, *tell the truth on 'em.*

Appendix
Your Turn—Resources For Action

Here's what you can read, listen to, act on, join and get in trouble with.

Start at www.GregPalast.com. Sign up for news reports, watch my BBC *Newsnight* television reports in streaming video, join the research collective and check out expanded and updated links to the organizations and news sites listed below.

Media: You're Not Stupid, They Just Talk to You That Way

Here's just a few of the terrific Internet outlets that don't treat you like a fool. Get your *samizdat* news from: MediaChannel.org, consortiumnews.com, Guerrilla News Network (GuerrillaNews.com), Buzz-Flash.com, and become a member of the *real* Radio Free America, The Pacifica Radio Network, Salon.com, Fairness and Accuracy in Reporting (FAIR.org), BBC.co.uk (where all BBC television and radio programs are archived) and GuardianUnlimited.co.uk for *Guardian* and *Observer* reports. And sign up for Russell Mokhiber's *Corporate Crime Reporter* and Jim Hightower's *Lowdown* newsletters.

Here are sources for more information and ideas for action . . .

Chapter 1–Jim Crow in Cyberspace

The Alliance for Democracy, Boston, headed by Ronnie Dugger has been fighting against computerized elections theft for years. People for the American Way is acting as law firm of record for plaintiffs in *NAACP vs. Harris*. Voter March, chaired by Lou Posner, New York, and Citizens for Legitimate Government, based in Pittsburgh, won't forget the theft of the election of 2000 or the theft of the 2004 election.

Chapter 2–The Best Democracy Money Can Buy

For (declared) listings of which corporations invested in which politician, go to the Center for Responsive Politics Web site (opensecrets.org) and Chuck Lewis' Center for Public Integrity (publicintegrity.org) of Washington. For doings in the Lone Star state, go to Craig McDonald's group with the vigilante name, Texans for Public Justice (tpj.org). Regarding pollution both environmental and political in Texas, check out Paul Orem's group, Working Group on Community Right-to-Know (rtk.net), and Public Citizen of Texas (texascitizen.org). For taking on George Bush's gold-digger buddies, go to the Council of Canadians (canadians.org), the heroic Tundu Lissu's Lawyers' Environmental Action Team in Dar es Salaam (LEAT.or.tz) and BothEnds.org (affiliated with Friends of the Earth, Holland). For no-BS info on the war on terror, contact the National Security News Service, Washington (PublicEdCenter.org).

Chapter 3—California Reamin'

Join your state's Citizen Utility Board or other activist group—in California, The Utility Action Network (TURN.org) and Dan Berman's Public Power advocacy group (publicpowernow.org). In Texas, sign up with the Consumers' Union. Outside the United States, contact Public Services International (world-PSI.org), the electricity, water and gas workers confederation in Brussels. For the real skinny on Enron, contact the Sustainable Energy & Economy Network (SEEN.org). Government officials and activists should check out DemocraticRegulation.com, the Web site I've set up with Jerrold Oppenheim and Theo MacGregor to fight the deregulation dragons.

Chapter 4—Sell the Lexus, Burn the Olive Tree

GregPalast.com has a transcript of two hours of my talks with Nobelist Joe Stiglitz as well as copies from pages of World Bank and IMF confidential documents. For more info, three globalization watchdogs stand out: Citizens' Network On Essential Services (ServicesForAll.org), the Center for Economic and Policy Research (CEPR.net) and Lori Wallach's Global Trade Watch (Citizen.org/trade/)—all Washington based. For Latin American issues, go to Resource Center of the Americas (Americas.org). Then put on your gas mask and contact the affiliates of the International Forum on Globalization (IFG.org), the groups that planned the unplanned Seattle demonstrations. On AIDS and trade, contact Jamie Love's group, Consumer Project on Technology (cptech.org).

Chapter 5–Inside Corporate America

To respond to those who take away your day in court, join with the Center for Justice & Democracy founded by Michael Moore with Joanne Doroshow (CenterJD.org). Want to sue the bastards? Find out about some of the most important class-action suits at the site of Cohen, Milstein, Hausfeld and Toll (CMHT.com) of Washington. Want to find out what your green group's doing with your green? Check out the PIG reports by the Non-Profit Accountability Project, Washington. For info on private prisons, see The *Prison Privatisation Report International (PPRI)* (psiru.org/justice/), edited by Stephen Nathan.

Chapter 6–Pat Robertson, General Pinochet, Pepsi-Cola and the Anti-Christ

For more on the vicious vicar, contact Americans United for Separation of Church and State (au.org) headed by the Reverend Barry Lynn. On "President" Pinochet and his running mate, Henry Kissinger, see the CIA's own documents at the National Security Archives at George Washington University in the District of Columbia (gwu.edu/~nsarchiv/). To prevent the next oil spill in Alaska, join the Alaska Forum for Environmental Responsibility (alaskaforum.org). Had enough of money-mad scientists? Support the Center for Science in the Public Interest (CSPInet.org).

Chapter 7–Small Towns, Small Minds

To take on Wal-Mart or McDonald's, contact Sprawl-Busters (sprawl-busters.com).

Chapter 8—Kissing the Whip

At Cryptome.org, read the latest in MI5, CIA and other documentation you're not supposed to see. For the latest on speaking truth to power, subscribe to *Index on Censorship* and ProjectCensored.org. Whistleblowers, contact the Government Accountability Project (whistleblower.org) for the rules on letting it all hang out. To rid yourself of Big Bank blues, check out the National Federation of Community Development Credit Unions (NatFed.org) to find the credit coop near you. To join a labor union, I'd like to direct you to the Web site that tells you how to sign up to organize your shop, but the AFL-CIO is too unimaginative, exhausted and defeated to have one.

Acknowledgments

Investigative reporting in America is virtually a crime these days, so getting out the word when Corporate Media just would not cover these stories required the time, grit, and talents of hundreds of supporters who shared my dislike for swallowing the usual news goo.

Unless I can attach a Volume 2 to this book, I can't list all these helpers. To those who have given their time compensated only by my crankiness and procrastinations, special thanks . . .

. . . to Oliver Shykles, researcher-writer extraordinaire for lending me the Dead Kennedys T-shirt when I most needed it, and Fredda Weinberg, cyber-genius, organizer, digger-outer and flack-catcher at GregPalast.com. To Meirion Jones, gonzo producer at BBC Television *Newsnight*, for making me wear that hat and George Entwistle for telling me to take it off. To the Salon.com and *American Prospect* Table Talk volunteers who broke down the wall between author and reader to pour in the info when I was under the deadline gun. To my editors at the *Guardian* and *Observer*, Will Hutton, Alan Rusbridger, Roger Alton and especially Ben Laurance, who would tell me to stay out of trouble then assign me into it. To my co-investigator Antony Barnett in London, who suggested I carry a wire. To Lenora Stewart, gumshoe and author, for finding the documents Exxon and the power pirates wish you hadn't.

To the Hon. Cynthia McKinney for defending me when she could have been defending herself.

To Joe Conason and E. J. Dionne for demanding I bring my words back home to America; and to Joe, Bob Herbert, Bob Kuttner, Dave Ruppe, Noam Chomsky, John Pilger, Bill Spain and Smart White Man Michael Moore for introducing me to your readers when, in darkest hours, I thought no one could hear me shouting from across the Atlantic. To Katrina Vanden Heuvel at *The Nation* and Rick MacArthur at *Harper's* for breaking the embargo on my printed words; and to Luis Bredow of *Gente*, Bolivia, for translating and publishing my investigations and losing his job for it.

To the Internet publishers who got out my words when U.S. mainstream media barricaded the newsroom doors: Emily Bell of *Guardian Unlimited*, Joan Walsh and Kerry Lauerman of Salon.com, Anthony Lappe of Guerrilla News Network, Media Channel.com, the whole Buzzflash.com gang, Bev Conover and Linda Starr of *OnLine Journal*, Marc Ash of Truthout.com, TomPaine.com, Julie Light of CorpWatch.com, BBC.co.uk, Americas.org, bartcop.com, Commondreams.com, Meria Heller and other dot commies—may you all one day dance on the graves of the newsprint dinosaurs.

To Winston Smith for painting the murals inside my head. To Diana Finch, agent and friend, and to publishers Roger Van Zwanenberg at Pluto, Kelly Notaras at Plume and Richard Eion Nash at Softskull for your patience with my perfectionism.

To Amy Goodman, Michael Jackson, Jim Hightower, Nancy Skinner, Alex Jones, the *CounterSpin* crew, Jeff Cohen, Phil Donahue, Wilmer Leon, Louie Free, Rob Lorei, Randi Rhodes, Alec Baldwin, Jim Bohannon, Mike Malloy, *This Is Hell Radio*. Annie Azzariti, Tom Jacobs, Dennis Bernstein, C-Span, and especially the Pacifica Radio Network for smashing the electronic Berlin Wall.

To Richard Ray Perez and Joan Sekler for filming *Unprecendented*, and deepest appreciation and thanks to the media's nagging conscience, Danny Schechter, for filming *Counting on Democracy* and for being my Virgil through the lower rings of the television Inferno.

To Lou Posner, Carla Itzkowich, Kat L'Estrange and Kim Tarner of Voter March; Nancy Newell, Deb St. John, Carolyn Kay, Bob Fertig, Mike Richtenwald, Sherry Wolf, Martin L. King III, People for the American Way, Project Censored, Alliance for Democracy, and so many others for taking the Best Democracy crusade on the road. To Nick Hilyard and Bianca Jagger for standing up for me in the Queen's bloody courtroom, speaking truth to power.

To Robin Simpson, Rob Weisbrot, Nancy Alexander, Sara Grusky, Joe White, Larry Ottinger, Jerry Oppenheim, Theo MacGregor, Paul Robbins, Joel Swadesh, Brod Bagert Jr, Brod Bagert Sr, Liz Macall and Geri Palast for research and investigative materials shared freely; and to Joe Stiglitz for sharing uncomfortable truths. And to all the whistleblowers, witnesses, sources, gadflys, troublemakers, investigators, enraged citizens, experts, insiders and researchers who produced so many of the documents, facts, photos and damning evidence on which these tales are based—especially those of you who cannot be named.

To Gil and Gladys Palast and Frank Rosen for teaching me that a life spent saving this sad species from itself is not wasted.

To the memories of Lois Rosen, Ron Ridenhour and Gary Groesch, whose admonitions keep me at the typewriter every night.

To David Shayler, jailed in the Queen's dungeon, for the words I quote here.

And finally, to the inestimably courageous human rights lawyer Tundu Lissu, who for providing me documentation of a massacre will probably be reading this from a jail cell in Tanzania, charged with the world's most honorable crime, sedition.

Index

(Photograph copyright © Daniel Morduchowicz 2002)

About the Author

"The most important journalist of our time—dominating journalism on two continents," says Britain's *Tribune* magazine—but in his native America, **Greg Palast's** into-the-gut investigative reports for BBC Television's *Newsnight* and *The Guardian* papers are all but banned. Palast has broken some of the biggest stories of recent years: how Katherine Harris stole the 2000 election for Bush by illegally removing African Americans from voter rolls (named *Salon*'s Politics Story of the Year) and how Bush killed off the FBI's investigation of the bin Laden family prior to the September 11 attack (awarded California State University's Project Censored Prize for a report too hot for U.S. media). Palast went undercover to investigate Enron's manipulations years before American papers would touch the topic—recognized as Britain's Story of the Year in 1999. Winner of the *Financial Times'* David Thomas Prize, Palast is a mainstream favorite in Europe, but in the United States he's the "cult fave" (*The Village Voice*), Guerrilla News Network's 2002 Reporter of the Year and the "journalist hero of the Internet" (Alan Colmes, *Fox TV*).

An internationally recognized expert on the control of corporate power, before picking up pen and camera Palast worked with labor unions and consumer groups in the United States, South America and Europe investigating corporate corruption. In America, among his more noted cases, he directed government investigations and prosecution of racketeering by nuclear plant builders and, for the Chugach natives of Alaska, probed charges of fraud by oil companies in the grounding of the *Exxon Valdez*.

Palast's lectures at Cambridge University and the University of São Paulo are contained in the book *Democracy and Regulation*, written with Jerry Oppenheim and Theo MacGregor, published by the United Nations and Pluto Press (2003). He divides his time between New York and London.

For updates, to view Palast's video reports, or to contact the author, visit www.GregPalast.com

About the Illustrator

Winston Smith's wickedly satirical art has appeared on the albums of dozens of malcontents, including **DEAD KENNEDYS, D.O.A., GREEN DAY** and **GEORGE CARLIN.** His works have also decorated the pages of distinguished rags such as *SPIN, FLIPSIDE, DETAILS, JUXTAPOZ, THE ATLANTIC MONTHLY, PLAYBOY* and *THE NEW YORKER.*

Please visit

WWW.WINSTONSMITH.COM

to collect posters, T-shirts, fine art prints and original art. Winston's two books *THE MONTAGE ART OF WINSTON SMITH, Vol. I: Act Like Nothing's Wrong* and *THE MONTAGE ART OF WINSTON SMITH, Vol. II: Artcrime* are published by **Last Gasp of San Francisco.** Each 96-page volume contains a rich selection of full-color montage compositions guaranteed to amuse and inspire.

Also be sure to check out
"New World Disorder," an outrageous 24" x 15" color poster made especially for
Greg Palast's *THE BEST DEMOCRACY MONEY CAN BUY*